Real-Time Animation with Adobe Character Animator

Animate characters in real time with webcam, microphone, and custom actions

Chad Troftgruben

BIRMINGHAM—MUMBAI

Real-Time Animation with Adobe Character Animator

Copyright © 2022 Packt Publishing

All rights reserved. No part of this book may be reproduced, stored in a retrieval system, or transmitted in any form or by any means, without the prior written permission of the publisher, except in the case of brief quotations embedded in critical articles or reviews.

Every effort has been made in the preparation of this book to ensure the accuracy of the information presented. However, the information contained in this book is sold without warranty, either express or implied. Neither the author, nor Packt Publishing or its dealers and distributors, will be held liable for any damages caused or alleged to have been caused directly or indirectly by this book.

Packt Publishing has endeavored to provide trademark information about all of the companies and products mentioned in this book by the appropriate use of capitals. However, Packt Publishing cannot guarantee the accuracy of this information.

Group Product Manager: Rohit Rajkumar
Publishing Product Manager: Ashitosh Gupta
Senior Editor: Keagan Carneiro
Senior Content Development Editor: Adrija Mitra and Feza Shaikh
Technical Editor: Joseph Aloocaran
Copy Editor: Safis Editing
Project Coordinator: Manthan Patel
Proofreader: Safis Editing
Indexer: Rekha Nair
Production Designer: Shankar Kalbhor
Marketing Coordinator: Nivedita Pandey

First published: December 2022

Production reference: 1251122

Published by Packt Publishing Ltd.
Livery Place
35 Livery Street
Birmingham
B3 2PB, UK.

ISBN 978-1-80324-694-9

www.packt.com

*To my son, Halfdan, may you never see the limit of your potential and imagination.
To my wife, Stephenie, may this incredible journey never end.*

– Chad Troftgruben

Contributors

About the author

Chad Troftgruben is a freelance animator who has spent several years learning about animation software while working on personal and commercial projects. Chad has worked with several companies for over a decade creating e-learning content. Some of these companies are Smith Micro, Lost Marble, Virtual Training Company, Packt Publishing, Train Simple, and Pluralsight.

Presently, Chad spends his time being a father and expanding his animation knowledge through the creation of original works. Chad also offers a series of animation video courses through Udemy, Skillshare, and his own website.

I want to thank the great team at Packt, especially Adrija, Keagan, and Feza. Writing a book is a challenge, but it's always easier when you work with awesome people. I'm also grateful for our thoughtful reviewers. Your insights helped mold the book to be more user-friendly and informational. Finally, thanks to all the supporters who have shown so much love and support for my work over the years. Without you, this book wouldn't be possible.

About the reviewers

Calvin O'Connor always knew he wanted to go into animation at a young age, and as he progressed through his academic studies he realized there was a plethora of avenues to explore. He had a soft spot for 2D animation, and one of his first jobs in the industry was a show that was made using Character Animator. Despite production starting at the beginning of the pandemic with the entire team working remotely, Calvin really took a shine to the program, and he began experimenting with puppets and finding new methods of animating. Since then, Calvin has used the software for design and rigging for various clients, such as Adobe, Octopie, and, Quibi. He also used Character Animator to create his own personal avatar for streaming games on Twitch, bridging his love of gaming with animation. He's always looking for new techniques and ventures with the software to make his own personal content.

Yogender Kumar serves as a senior UI/UX designer at Indegene Pvt. Ltd., Bangalore. He has strong hands-on experience in branding and advertising. He has been working in the creative field for more than seven years. He has worked with different clients worldwide as a graphic designer, animator, and video editor, and he is now working as a UI/UX designer. Yogender Kumar completed his education in graphics and animation at Kurukshetra University, Kurukshetra, India.

Table of Contents

Preface	xiii

Part 1: Preparing Character Art for Rigging

1

What You Need to Know Before Rigging and Animating — 3

System requirements for Character Animator	3	Testing your webcam	11
		Testing your microphone	13
Downloading Character Animator	4	Playing with samples and the characterizer	14
Character Animator Pro versus Starter	7		
Calibrating equipment in Character Animator	8	Playing with a sample rig	14
		Recording animation	16
Creating a new project	9	Animating with Characterizer	17
Saving project versions	9	Summary	19
Loading and renaming project versions	10		

2

Comparing Adobe Character Animator to Other Animation Apps — 21

What is Adobe Animate?	21	A brief history of Adobe After Effects	34
Brief history of Adobe Animate	22	The strengths of After Effects	34
The strengths of Adobe Animate	24	Using After Effects with our Character Animator productions	36
Using Animate with Character Animator productions	26		
		Other popular animation apps	36
What is Adobe After Effects?	34	Summary	37

3

Preparing a Character Rig in Photoshop 39

Designing your character	39	Creating main groups	58
Streamlining and renaming layers	41	Adding eyebrow phases	60
Creating a character group	43	Arranging the eye groups	62
Removing unneeded layers	44	Separating out the hair	66
Merging and renaming the limbs	45	Cleaning up PSD layers	69
Reorganizing the eye layers	49	Summary	71
Organizing with normal and independent groups	57		

Part 2: Rigging Character Art for Animation

4

Importing and Tagging Your Character 75

Technical requirements	75	Switching the tag view	84
Adjusting the rig in Character Animator	75	Understanding left and right tags	85
		Tagging head layers	87
Importing Chaz into Character Animator	76	Tagging mouth layers	91
Making layer changes in Character Animator	77	Tagging the body layers	92
Creating PSD versions	81	Summary	97
Tagging the head and mouth	84		

5

Creating Control Handles and Behaviors 99

Technical requirements	99	Assigning layers as Independent	108
Adding modifiers for mouse control	99	Welding Independent groups to the body	110
Adjusting the layer and mesh properties	101	Refining limbs with the stick tool	114
Adding draggers and fixed modifiers	102	Adjusting limb rotation	116
Linking Independent groups	108	Summary	119

6

Physics, Behaviors, and Meshes — 121

Technical requirements	121	Creating layer-specific behaviors	127
Adding physics and danglers	121	Refining animation with meshes	128
Modifying universal behaviors	124	Summary	130

7

Assigning Mouths and Props with Triggers and Swap Sets — 131

Technical requirements	131	Further exploring triggers and swap sets	140
Creating triggers for props	131	Creating visual controls for triggers	140
Importing props	132	Other tips for using triggers and swap sets	142
Creating triggers	135		
Creating swap sets for hands	137	Summary	142

8

Refining Layers and Exploring Optional Rig Features — 143

Technical requirements	143	Implementing head turns	150
Animating eyelids	143	Tagging the head phases	151
Importing a character with eyelids	144	Testing the head turns	152
Tagging the eyelids	145	Summary	153
Animating breathing and jaw animations	148		

Part 3: Animating and Refining Your Scene

9

Working with Preset Actions — 157

Technical requirements	157	Mixing actions on the timeline	166
Creating a walk cycle	157	Summary	167
Modifying a walk cycle	164		

10

Animating a Simple Sequence — 169

Technical requirements	169	Importing and positioning the alien guest	175
Assembling the set	170	Recording dialogue	177
Importing the background assets	170	Using a screenplay or outline	177
Getting started with building the set	171	Recording Chaz's dialogue in real time	177
Positioning the characters in the scene	172	Importing and lip-syncing the alien's dialogue	179
Importing and positioning Chaz	173	Summary	182

11

Rearranging, Polishing, and Enhancing Our Sequence — 183

Technical requirements	183	Setting automatic blinks for the alien	192
Using PNG sequences for external animations	183	Adding arm movement to the alien	193
Importing PNGs for the sequence	184	Arranging character actions in sequence	195
Adding Cycle Layers behavior	186	Correcting flaws and enhancing animations	200
Adjusting the audience in the scene	188	Summary	205
Adding more character actions	190		
Adjusting the alien's gaze	190		

12

Exporting, Editing, and Sharing Your Character Animator Sequence — 207

Technical requirements	207	Editing in After Effects with Dynamic Link	214
Export options in Character Animator	208	Why use After Effects?	214
Setting export duration	208	Importing and understanding Dynamic Link	214
How to export files	209	Layering	217
Exporting Character Animator scenes as videos	210	Adding special effects	222
		Adding camera features	228

| Editing in Premiere | 235 | Summary | 244 |
| Color grading and filters | 238 | | |

13

Additional Character Animator Tools and Features — 245

Technical requirements	245	Tracking body turns	264
Puppet Maker	246	Using the Stream workspace	267
Character Animator scene cameras	253	Summary	269
Tracking body animations	260		

Index — 271

Other Books You May Enjoy — 278

Preface

Adobe Character Animator is 2D-character animation software aimed at non-animators looking for a fun way to create entertainment and business presentations or videos. Character Animator relies on live interaction from the user using a webcam, microphone, keyboard, and mouse to control the puppets or character rigs on screen.

This book introduces you to the world of Character Animator by taking a designed character and properly rigging it. We will show proper layer structure for our character PSDs and what to look out for when importing and rigging in Character Animator.

From there, you will learn how to enhance characters through physics and behaviors, which are automatic or context-sensitive-based actions that can be easily changed in Character Animator. Triggers and swap sets allow for image sequence-based animations. Working with preset animations, lip-syncing, and head movements will make the rig more dynamic.

Finally, with all this knowledge, we will build a more complex scene using two characters and background elements. We will bring our work into After Effects and Premiere for a final polish before publishing it in Media Encoder.

By the time you're done animating along with us, you will be able to take this knowledge and start creating your very own animated productions. Whether you want to build a sitcom, business presentation, or a cartoon presence through a streaming app, this book is here to help guide you on the right path.

Who this book is for

This book is for beginners looking to set up and animate cartoon characters using a webcam and microphone. This can then be the basis to build fully edited productions or stream on various platforms. The book is also useful for animators looking to learn Character Animator's non-traditional approach to animation.

What this book covers

Chapter 1, *What You Need to Know Before Rigging and Animating*, teaches you the system requirements for Character Animator, where to download the app, and how to play around with sample files to get a feel for the software's basic features.

Chapter 2, *Comparing Adobe Character Animator to Other Animation Apps*, delves into Character Animator's unique abilities, which allow for the creation of awesome work, although there are other applications out there with their own strengths. Here, we will go over some of those animation applications while also explaining the link these can have to Character Animator's workflow.

Chapter 3, *Preparing a Character Rig in Photoshop*, looks at taking a completed character and reorganizing the layers in Photoshop to ensure a smooth process when rigging and animating. While Character Animator makes it possible for any art style to be used, it's important to understand proper layer structure and independence for your characters. We will also learn about proper labeling to help Character Animator tag body parts appropriately.

Chapter 4, *Importing and Tagging Your Character*, explores tagging, which is a process where we identify layers and points so that Character Animator knows what to do with them. Some of the work we did in the previous chapter will help us here, as Character Animator will automatically tag some layers, but here we will go over how to tag each layer to assure no asset is left behind.

Chapter 5, *Creating Control Handles and Behaviors*, examines control handles, which are points on the character we set up for various interactions and can be equipped with behaviors to create a variety of effects. This includes dragging limbs, adding bend refinements, and working with independent groups for advanced rigging. This chapter is about honing in and refining the controls of your character rig.

Chapter 6, *Physics, Behaviors, and Meshes*, delves further into Character Animator's strengths after putting a workable rig in place. We can set up a rig to not only interact with movement or other entities but also layer-specific and universal behaviors that can add more interactivity and realism. We will also look at meshes and how they can help change the rig further.

Chapter 7, *Assigning Mouths and Props with Triggers and Swap Sets*, introduces triggers and swap sets. As you continue to develop your characters and build scenes, you may find you need more flexibility with your rigs. Triggers and swap sets allow you to call in objects that may be invisible, swap props on the fly, or even create a series of mouth poses controlled with any device. This chapter goes over how to set these up and what to look out for.

Chapter 8, *Refining Layers and Exploring Optional Rig Features*, covers additional features that we can take advantage of once our rig is almost ready to be put into an animated scene. Some of these are style choices, while others can enhance any rig you're using. Eyelids, breathing, and head turns are covered in this chapter.

Chapter 9, *Working with Preset Actions*, explores preset actions. While you can make all of your character animations from scratch, preset actions are included to help you get your character moving. Walk cycles, running animations, and more can easily be added with a click of a button. We will learn about this as well as combining actions when animating on the timeline.

Chapter 10, Animating a Simple Sequence, looks at animating a sequence. We will import our character into a scene, move them around and interact with a second character. We will lay down key moments and actions to plug into the scene. We will record dialog using our camera and mic as well as use the external audio lip-sync feature. This will set us up for editing and polishing the sequence in Chapter 11.

Chapter 11, *Rearranging, Polishing, and Enhancing Our Sequence*, covers taking the animations and audio laid down in the previous chapter and uses the timeline to piece the tracks together to create a cohesive narrative. This will also be the time to go through and add any flourishes or additional content to the scene before we send it to After Effects and Premiere for export.

Chapter 12, *Exporting, Editing, and Sharing Your Character Animator Sequence*, explores the next step after you have animated a complete sequence in Character Animator. You can choose to export the sequence as is to share it with friends or on social media, or you can take it over to After Effects or Premiere to add effects or make edits to help with the flow. We can use Character Animator for many projects, so we will try to cover as much ground as logically possible.

Chapter 13, *Additional Character Animator Tools and Features*, delves into additional Character Animator features. While we have covered a lot of what it offers, there are still more features to explore. At the time of writing, some of these features didn't work within the planned workflow. Character Animator even introduced some features as the book was being written, which is a great example of how Adobe supports its products. Therefore, we want to highlight these features, as they can enhance your animations, save time, or even help you to perform live on a variety of streaming platforms.

To get the most out of this book

It's recommended you purchase a copy of Adobe Character Animator under a Pro license. This app is also included under the Adobe Creative Cloud subscription plan. We will also be using other apps within the Adobe Creative Cloud to help produce our animation. While you don't need these apps to work with Character Animator, it is highly recommended for an optimal learning and production experience.

Software/hardware covered in the book	Operating system requirements
Character Animator v23.0	Windows or macOS
Photoshop v24.0	Windows or macOS
After Effects v23.0	Windows or macOS
Premiere Pro v23.0	Windows or macOS
Animate v23.0	Windows or macOS

Be sure to have a webcam and microphone plugged into your computer, as this is the primary way we will be interacting with Character Animator. It's also recommended you have nice even lighting to get the best results. If you plan to do a full-body motion, be sure to have plenty of room.

The supporting files for this book are available at `https://packt.link/GdF1Z`.

Download the color images

We also provide a PDF file that has color images of the screenshots and diagrams used in this book. You can download it here: `https://packt.link/C2J50`.

Conventions used

There are a number of text conventions used throughout this book.

`Code in text`: Indicates code words in text, database table names, folder names, filenames, file extensions, pathnames, dummy URLs, user input, and Twitter handles. Here is an example: "Be sure to have your tagged character open in Character Animator. Or you can access `Chat_with_Chaz.chproj`. Also, we will do a little work in Photoshop. The modified file from that task will be labeled `Chaz_Host_v3.psd`. Let's get going!"

Bold: Indicates a new term, an important word, or words that you see on screen. For instance, words in menus or dialog boxes appear in **bold**. Here is an example: "Load **Version 2** from the **History** panel if you wish to work with the book's example."

> **Tips or important notes**
> Appear like this.

Get in touch

Feedback from our readers is always welcome.

General feedback: If you have questions about any aspect of this book, email us at `customercare@packtpub.com` and mention the book title in the subject of your message.

Errata: Although we have taken every care to ensure the accuracy of our content, mistakes do happen. If you have found a mistake in this book, we would be grateful if you would report this to us. Please visit `www.packtpub.com/support/errata` and fill in the form.

Piracy: If you come across any illegal copies of our works in any form on the internet, we would be grateful if you would provide us with the location address or website name. Please contact us at `copyright@packt.com` with a link to the material.

If you are interested in becoming an author: If there is a topic that you have expertise in and you are interested in either writing or contributing to a book, please visit `authors.packtpub.com`.

Share Your Thoughts

Once you've read, we'd love to hear your thoughts! Scan the QR code below to go straight to the Amazon review page for this book and share your feedback.

`https://packt.link/r/1803246944`

Your review is important to us and the tech community and will help us make sure we're delivering excellent quality content.

Download a free PDF copy of this book

Thanks for purchasing this book!

Do you like to read on the go but are unable to carry your print books everywhere? Is your eBook purchase not compatible with the device of your choice?

Don't worry, now with every Packt book you get a DRM-free PDF version of that book at no cost.

Read anywhere, any place, on any device. Search, copy, and paste code from your favorite technical books directly into your application.

The perks don't stop there, you can get exclusive access to discounts, newsletters, and great free content in your inbox daily

Follow these simple steps to get the benefits:

1. Scan the QR code or visit the link below

`packt.link/free-ebook/9781803246949`

2. Submit your proof of purchase
3. That's it! We'll send your free PDF and other benefits to your email directly

Part 1: Preparing Character Art for Rigging

Before we take our character and start animating, there are some considerations. First, it's best to know how the app works, and this chapter will highlight key points. When it comes to art, our character's layers will need to follow a specific pattern. Character Animator works best when you name layers as well as organize groups a certain way, which you will learn. Photoshop will be featured heavily here, as it's the best choice for organizing .psd files.

This part includes the following chapters:

- Chapter 1, *What You Need to Know Before Rigging and Animating*
- Chapter 2, *Comparing Adobe Character Animator to Other Animation Apps*
- Chapter 3, *Preparing a Character Rig in Photoshop*

1
What You Need to Know Before Rigging and Animating

In order to ensure a smooth experience, we will first talk about the system requirements and how to download Character Animator. We will touch on the differences between the Starter and Pro versions of the app and make sure your equipment is compatible with Adobe Character Animator. Character Animator works differently from other animation apps in that you act out sequences using your webcam and microphone to record animation, so it's important we have those pieces of hardware ready. Once your equipment is confirmed to be functioning, we can test some sample files out to get a handle on what the software is capable of. We will also take a look at **Characterizer**, an easy and fun way to quickly bring yourself into a scene.

In this chapter, we're going to cover the following main topics:

- System requirements for Character Animator
- Downloading Character Animator
- Calibrating and setting a rest pose in Character Animator
- Playing with sample files and **Characterizer**

Technical requirements

The supporting files for this book are available at `https://packt.link/GdFlZ`.

System requirements for Character Animator

To get the most out of this book, it's recommended you have the following:

- An updated copy of Adobe Character Animator
- A webcam

- A microphone
- A well-lit room to record in

Adobe Character Animator comes with a few requirements if you're looking to maximize your project's potential. A nice computer will allow for faster processes. This can be useful, especially as projects take up more resources.

While traditional methods used in other applications are achievable here to some extent (such as controlling animation using a mouse and keyboard), you will find it's best to interact using a microphone and webcam. This not only allows for real-time expressions and lip-syncing but also full body tracking if desired. For a more detailed breakdown, here are Character Animator's requirements according to Adobe: `https://helpx.adobe.com/adobe-character-animator/system-requirements.html`.

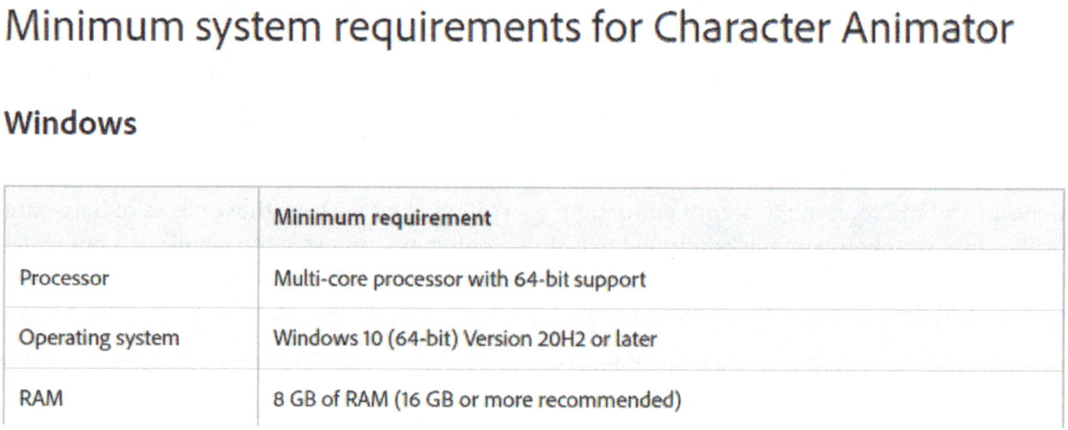

Minimum system requirements for Character Animator

Windows

	Minimum requirement
Processor	Multi-core processor with 64-bit support
Operating system	Windows 10 (64-bit) Version 20H2 or later
RAM	8 GB of RAM (16 GB or more recommended)

Figure 1.1: A preview of the requirements for Windows (the page contains Mac specs as well)

It's advised you record in a well-lit room. This will ensure your webcam can pick up on your expressions. If you plan to take advantage of the body tracking feature, make sure you have enough room to move freely and safely. The camera will also need to be placed at a distance, but we will go over that in detail when we get to body tracking later on.

All the images in this book will showcase the Windows UI. However, the macOS and Windows versions are identical except for the UI and shortcuts. All the shortcuts given in this book will be for both Windows and macOS.

Downloading Character Animator

You can download Character Animator via the Adobe Creative Cloud or the Adobe website. The Pro version, which is what we will be using, requires a subscription that comes with a monthly fee. You can gain access to the app for free under the Starter UI, but this will limit your features and ability to follow along with the book.

If you wish to download Character Animator through the Adobe Creative Cloud, follow this link: `https://www.adobe.com/creativecloud/desktop-app.html`.

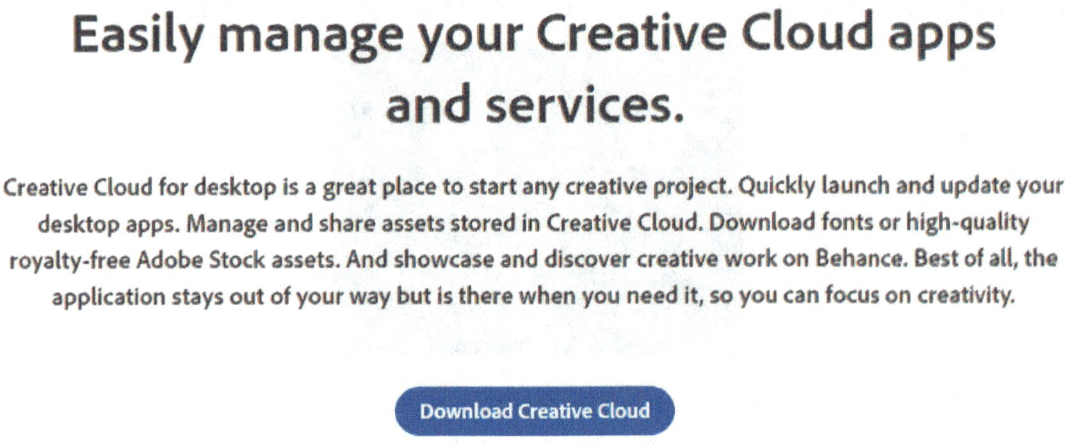

Easily manage your Creative Cloud apps and services.
Creative Cloud for desktop is a great place to start any creative project. Quickly launch and update your desktop apps. Manage and share assets stored in Creative Cloud. Download fonts or high-quality royalty-free Adobe Stock assets. And showcase and discover creative work on Behance. Best of all, the application stays out of your way but is there when you need it, so you can focus on creativity.
Download Creative Cloud

Figure 1.2: Downloading Creative Cloud for desktop not only grants access to Character Animator but also all of Adobe's amazing apps

If you wish to download Character Animator without the Adobe Creative Cloud, follow this link and click **Buy Now** next to Character Animator: `https://www.adobe.com/products/character-animator.html`. Follow the on-screen instructions, download, and install. You will also be prompted to create an Adobe account if you don't already have one.

Ch
Animate in real time. Really.
Use your expressions and movements to bring your characters to life with Character Animator. Get it in the Creative Cloud All Apps plan for US$54.99/mo.
Start for free
Buy now

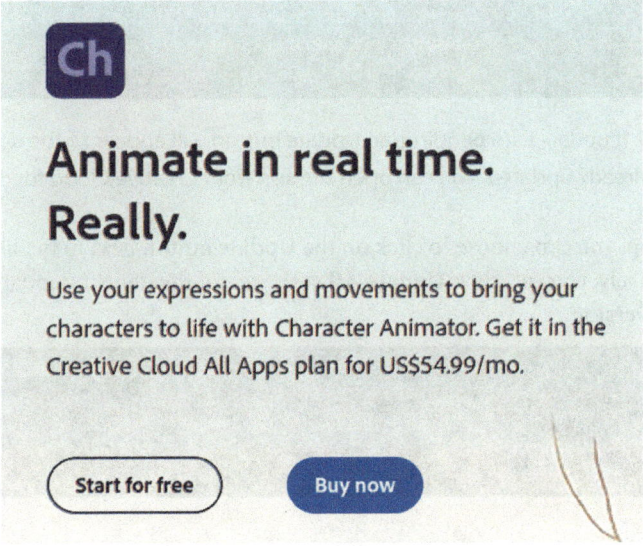

Figure 1.3: You can now use the app for free with Starter mode, but we will be using the Pro version for this book

This book is being written according to v23.0 and it's recommended you update to the latest version of Character Animator before following along. To update, you can use the Adobe Creative Cloud, click **Updates** on the left-hand side of the panel, and look for Character Animator in the list.

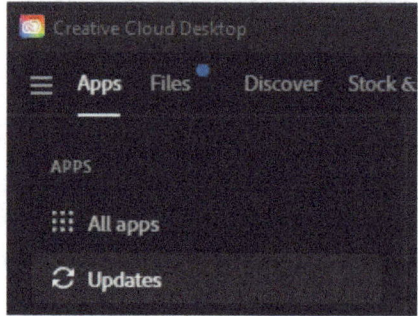

Figure 1.4: Under Apps, you will find Updates, the section that will check for any updates for installed Adobe apps

If the app has an update pending, you will see an Update button on the right. If the app is updated, you can directly open the app from the Creative Cloud using the Open button.

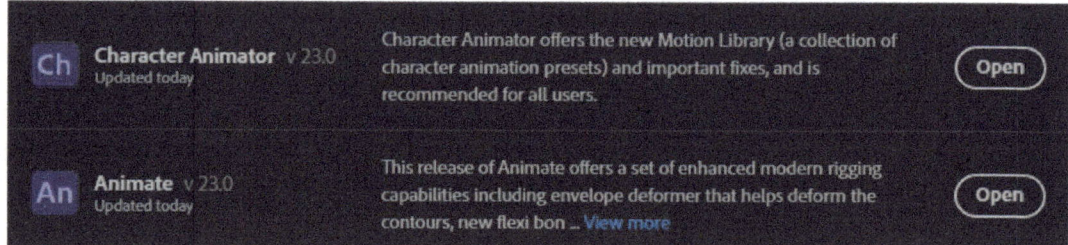

Figure 1.5: If updates are pending, an Update button will appear to the right of the app. If already updated, you can open the app from Creative Cloud for desktop

Once you find the app, you can choose to click on the **Update** button next to the listing if a new update is available. Alternatively, you can click **Update All** at the top of the panel to update all installed Adobe apps to the current version:

Figure 1.6: If using the Creative Cloud for desktop, click Update All on the left to ensure you're up to date

Once you have successfully installed and launched the app, we can talk about the differences between the **Pro** and **Starter** UIs.

Character Animator Pro versus Starter

As of v23.0, you now have the option to use Character Animator for free under the **Starter** UI. This simplified format limits many of Character Animator's useful features. It does have its uses, especially if you want to explore how the motion capture tool works, or if you quickly want to animate and export a preset character:

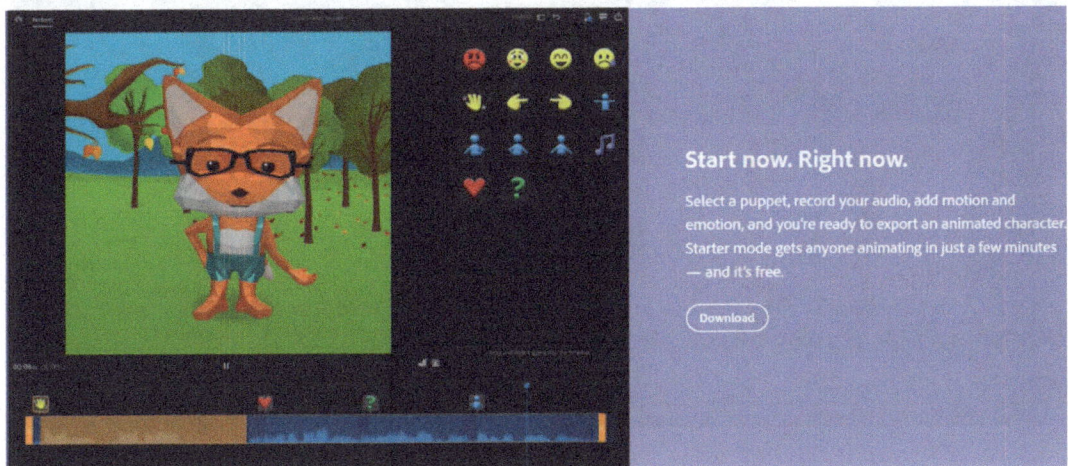

Figure 1.7: Starter mode is great for those curious about the functionality of Character Animator, but it lacks many great features

However, for the purposes of having more control and tools, it's recommended you purchase a copy of the **Pro** version to get the most out of this book. With the **Pro** version, you can also switch to the **Starter** UI, if you feel the need. You can do this by toggling the UI button at the top right:

Figure 1.8: Clicking PRO will allow you to switch to STARTER mode

Before you confirm your choice, you will also be given an explanation of how **Starter** mode differs from **Pro**.

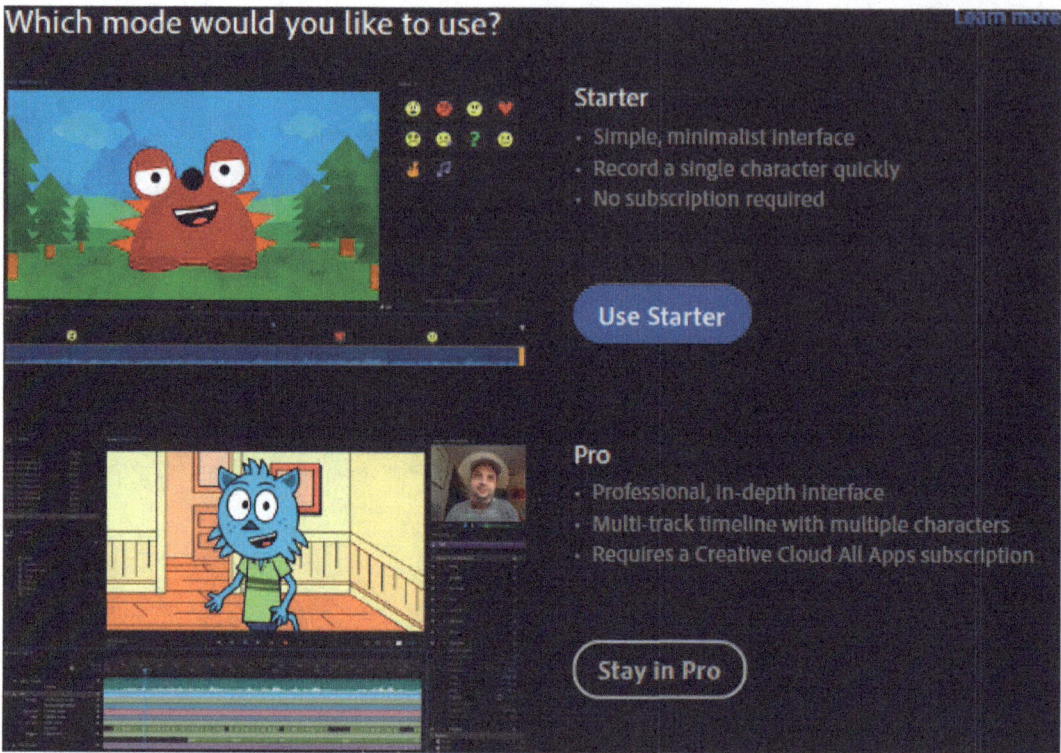

Figure 1.9: Here is the official breakdown of the modes according to Character Animator

The **Starter** mode is great if you want to get your feet wet with the basics of the app, but Character Animator offers a lot of features that can only be found in the **Pro** version, and that's the version of the app we will be using for this book. With that said, let's look at how to calibrate our equipment for optimal animation.

Calibrating equipment in Character Animator

Before we go any further, let's test out our webcams and microphones to ensure everything is in working order. We will also look at how Character Animator saves projects, which is different from most mainstream animation software. At the end of this section, we will have covered the following:

- Creating a new project
- Saving project versions
- Loading and renaming project versions
- Testing and calibrating your webcam and microphone

Launch the Character Animator app. Once loaded, if opening the app for the first time, a welcome screen showcasing sample files and other options will display. If you don't see this, click on the **Home** button on the top left:

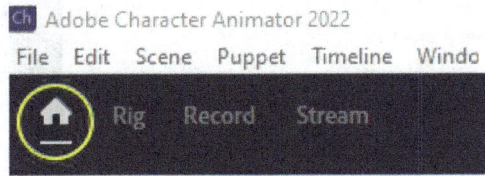

Figure 1.10: The Home button is always on the top left in case you get lost

Now, let's create a new project and dive deeper.

Creating a new project

While playing with **Sample Files** is beneficial, let's focus on the webcam and microphone settings first:

1. Click on the **New Project** button and it will prompt you to save the project file.

Figure 1.11: You can easily open or create new projects from the home screen

2. Locate a safe place on your computer and save the file as `ch_book_project`.
3. Once saved, a new blank workspace will pop up.

We will use this one project file for the duration of this chapter.

Saving project versions

Character Animator saves automatically any time we change the project file. While this offers peace of mind on some level, you may find it beneficial now and then to save a state in the **History** panel by going to **File** > **Save Project Version** (*Ctrl + S* or *⌘ + S*).

What You Need to Know Before Rigging and Animating

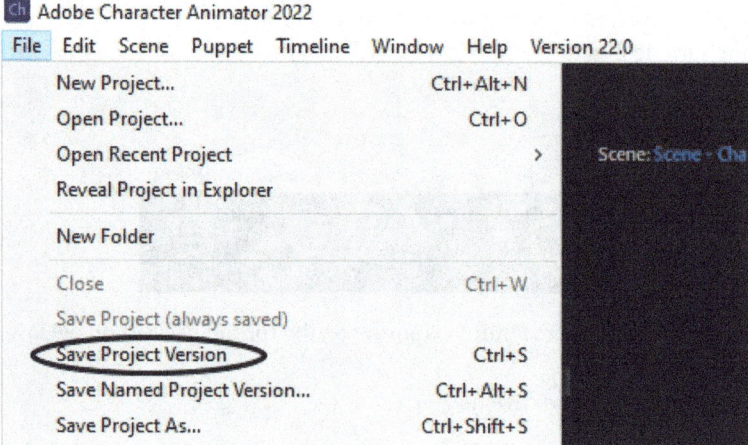

Figure 1.12: Manually saving a project version

This will create a saved state of the project in the **History** panel that you can jump back to at any point.

Loading and renaming project versions

Let's take a closer look at the **History** panel:

1. To access the **History** panel, go to **Window > History**. We can reinstate the versions saved here.
2. To load a state, simply double-click on it. Using versions is a great way to create backups or states of your file in case future changes cause errors or undesired results.

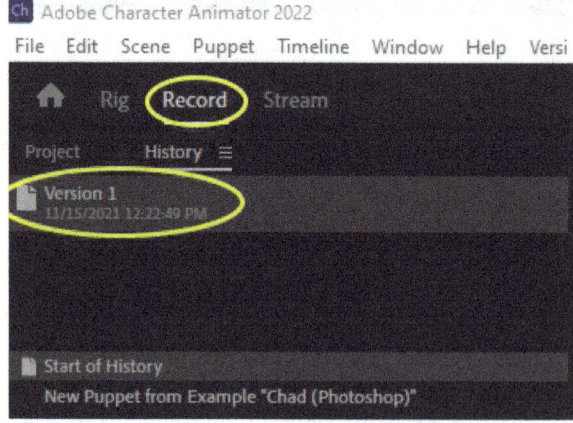

Figure 1.13: Double-clicking on any saved version will restore that file's state

3. You can right-click on **Version 1** and choose **Rename "Version 1"** from the list if you wish to create a more descriptive save state.

4. You can also create a save state with a new name by going to **File** > **Save Named Project Version** (*Ctrl* + *Alt* + *S* or ⌘ + ⌥ + *S*).

If you prefer to separate project files entirely as you save backups, you can also duplicate the project file itself by going to **File** > **Save Project As** (*Ctrl* + *Shift* + *S* or ⌘ + *Shift* + *S*).

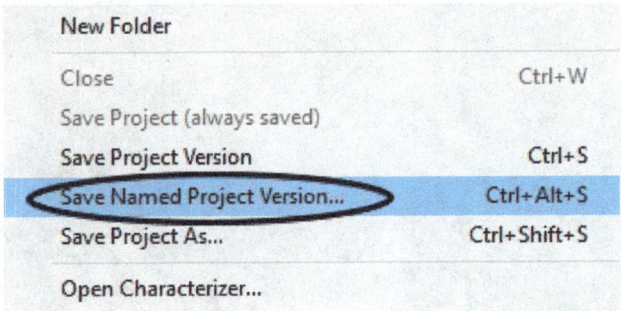

Figure 1.14: Creating a backup with a new name in one step

For the main project in this book, we will use one project file with several versions available via the **History** panel. This will allow you to go through the rigging and recording example files step by step as we call them out in the book. It's also less messy than creating multiple project files.

Testing your webcam

Getting back to our new file, this blank screen we are looking at is the **Record** tab. It's blank because we have yet to insert any puppets into this project. We will get there in due course:

1. If you're not on the **Record** tab, you can access it by clicking **Record** in the top left:

Figure 1.15: The Record tab is always accessible at the top

2. Direct your attention to the top right. The **Camera & Microphone** tab should be visible. If not, go to **Window > Camera & Microphone**.

3. Click on the **Webcam** button at the bottom of the panel. This should activate your connected webcam and show a preview in the window:

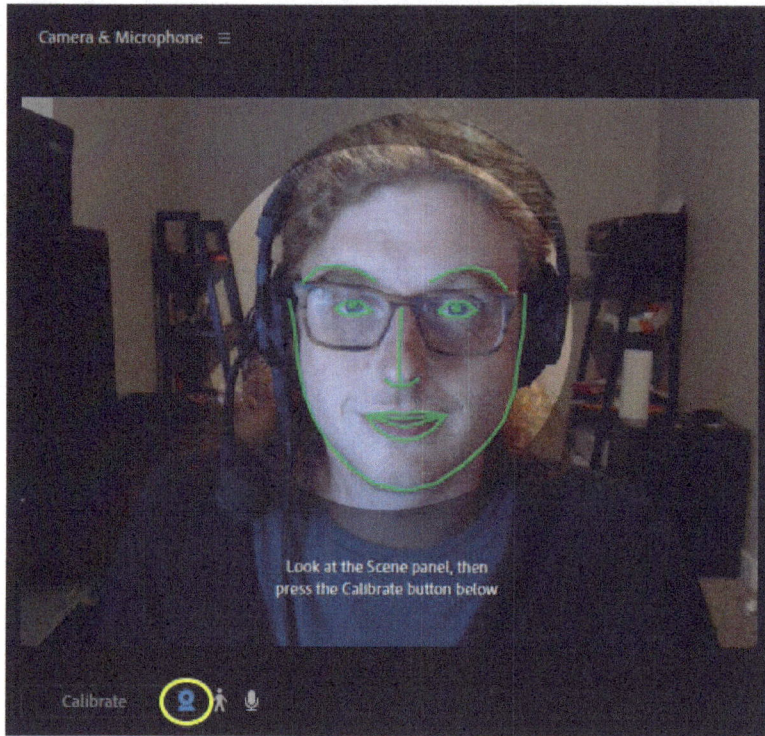

Figure 1.16: Previewing by clicking the webcam icon

4. What's important next is situating your face within the highlighted area. You will also want to look straight at the camera, keeping your expression relaxed and neutral.

5. Once you have situated yourself, click the **Calibrate** button below the preview window:

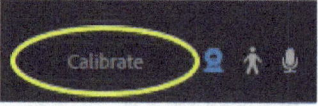

Figure 1.17: The Calibrate button lies below the preview window

6. This will allow the app to detect your face more accurately and know when it should be neutral during your emotions and actions. **Rest Pose** is used to refer to this neutral state, as well.

Test the camera by turning your head left and right and moving your head within the preview space. Blinking, raising and lowering your eyebrows, and opening and closing your mouth should also track. If the green tracking lines follow along, calibration is complete!

Testing your microphone

You can enable and disable your microphone by clicking on the microphone button at the bottom. Enabling it will allow you to preview your audio level on the histogram, but nothing else will happen since no puppets are present.

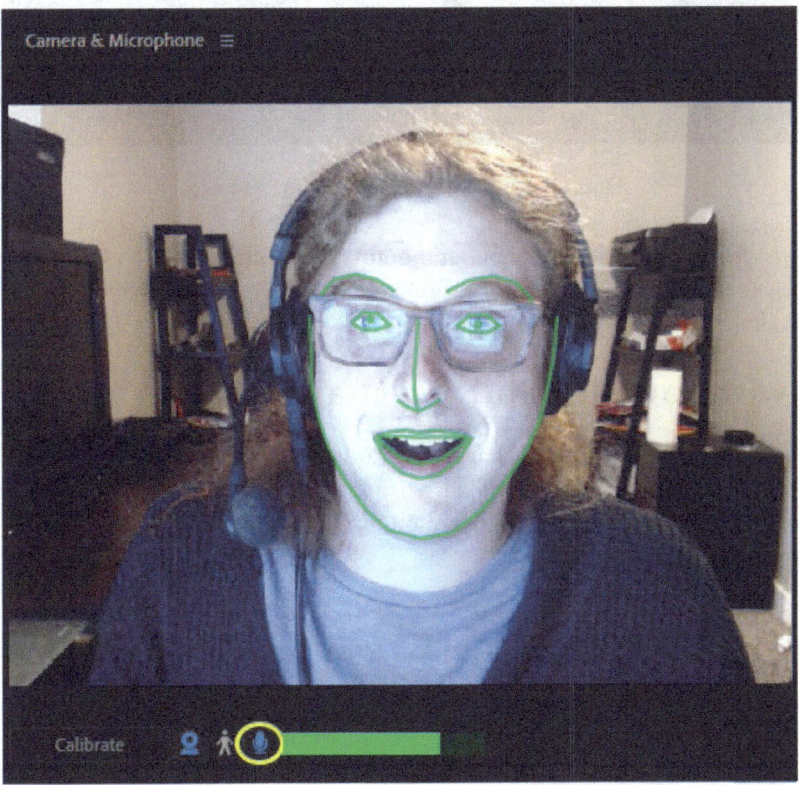

Figure 1.18: Clicking on the microphone will reveal the histogram, a meter used to judge audio levels

Now, let's say you have multiple microphones or maybe something isn't detecting correctly. You can configure your audio hardware by going to **Edit** > **Preferences** (*Ctrl + K*) on Windows or clicking on the Apple logo and choosing **Preferences** (⌘ + ,) on macOS. **Audio Hardware**, the top option on the left, will give you access to all audio equipment connected to the computer.

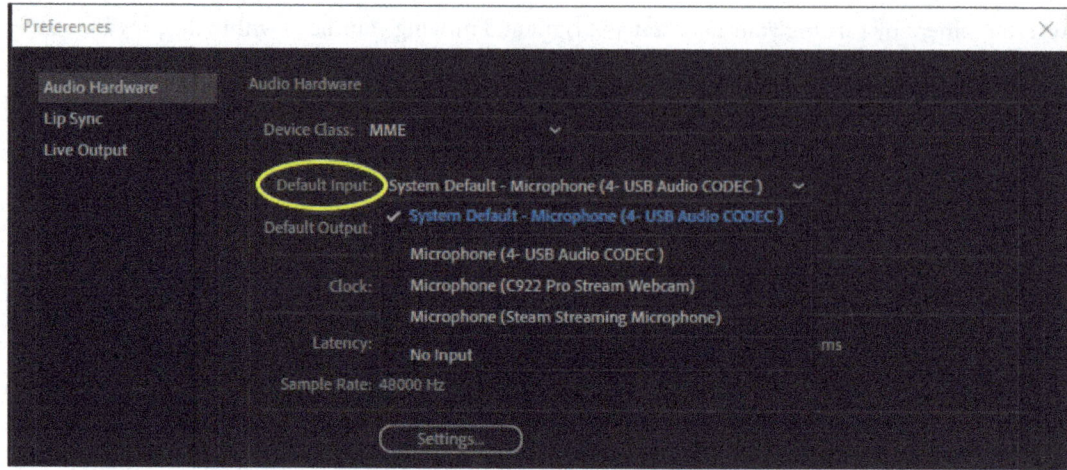

Figure 1.19: Setting up your audio hardware

Once you have selected your desired input and output audio choices, click **OK** and try to test the mic again to ensure the histogram below the preview is detecting audio. With your equipment now detected and calibrated, let's play with some sample files!

Playing with samples and the characterizer

This is a good way to experience how Character Animator functions. It also allows us to see if any further calibration needs adjusting. We will also use **Characterizer**, which is an easy and quick way to bring an animated version of yourself, or a picture of someone, into the production. Here's what we will be covering specifically:

- Playing with a sample rig
- Recording animation
- Animating with Characterizer

Playing with a sample rig

To begin, let's go back to the home screen:

1. To do this, click on the **Home** button on the top left of the app. We want to direct our attention back to the sample files being showcased.
2. Let's choose the first puppet on the list. **Chad**, which is the name of the puppet, is a simple head rig that can track our head, mouth, and eyes.
3. When you select the puppet, it will bring you to the **Recording** tab with the **Chad** head in the workspace:

Figure 1.20: Sample puppets

4. Let's turn the webcam and microphone on by clicking on the webcam and microphone buttons under the upper-right preview window. If you need to calibrate again, do that.
5. Now, try opening your mouth. The puppet should correspond and show an open-mouth pose. The same goes for head tilts, eyebrows, eye blinks, and pupils.

It tracks facial features through the camera, allowing us to animate the head (although nothing is being recorded on the timeline yet). This is useful when rigging a puppet, as we can test the actions before committing any animation to the timeline:

 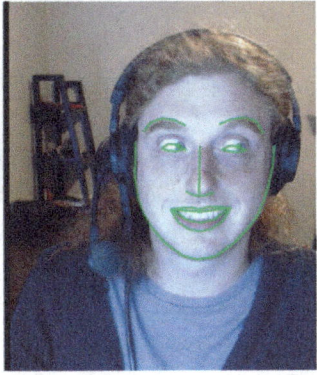

Figure 1.21: Looking right and smiling causes the puppet to do the same thing

Now, try saying something and pay attention to the puppet's mouth. The puppet should approximate the phonemes you are producing and try to fill in the poses that most make sense:

Figure 1.22: The puppet should track your voice, creating phonemes to lip-sync

If the puppet isn't detecting your video or audio, go back to **Preferences** and ensure your input and output are correct.

Recording animation

If you'd like to try recording some animation, you will find a red record (*Ctrl + R* or ⌘ *+ R*) button below the puppet preview. Clicking this will start a 3-second countdown and start moving the timeline and any movement or words will record:

Figure 1.23: Your recording will count down once you hit the red record button

You can hit the stop button, scroll the timeline scrubber back to the beginning, and hit play. You will see what you just did play back:

Playing with samples and the characterizer 17

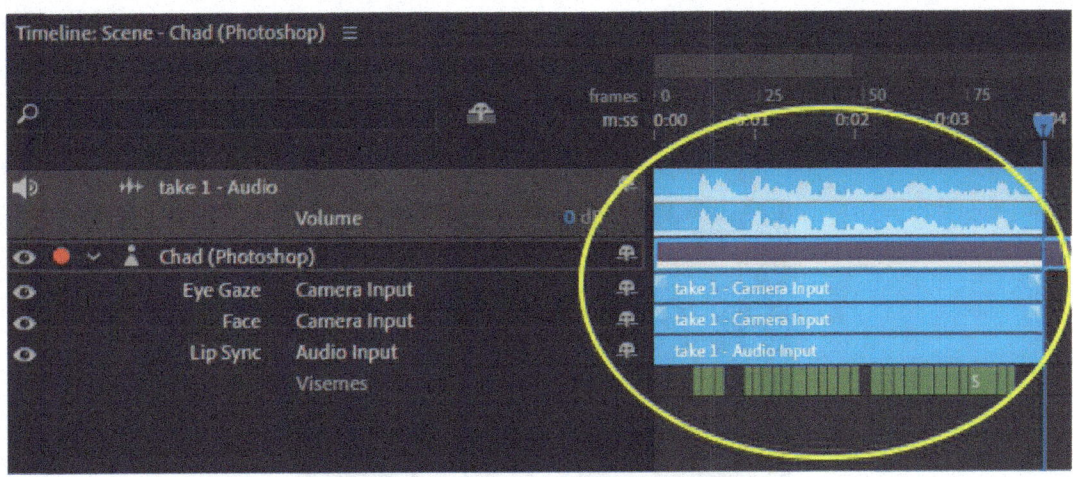

Figure 1.24: All of this content was created through the webcam and mic

We can also edit the timeline, allowing us to hone in and alter segments. We can even work with multiple characters, sets, and props! All of this will become clearer later on.

Animating with Characterizer

To begin, go to **File** > **Open Characterizer**. A new window will open up with a big plus symbol button with **Create New Capture…** written below it. You may also see other captured projects if any work has been done in this panel before. Click on the plus symbol to get started:

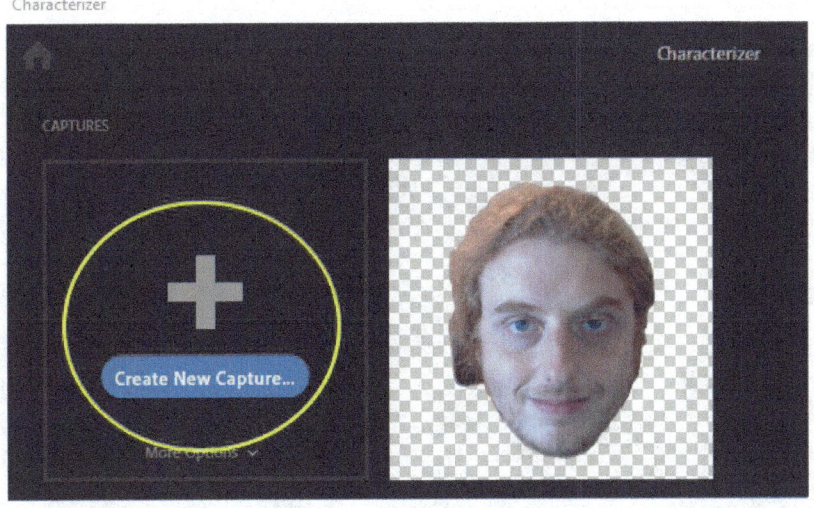

Figure 1.25: Clicking on the Create New Capture… button to begin

A new window will show your camera preview and some on-screen instructions will be present. You may also hear a narrator explaining the process. Be sure your head is in the center highlighted area. Face forward and then hit **Start**. You will hear an instructor prompting you to do a few tasks: close your eyes, smile, frown and say various words. What this is doing is capturing all the phases needed to create animation for your head in Character Animator.

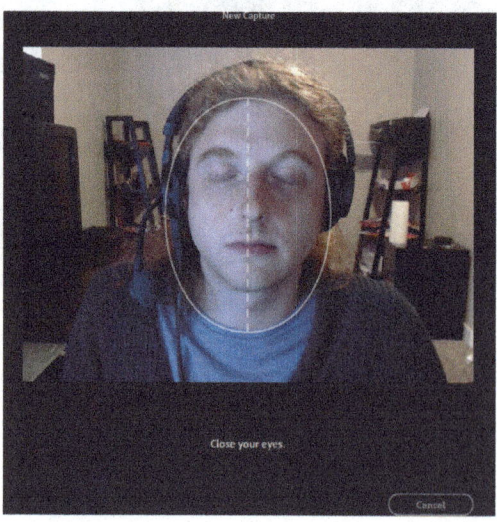

Figure 1.26: Just follow the prompts on the screen and Character Animator will do the rest

On the next screen, you can page through the poses that the app has generated. If anything is amiss or doesn't look correct, you can click on the back button on the top left and redo the process.

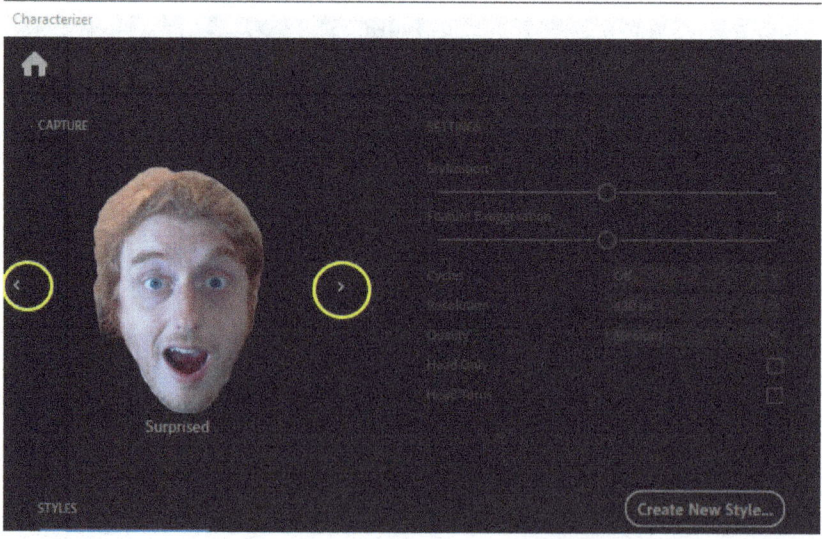

Figure 1.27: You can page through each pose to make sure everything is correct

Once satisfied with the poses, you can decide whether you want to stylize your capture. Each style option allows you to tweak various aspects, such as **Stylization**, **Feature Exaggeration**, sketch-like animation effects, and much more. Once satisfied, you can click **Generate** and it will place the puppet into the **Recording** workspace.

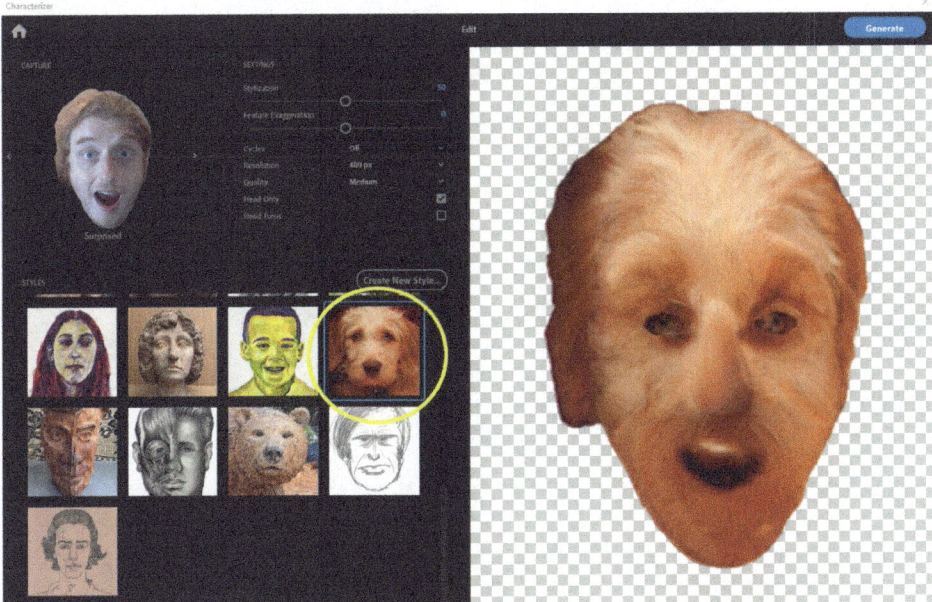

Figure 1.28: You can stylize your character in a variety of fun ways

Other things you can do is import outside images to create the character and import new styles. For this book, we are going to focus on using original artwork and rigs. But it's good to know **Characterizer** is there, as you never know – a future project could be perfect for it.

Summary

Feel free to play around until you're comfortable with the UI and the **Recording** tab. What's important here is you know how to do the following:

- Download the app and use the Pro UI
- Make new projects
- Save versions
- Calibrate your equipment

Up next, we're going to take a look at some of the other animation apps in Adobe Creative Cloud, how they differ, and how we can combine software to create unique effects.

2
Comparing Adobe Character Animator to Other Animation Apps

Adobe Character Animator is unique and comes equipped with features that are accessible to newcomers to animation. But Character Animator isn't the only animation app out there. In fact, if you're accessing Character Animator through Adobe Creative Cloud, you also have access to Adobe Animate and After Effects. There are also apps from other companies that offer unique features.

If all of this software can create animation, why choose Character Animator? Can you use more than one piece of software? To help make this easier to understand, this chapter will cover the following:

- What is Adobe Animate?
- What is After Effects?
- Other popular animation apps

The focus of this book is on Character Animator, and so we will only cover topics necessary for working in the app. If you don't have access to Animate or After Effects, don't worry. Any files we create with these apps in the book will be exported and made import-ready for Character Animator. With that said, let's get going!

What is Adobe Animate?

Adobe Animate is one of the most well-known animation apps. You may know of it under a different name, but it cemented its popularity in the 1990s. In this section, we will cover the following:

- A brief history of Adobe Animate
- The strengths of Animate
- Using Animate with our Character Animator productions

With that said, let's take a quick trip back in time.

Brief history of Adobe Animate

Adobe Animate is one of the longest-running 2D animation apps to exist, at least for the average consumer. While we won't spend much time on its history, it's always good to have a bit of context.

Created in 1996 under the name FutureSplash Animator, the app has undergone name changes and ownership changes from FutureWave Software, to Macromedia, and finally, to Adobe. The most popular name for this app was Flash.

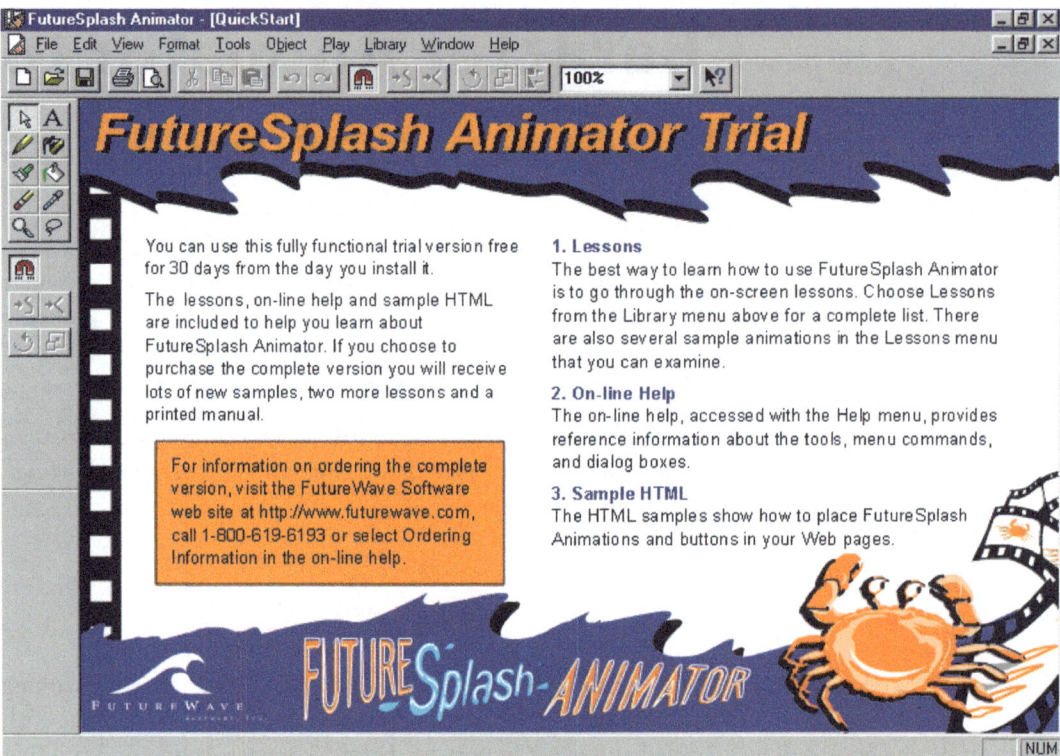

Figure 2.1: Trial splash screen for the original FutureSplash Animator

The app saw a golden age of sorts under Macromedia in the late 1990s and early 2000s with its lightweight .swf file format. These interactive browser-based animations and games lead to a wealth of content, even helping to create the likes of Newgrounds, a popular animation community that has existed for over two decades.

Figure 2.2: Newgrounds is responsible for the popularity of Flash in the early 2000s

Many today refer to animations created in any consumer software as Flash animations. While perfect for older browsers and slower internet speeds, Flash, or rather Flash-based browser media, eventually fell out of vogue when faster and more secure content streaming went mainstream.

Figure 2.3: An early Flash cartoon created in 2002 by the author

It's primarily used now as a traditional animation app, which is why Adobe changed the name to Animate a few years ago. Steady updates have added new tools and features, making it more in line with other popular animation apps.

The strengths of Adobe Animate

There are a few things Animate can do to help with modern animations. Here, we will be covering the following strengths of the app:

- Frame-by-frame animation
- Symbols
- Drawing tools

Arguably, there are more strengths to the app than listed here. But these are some of the main features.

Frame-by-frame animation

Because of the way you can add keyframes and use the draw tools, Animate is one of the best apps out there for frame-by-frame animation. This is the art of literally going frame by frame, using onion skins (or references from previous frames) to draw and design your animation.

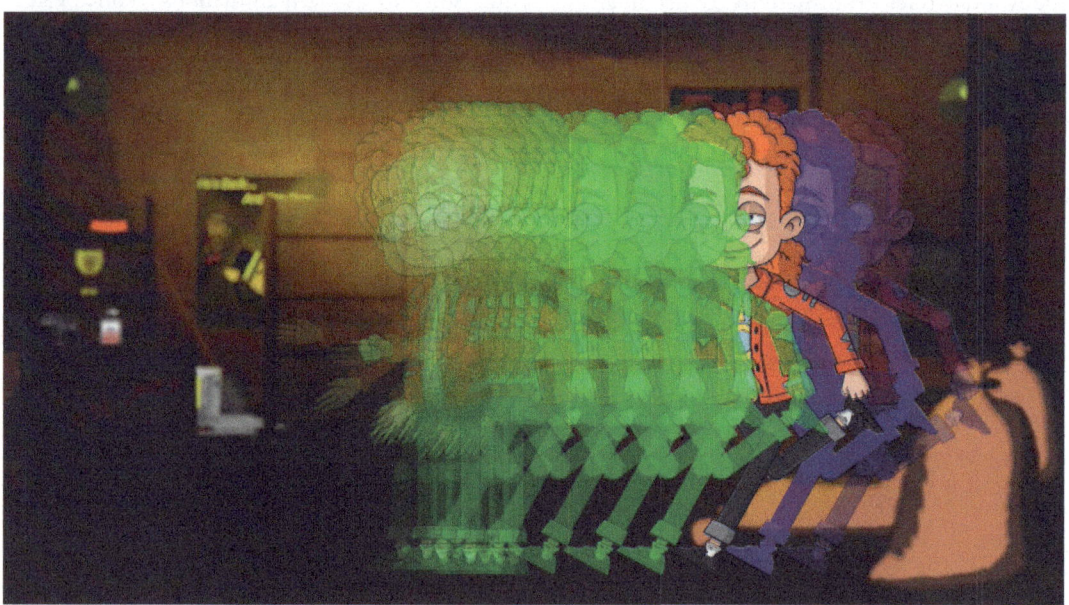

Figure 2.4: An example of onion skinning in Animate

This is a traditional way of working. It's time-consuming, but the payoff is worth it if your patience and skills are up to the task. A great example of this type of animation is the work of Harry Partridge, a prolific YouTube animator. Check out his work here: `https://www.youtube.com/user/HarryPartridge`.

Symbols

Symbols allow the user to create reusable looping animations and dictate when an animation should jump to a certain frame, stop playing, and other helpful tasks.

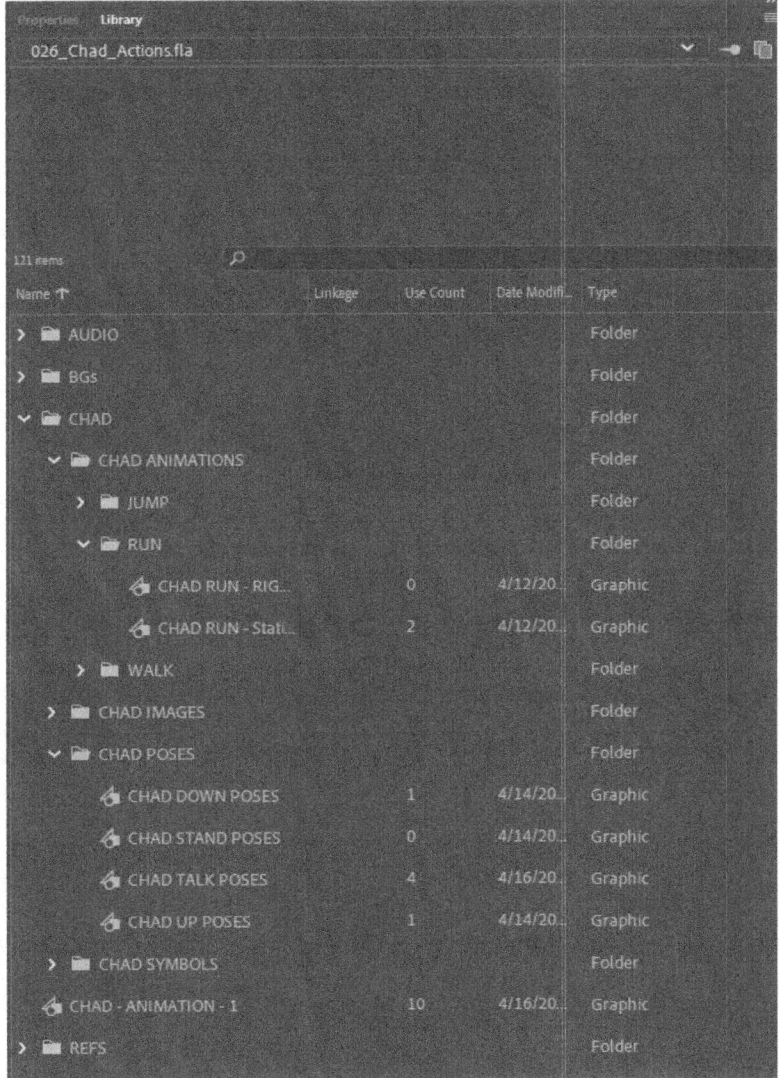

Figure 2.5: An example of an Animate project's library

The Library also allows for the easy transfer of assets between Animate projects. These libraries can be used across multiple episodes in a series, as an example.

Drawing tools

Animate has some nice freehand-based drawing tools. The vectors you create can be shaped and molded through beziers and points.

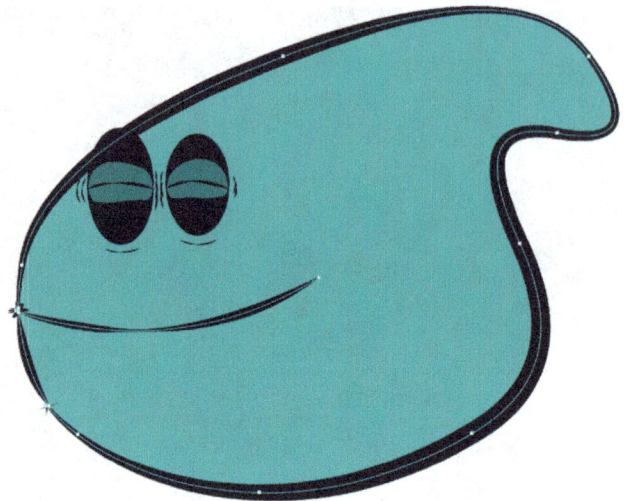

Figure 2.6: Vectors allow for smooth lines and moldable shapes

The app is also compatible with most popular tablets, allowing for pressure sensitivity.

Using Animate with Character Animator productions

So, that leads us to the important topic for this section: why should we consider adding Animate to our toolset when using Character Animator? Here are a few of the things that Animator can help you with:

- Designing characters and assets
- Creating animations and effects
- Bringing character animator assets into animate

Animate can intake rendered Character Animator files as well, allowing for two workflows.

Designing characters and assets

As discussed previously, Adobe Animate has a strong lineup of drawing tools, allowing for both freehand and shape-based art. With the ability to export images, vectors, and PNG sequences, we can bring both animated and still art into our Character Animator productions.

What is Adobe Animate? 27

Figure 2.7: An example of a more complicated character design in Animate

Alternatively, we can export our Character Animator animations and bring them into Animate. This is once again done by exporting the Character Animator content as a PNG sequence.

Importing Animate art into Character Animator

If you have a copy of Animate installed, you can access the `Blob_fla_example.fla` file inside of the book's example files. This is a really simple file as we just need some context before importing it into Character Animator. If you don't have a copy of Animate installed, don't worry! We have the exported file needed to import into Character Animator available in the exercise files.

This is a simple vector-based creation using Animate's draw tools. We have two groups housing eye and mouth phases. Here, is how we can get this creation over to Character Animator:

1. Go to **File** > **Publish Settings**.
2. Under **OTHER FORMATS** on the left side of the panel, click on the text **SVG Image**.
3. New options will appear on the right. Be sure to check **Optimize for Character Animator**.

28 Comparing Adobe Character Animator to Other Animation Apps

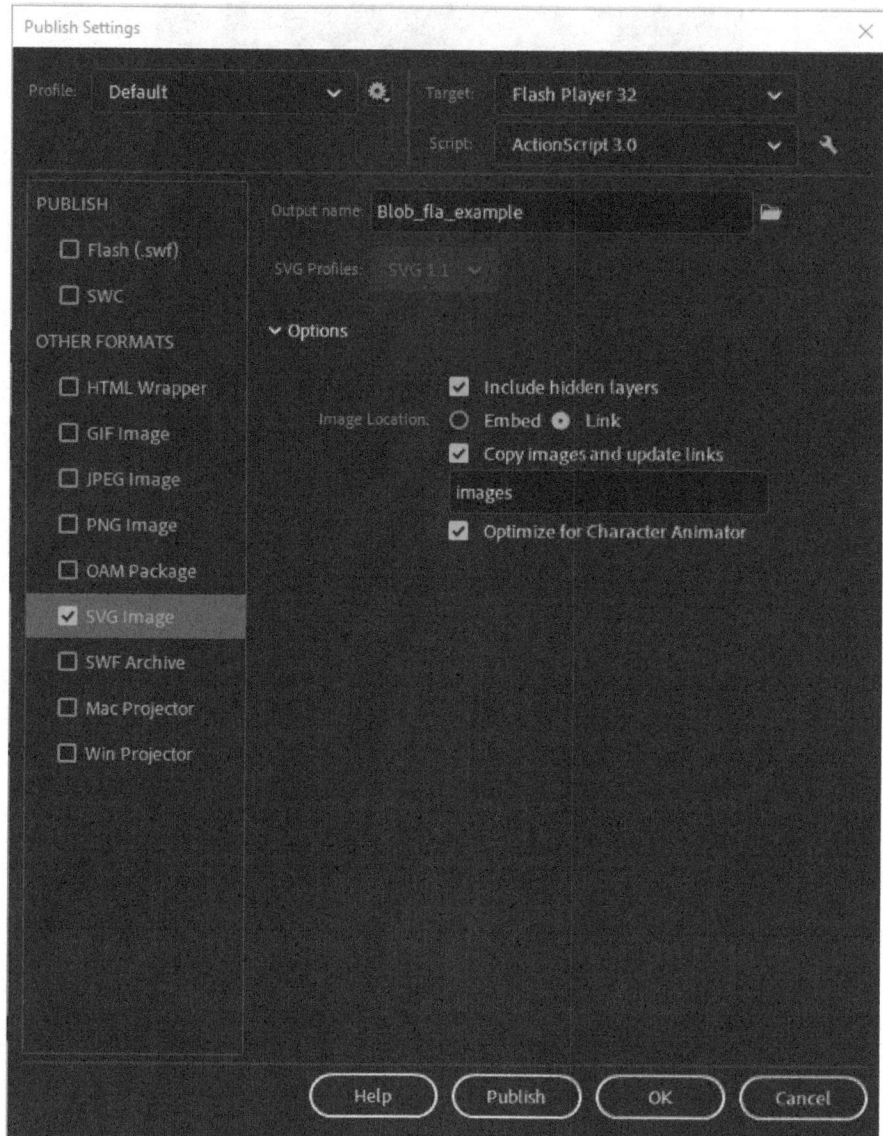

Figure 2.8: The Publish Settings panel

4. Press the **Publish** button.
5. Open Character Animator.

6. Make sure the **Rig** tab is open. The previous project we worked on will automatically open, which is fine.

Figure 2.9: The rig workspace in Character Animator

7. Double-click inside the upper left **Project** panel, or use *Ctrl + I* or ⌘ *+ I* to import a file.
8. Locate the .svg file you just exported from Animate and double-click to bring into Character Animator. Alternatively, you can look under the book's files and open `blob_fla_example.svg`.

Once imported, note how the Animate layers transfer over. This is useful, although it is lacking the groups in the original Animate file. While disappointing, we can still organize groups and other functions to properly set up the rig in Character Animator.

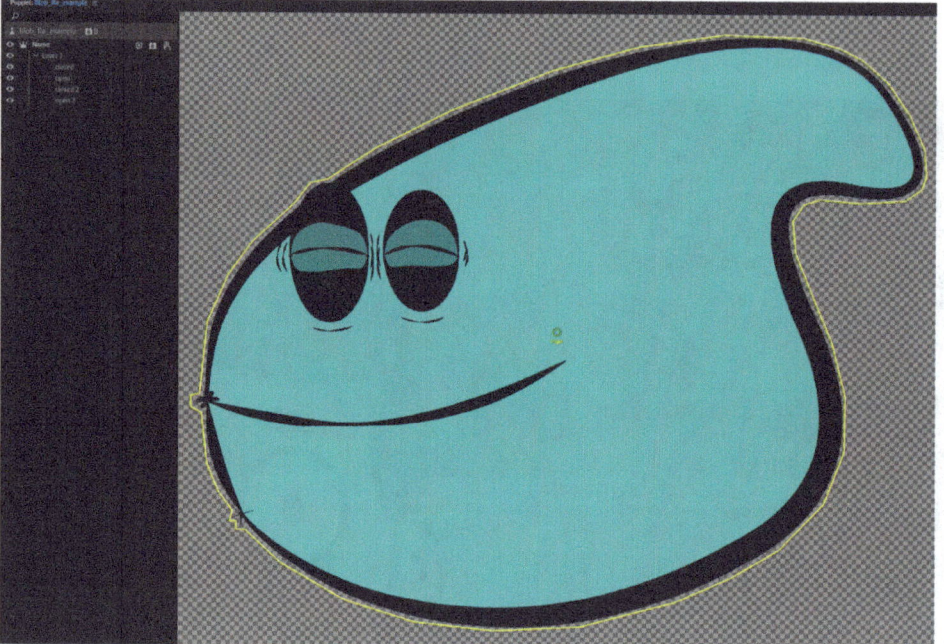

Figure 2.10: Our vector-based character imported into Character Animator

If we look at the **Puppet** panel, we will see the four poses that were brought over with the import. These will appear as layers.

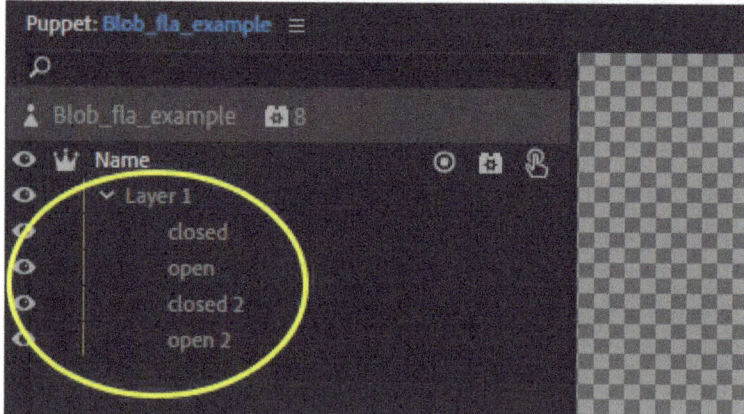

Figure 2.11: The .svg file will transfer layers over when properly exported – minus folders

We will learn more about the importance of layers in the next chapter.

Creating animations and effects

While Animate has some nice drawing tools, its primary function is to animate. It's easy to import these animated creations into Character Animator, adding even more life and detail to your productions.

Character Animator is for animating characters and building sequences. It doesn't offer much in terms of effects or particles, which is why we sometimes need to use other apps.

Once again, we will briefly look at Animate and if you don't have a copy, don't worry. The exported content is available in the book files.

Exporting and importing Animate content for Character Animator

If you open `Animated_smoke.fla` in the book files, you will see a simple puff of smoke animate across 20 frames. We are going to add this animated smoke to Character Animator.

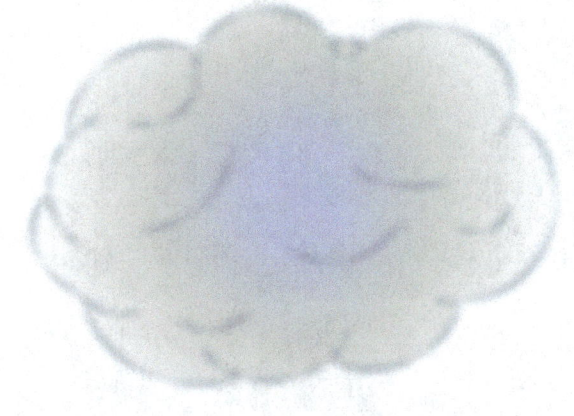

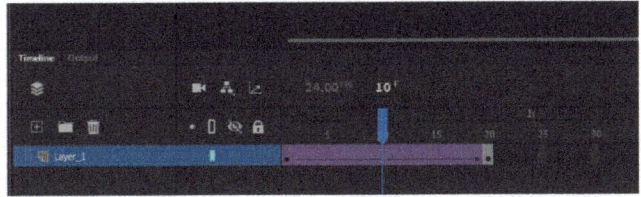

Figure 2.12: The animated puff of smoke in Animate

For importing animated content into Character Animator, image sequences will need to be exported. An image sequence is an exported sequence of frames, with each frame represented in an image. Lots of animation and video software, including Character Animator, recognize these sequences and put them together so they animate like a video clip when imported.

To export a PNG sequence of the smoke in Animate, you need to do the following:

1. Go to **File** > **Export** > **Export Movie** (*Ctrl + Alt + Shift + S* or *⌘ + ⌥ + Shift + S*).

2. Here you can choose a name and where to save the sequence. It's recommended you create a new folder to place the images in to keep everything contained and organized.

3. Before saving, make sure **Save as type**, which is located at the bottom of the save panel, is set to **PNG Sequence (*.png)**. PNGs are preferable for quality, as well as their ability to use transparent backgrounds.

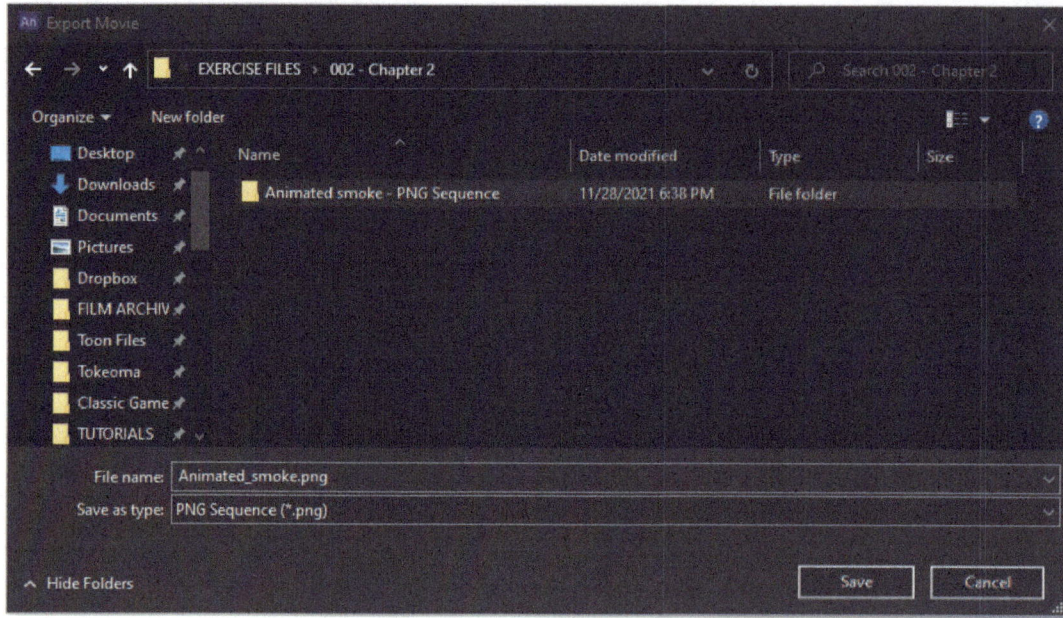

Figure 2.13: Choosing PNG Sequence (*.png) as the type

4. Once ready, press **Save** and Animate will export each frame of animation as a PNG.

How do we import this sequence into Character Animator? Unlike puppets, we can't use the traditional import method as doing so will just bring in a single image. To import a PNG sequence, you need to do the following:

1. Open Character Animator.
2. Go to **File** > **Import Cycle**.
3. A new file browser window will appear. Locate the first image of the sequence and click on it. To ensure it's the first frame, organize the files by name and select `Animate_smoke0001.png`.

What is Adobe Animate? 33

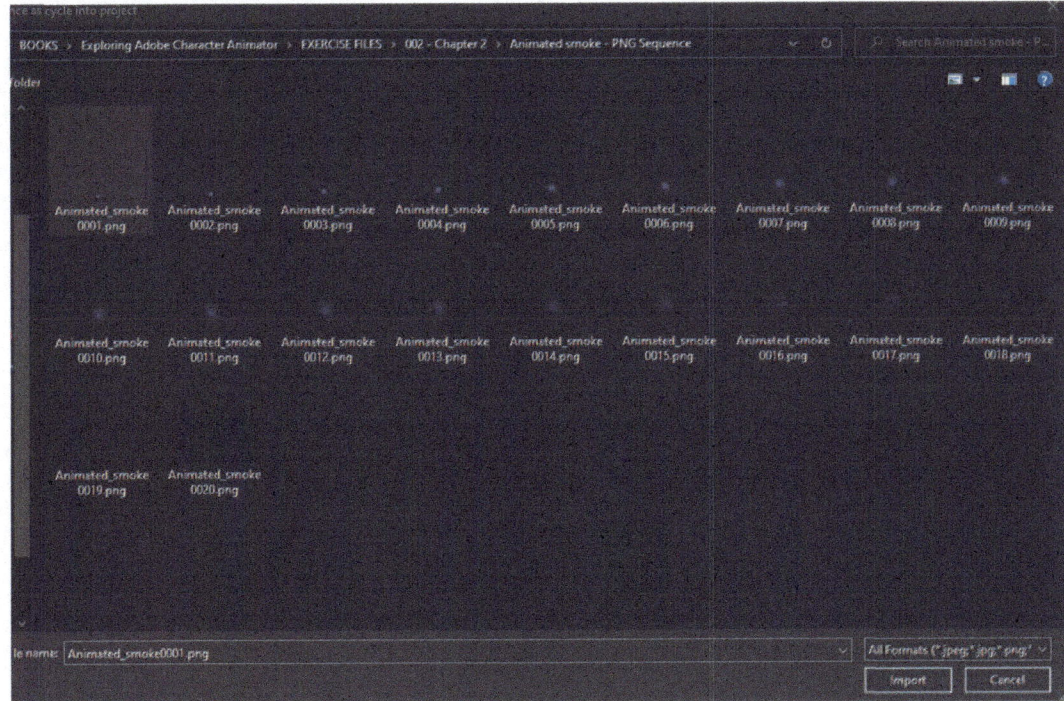

Figure 2.14: Selecting the first image is the best way to ensure all files are accounted for

4. After processing, the sequence will appear in your project browser.
5. Click the **Record** tab on the top.
6. Click and drag the sequence from the project panel to the bottom of the screen (this is where the timeline is located).
7. With the sequence on the timeline, you should be able to hit the **Play** button and see the smoke animate out. Make sure you're at the beginning of the timeline before hitting play to see the result.

This not only works with smoke effects but also with anything else you may choose to animate. As long as the file result ends up as an image sequence, Character Animator can decipher the cycle.

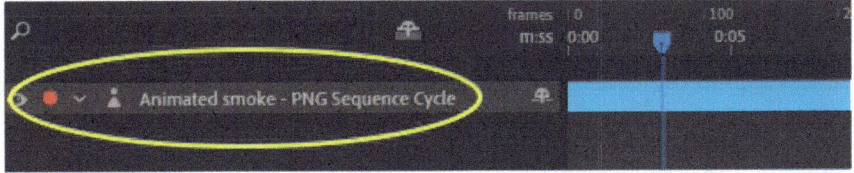

Figure 2.15: The smoke PNG sequence on the Character Animator timeline

To sum up this part, Adobe Animate is a great app and can create amazing content all on its own. But it can also be a great companion app for Character Animator. Keep this in mind if one of your productions needs outside content.

What is Adobe After Effects?

After Effects has lots of applications. Many people don't use it only for animation, but rely on its powerful video editing tools to create stellar pieces of media. In terms of functionality, it shares some similarities with Animate. But with After Effects' wide range of uses, there are more tools and menus to rummage through. We're just going to touch on some basics in terms of how these additional tools and menus can bolster Character Animator productions. In this section, we will cover the following:

- A brief history of Adobe After Effects
- The strengths of After Effects
- Using After Effects with our Character Animator productions

A brief history of Adobe After Effects

Like Animate, After Effects started its life in the early 1990s, under the Company of Science and Art. Originally, the application gained attention for its use of layers, masks, and keyframes, with very humble beginnings compared to how big it grew.

Figure 2.16: The After Effects app logo

As the app continued to develop and undergo changes in ownership, After Effects built up its reputation as a high-tier consumer video compositing application with a suite of animation tools.

The strengths of After Effects

After Effects has a lot of uses and like Animate, it can be a bit overwhelming to get a handle on. Breaking it down, After Effects is effective in the following areas:

- Compositing and grading media
- Motion graphics
- Expanding toolset and capability

Compositing and grading media

After Effects allows for limitless creative control with masking, coloring, and adding special effects to video or animation. If you have a copy of After Effects installed, you can open the included file, `blob_ae_example.aep`. As you can see in the following figure, our blob character got an upgrade: a blur, glow, and gradient were added.

Figure 2.17: Left – No effects. Right – glow, blur, and gradient effects

That's not even scratching the surface of what we could do. You can target individual layers, create compositions, use keyframe animation for custom dynamic effects, and so much more.

Motion graphics

After Effects is great for creating animated titles or moving shapes. With the ability to work in 3D space and a camera, plus dozens of helpful tools, creating eye-catching animated shapes and text is a pretty simple process. If you wish to view an example, check out `hello_3D_text.aep`.

Figure 2.18: After Effects allows for rudimentary 3D, light, and camera effects

Drawing meshes allows for morph effects and rudimentary character rigging. Add functionality with Cinema4D, a 3D modeling app, and you have a lot to dig into, if you wish.

Expanding toolset and capability

After Effects has hundreds of free and paid plugins, you can use to expand the app's capabilities. This includes the ability to create frame-by-frame animations (similar to Animate), add bone tools for true character control, and add custom or expanded effects.

Using After Effects with our Character Animator productions

Ultimately, what can After Effects do for our Character Animator productions? Here are a few basic examples:

- Grading a scene you animated in Character Animator
- Adding visual effects (such as a glow) to characters or props
- Creating animations for import into Character Animator
- Importing Character Animator animations to After Effects
- Camera movements in 3D space

Another nice thing about After Effects, is it can read Character Animator files and import them in. This means you can import animations for Character Animator directly into After Effects with no need for rendering beforehand. We will look at a few of these examples once we finish recording an animation in Character Animator.

Other popular animation apps

There are many animation apps from other developers with various strengths. The downside to these is they are not in Adobe Creative Cloud. However, some of these apps are free or offer trials, which is nice.

As you continue to learn animation, you may find it beneficial to check out some of these other apps to see if they can help with your productions:

- Moho (`https://moho.lostmarble.com`)
- Toon Boom (`https://www.toonboom.com`)
- Blender (`https://www.blender.org`)
- Cinema 4D (`https://www.maxon.net/en/cinema-4d`)
- OpenToonz (`https://opentoonz.github.io/e/`)
- TVPaint Animation (`https://www.tvpaint.com`)

Again, these are completely optional and something to keep in the back of your mind.

Summary

Remember, we require none of the previously covered apps to animate cartoons with Character Animator. They can enhance your production and with Animate and After Effects being available on Creative Cloud, it doesn't hurt to have some extra knowledge. Just remember the following:

- Animate is great for traditional animation, such as frame-by-frame
- After Effects allows us to add effects and polish to our productions
- You can use the previously covered apps with Character Animator, or vice versa
- Other applications have their own strengths and may be useful if the Adobe apps aren't a good fit

In the next chapter, we are going to begin our Character Animator production by preparing a PSD-based character for rigging!

3
Preparing a Character Rig in Photoshop

In the previous chapter, we imported a `.svg` file into Character Animator. While the app reads this file format, it's not the most ideal way to work. What's recommended is importing `.psd` files. Character Animator can read these files directly, bringing in not only the layers but also any groups and special tags as well.

It's also important to have access to an application that can read and edit these files. Luckily, if you have a subscription to Adobe Creative Cloud, you have access to Photoshop, which is what we will use in this chapter. Here is what we will cover:

- Designing your character
- Streamlining and renaming layers
- Organizing with normal and independent groups
- Putting the hair in its own layer
- Cleaning up PSD layers

Be sure to have Character Animator and Photoshop (or an app that can work with `.psd` files) ready to go. Once you're ready, we can begin!

Designing your character

This book will not go into the art of character design in depth. It's a vast topic that goes beyond what we're covering in this book, but there are some simple guidelines to follow if you do plan to design your own characters. Even if you have someone else design your characters, you may find that their way of dealing with layers doesn't quite fit the way Character Animator thinks. That means you may have to go in and adjust the layout before you can move over to the rigging phase.

Figure 3.1: A concept sketch of the character we will be animating

If you decide to design your own character, here are some tips to keep in mind:

- Draw all facial features on their own layers. This includes eyes, eyelids, and mouth poses.
- Create groups or folders for layers meant to trigger an animation. This includes things such as mouth poses, eye blinks, head turns, and hand poses.
- You can create toggle-able props or parts of the character, such as glasses, clothes, hairstyles, and so forth.
- Keep limbs separate and kept to one layer each.
- Naming your layers a certain way will help Character Animator interpret how parts of the rig react. We will see this soon when we look at the book's character .psd file.
- You can add physics to layers. So, if you want to allow fabric or hair to move, be sure to accommodate that when drawing.
- You can always look at the complete character .psd file in this book as a reference.
- We can add additional layers as long as names and order don't conflict.

As you move through this chapter and work with the book's character rigs, it should help develop an understanding of the art of character design.

Streamlining and renaming layers

Now is the time to look at our first character rig, Chaz the TV Host. Another artist designed this character, so we will need to go in and make sure the overall layer structure will work for our purposes.

You may find it easier to follow along with `body_part_guide_ch3.pdf`, which is included in the chapter's exercise files. This PDF is a screenshot of the character fully assembled for this chapter.

Open the `Chaz_Host_v1.psd` file so we can begin looking over this character design. Again, we will use Photoshop for this process.

Figure 3.2: Chaz is a TV show host who knows how to captivate an audience

Chaz is not only incredibly handsome but he also has a pretty complex layer list. This is how the artist originally laid out the file.

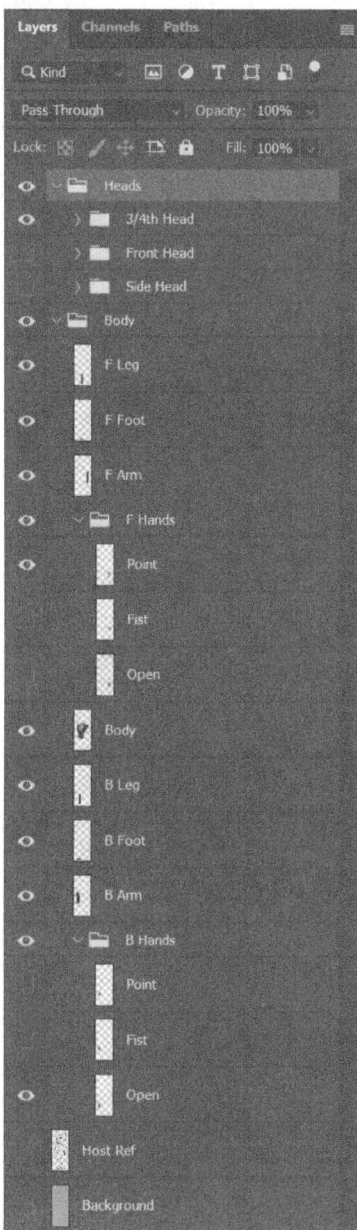

Figure 3.3: A preview of Chaz's layers

When using some other animation apps, the layout would work just fine, but here, we're going to need to do some streamlining to ensure this process goes as smoothly as possible when importing it into Character Animator.

Creating a character group

The first thing we are going to do is place the character inside its own group. Here's how we're going to do it:

1. Select the **Heads** group by clicking on it once.
2. Hold down the *Shift* key and click the bottom layer labeled **Background**.
3. Right-click and choose **Group from Layers…** from the options list:

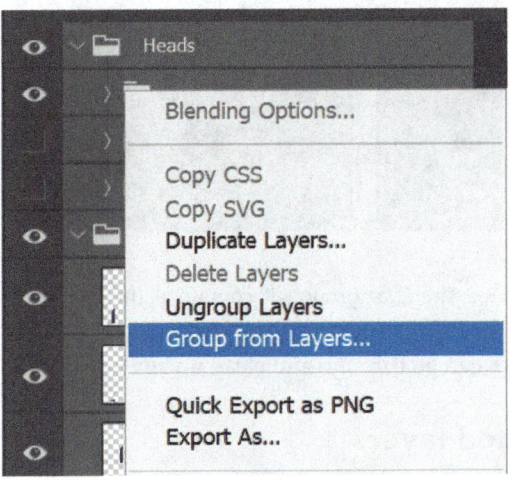

Figure 3.4: Along with Group from Layers…, we have other useful options too

4. A new dialog window will appear. Enter Chaz into the top **Name** field and click **OK**:

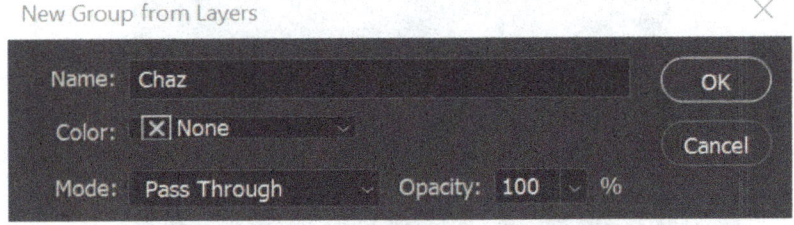

Figure 3.5: The New Group from Layers dialog box

You should now see a new group containing all other character layers:

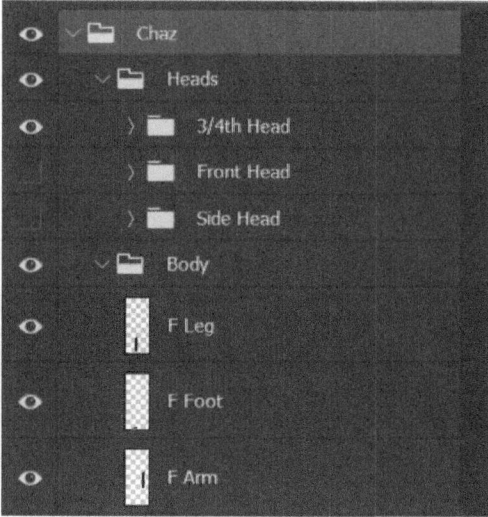

Figure 3.6: The Chaz group will contain all the character layers

With this group in place, we can go through and clean up any layers we don't need.

Removing unneeded layers

Depending on your character's design, there may be some layers left over. We can simplify our layer list and overall make rigging easier. With Chaz, the two bottom layers, **Host Ref** and **Background**, are unneeded:

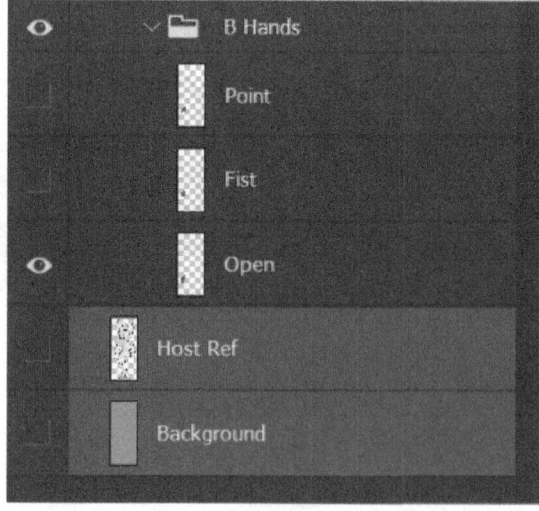

Figure 3.7: Host Ref and Background are currently hidden and not needed

The **Host Ref** and **Background** layers are leftovers from the design process. Let's remove these layers:

1. Click once on **Host Ref.**
2. Hold down the *Shift* key and click **Background**.
3. Press the *Delete* key on your keyboard (or click the trash can icon in the **Layers** panel):

Figure 3.8: The trash can icon is located on the bottom right of the Layers panel

Depending on the design of your characters, you may find that other layers are unneeded, but these two are the only ones for this rig. With that taken care of, we can focus on the next task.

Merging and renaming the limbs

It's best to make sure the limbs each sit on one layer – meaning that if you have separated an arm into two layers, let's say a bicep and forearm, you'll want to go in and merge those two layers.

Let's look at Chaz for this example. In the **Body** group, you will see four layers making up the arms:

- **F Bicep**
- **F Forearm**
- **B Bicep**
- **B Forearm**

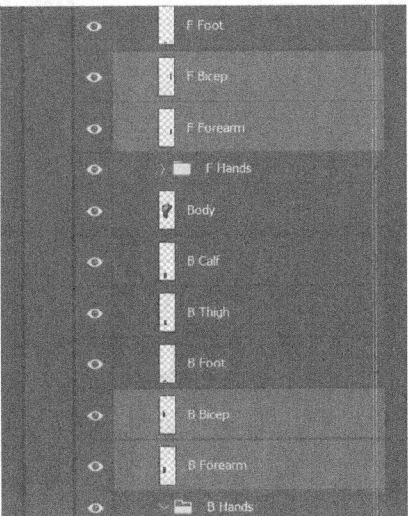

Figure 3.9: The arm layers

The layers labeled with **F** stand for the front while **B** is for the back. There are different ways you can label your layers to show order, such as left (**L**) or right (**R**). Since the body is a 3/4th view, it makes sense for us to use front and back labels. You will see this labeling with other layers as we continue to work.

The goal here is to merge the arm layers labeled **F** together and then do the same for **B**. We will start at the top of the layers list and work our way down. To do this, let's see the following steps:

1. Click on **F Bicep**.
2. Hold down the *Shift* key.
3. Click **F Forearm**.
4. Right-click and choose **Merge Layers** from the list:

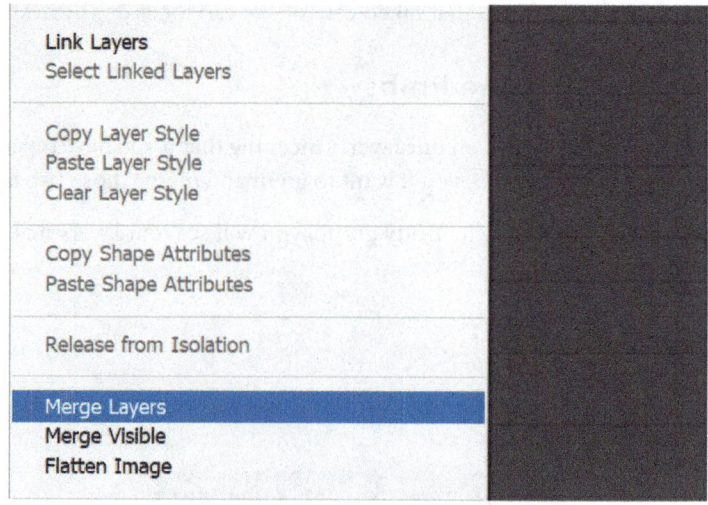

Figure 3.10: The menu when you right-click on a layer

You should now see a new layer combining the assets in each layer we selected. The layer will also adopt the name of the top layer from the merger. For us, that means the layer is now labeled **F Bicep**:

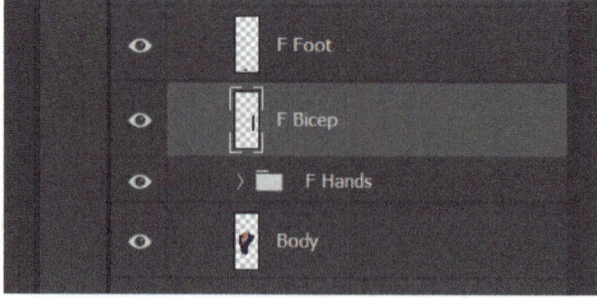

Figure 3.11: The two arm pieces are now one layer

Streamlining and renaming layers   47

Let's make this a more accurate name for now so that it's easier to identify. We will end up changing it again in the next section when we group items. To rename the layer, see the following:

1. Double-click on the name of the layer and the name should highlight in blue (don't double-click on the thumbnail of the layer or you'll open the **Layer Style** panel).
2. Rename the layer **F Arm** and hit *Enter* on your keyboard:

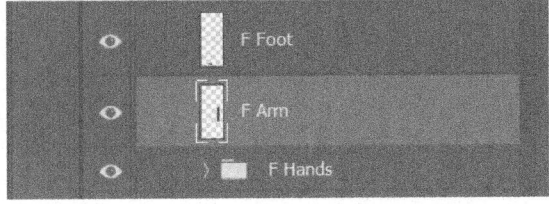

Figure 3.12: F Bicep changed to F Arm

You will now need to go in, merge the limbs, and rename them following the same steps. As a reminder, here's what you'll need to do:

1. Merge **B Bicep** and **B Forearm** and rename it **B Arm**.
2. Merge **F Calf** and **F Thigh** and rename it **F Leg**.
3. Merge **B Calf** and **B Thigh** and rename it **B Leg**:

Figure 3.13: The limbs are now reduced to four layers

Once you have finished merging, we will need to create four separate groups for each limb. Not only will we be placing limbs in these folders but also the feet and hands as well. Here's the easiest way to do this:

1. Click **F Leg**, hold the *Shift* key, and click **F Foot**. This will select both layers:

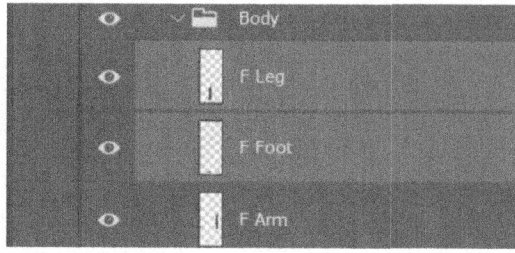

Figure 3.14: Legs and hands are separated

2. Right-click on one of the selected layers and choose **Group** from **Layers**.
3. A new panel will appear allowing us to name the new group. Choose **F Leg** and click **OK**:

Figure 3.15: F Leg is an appropriate name for this group

4. Repeat these steps for the remaining three limbs:

    I. Group **F Arm** and **F Hands** to create the new group, **F Arm**.

    II. Group **B Leg** and **B Foot** to create the new group, **B Leg**.

    III. Group **B Arm** and **B Hands** to create the new group, **B Arm**:

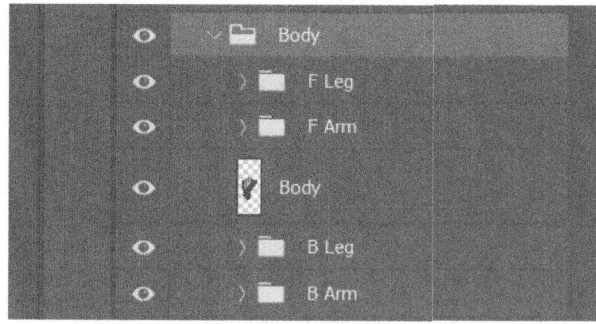

Figure 3.16: Four groups making up each limb

With those new groups in place, we can turn our attention toward the eyes.

Reorganizing the eye layers

If we look at the eyes, which are in the three head groups, you will find we have a few things going on. Let's focus on the **3/4th Head** group first. Be sure to press the arrow next to the group to expand the layers to see everything. Here are the elements that the artist included for the eyes:

- Whites of eyes
- Eyelids
- A blink phase
- Pupils

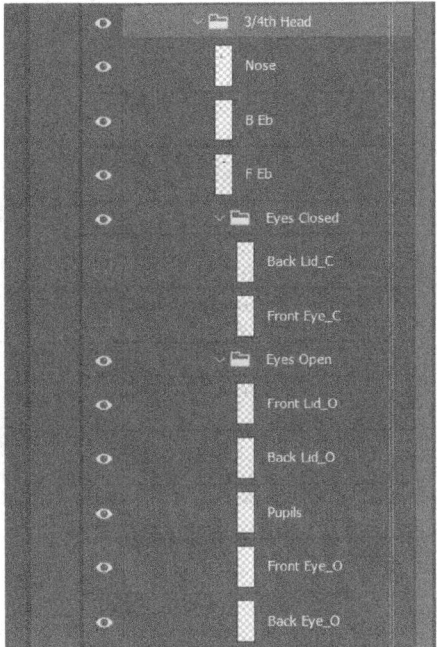

Figure 3.17: A preview of the original layer list for the ¾ Head

These layers live in two primary groups. This may be a good setup for other animation software, but Character Animator needs something a bit more streamlined to function properly.

Separating the pupils in the ¾ head phase

The artist has included both pupils on a single layer, but Character Animator can control each pupil separately. Plus, the software has an easier time understanding what the layers do when they're separated.

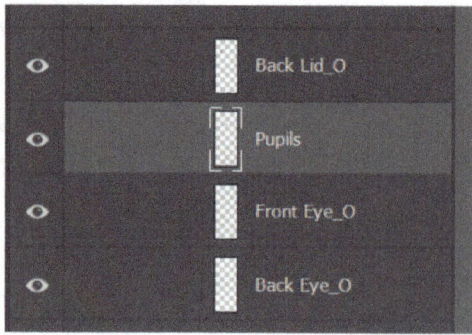

Figure 3.18: The pupils are currently sharing one layer

Here's what we need to do:

1. Click on the **Pupils** layer.
2. Select the **Rectangular Marquee Tool** option (*M* on the keyboard):

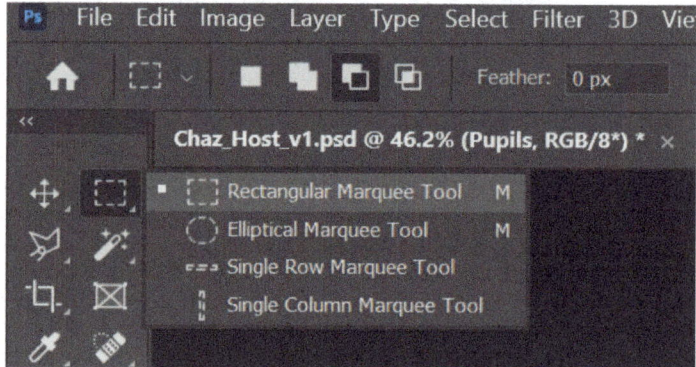

Figure 3.19: Holding down on the second tool grants you access to a variety of selection tools

3. Click and drag your selection area around the eye. This will ensure the pupil is fully selected:

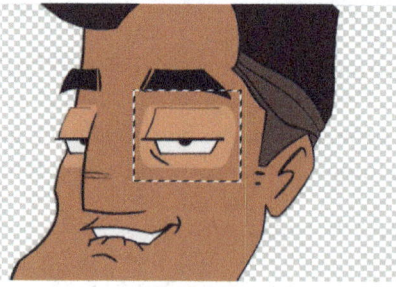

Figure 3.20: Selecting the entire area of the eye

4. Cut the pupil out of the layer by using *Ctrl + X* (or ⌘ + *X*).
5. Use *Ctrl + Shift + V* or ⌘ + *Shift + V* to **Paste in Place**.

This will remove the front pupil and place it in its own layer labeled **Layer 1** in the same spot as it was before.

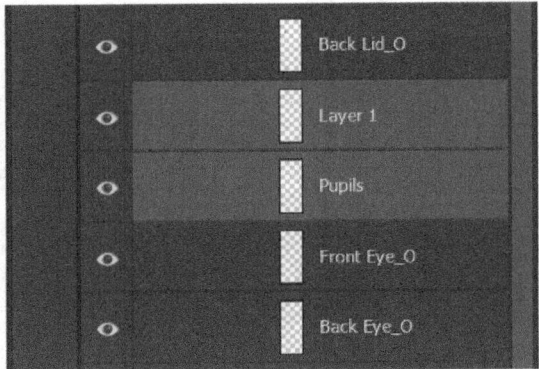

Figure 3.21: Layer 1 contains the newly pasted pupil

> **Note**
> There are two ways to paste in Photoshop. **Paste** will place the copied item in the center of the canvas while **Paste in Place** will place the item exactly where you had it before. That's why we use **Paste in Place** here, as it saves time and is more accurate.

Finally, let's rename the layers so they're easier to identify. Let's rename them as follows:

- **Layer 1** to **F Pupil**
- **Pupils** to **B Pupil**

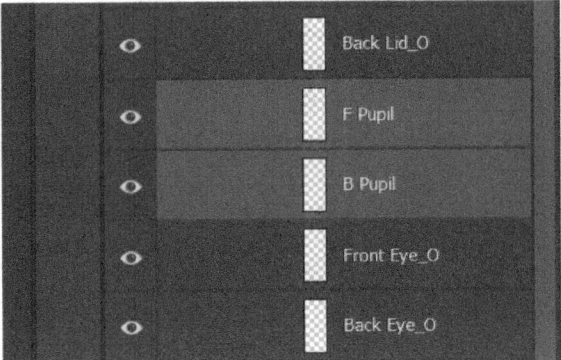

Figure 3.22: F Pupil and B Pupil are much easier to identify

With that complete, we can look at building a blink phase.

Correcting the 3/4th head blink phase

As with everything else we've covered, the blinking design is fine. It just requires some rearranging.

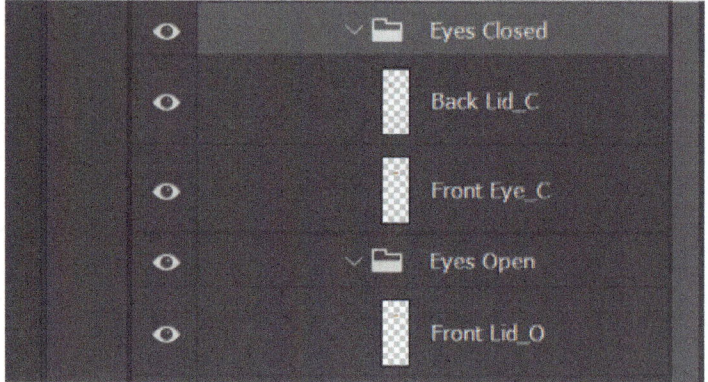

Figure 3.23: The original layout for the eyes in the ¾ head

Blinking is currently being simulated by overlaying lids on the eyes. Again, while sometimes effective, we need a different setup for Character Animator:

Figure 3.24: The blink layer overlays the open eyes with this design

As with the pupils, each closed eye will be on its own layer. To put this in working order, see the following:

1. Locate **Front Eye_O** and **Back Eye_O** on the layers panel. They're located under the **Eyes Open** group.
2. Duplicate the layers in place by using **Copy** with *Ctrl + C* or *⌘ + C* and **Paste in Place** with *Ctrl + Shift + V* or *⌘ + Shift + V*:

Figure 3.25: The duplicate eye layers

You should have two copies of each eye layer. Now, we want to take those lids that go over the whites of the eyes and combine them with these newly duplicated layers.

3. Drag **Front Eye_C**, which is located in the **Eyes_Closed** folder, right above the first **Front Eye_O** layer listed.

4. Drag **Back Lid_C**, also located in the **Eyes Closed** folder, above the first **Back Eye_O** layer listed:

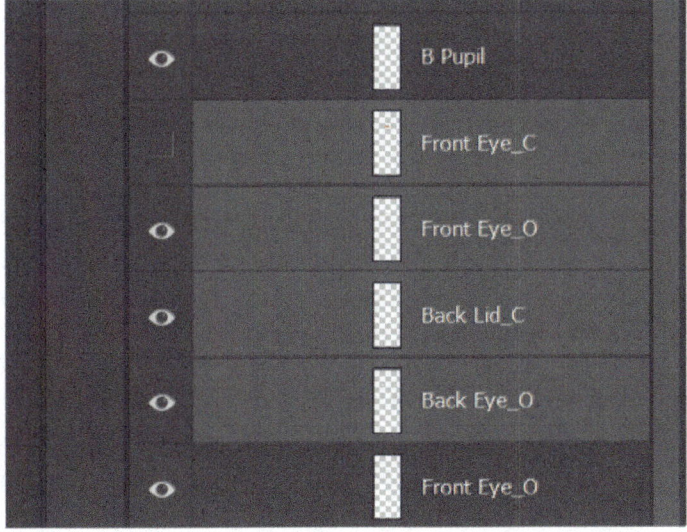

Figure 3.26: The eyebrow and eye layers properly lined up

5. Select **Front Eye_C** and **Front Eye_O**, right-click, and choose **Merge Layers**.
6. Rename the new layer **F Blink**.
7. Select **Back Lid_C** and **Back Eye_O**, right-click, and choose **Merge Layers**.
8. Rename the new layer **B Blink**.

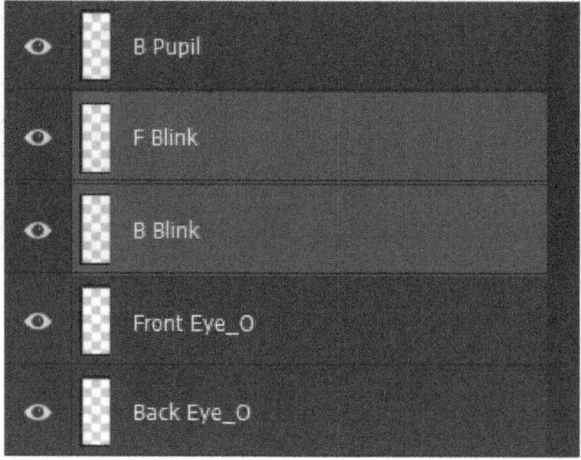

Figure 3.27: F Blink and B Blink after merging and renaming

With that, we now have two layers, each representing a blinking eye.

> **Note**
> When merging layers, always make sure they are all visible with **Opacity** set to 100%. If you merge an invisible or transparent layer with another, you will be unable to adjust after the fact.

Creating eyes for the front view

Now, we need to correct the eyes for the front view. This process will be similar to the previous one for correcting the 3/4th view blink and pupils. Here's what we need to do:

1. Collapse the ¾ **Head** group and hide it by clicking on the eye icon to the left of the layer.
2. Make sure **Front Head** is visible and expanded so we can see its contents.

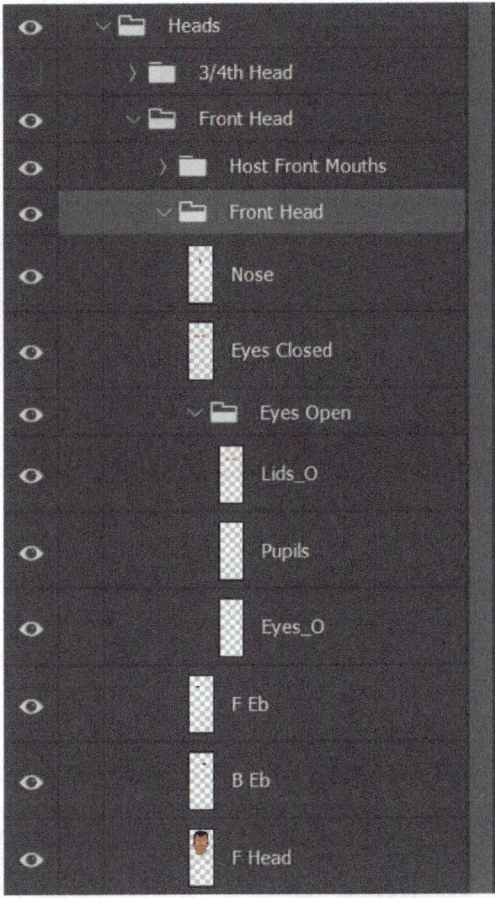

Figure 3.28: Front Head's current contents

3. Under **Front Head** is another folder with the same name, called **Front Head**. Let's expand that folder and locate **Eyes Closed**.
4. Select the left eye with the **Rectangle Marquee Tool** option (*M*).
5. Use *Ctrl* + *X* or ⌘ + *X* to cut and *Ctrl* + *Shift* + *V* or ⌘ + *Shift* + *V* to paste in place, putting the left eye on its own layer.
6. Rename the new layer **L Blink** and the original layer **R Blink**.

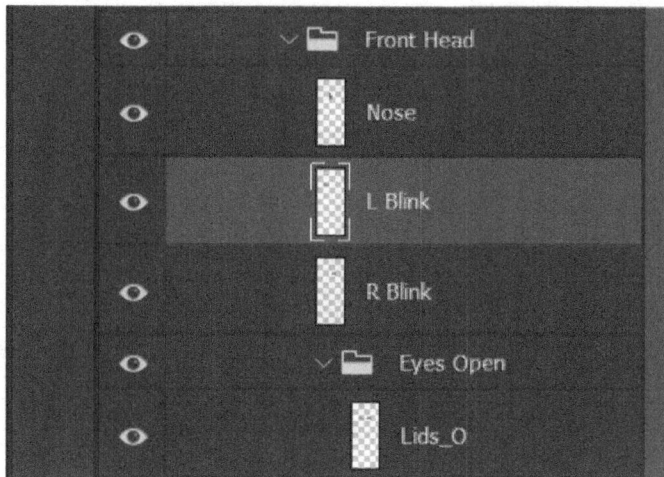

Figure 3.29: F Blink and B Blink after merging and renaming

7. Under the **Eyes Open** group, we will find three layers: **Lids_O**, **Pupils**, and **Eyes_O**.
8. Each of these will need to be separated into two layers using the same method as before:

   A. Select the left item on the layer.
   B. Cut and paste in place.
   C. Once this is complete, you should have six layers in the **Eyes Open** folder.

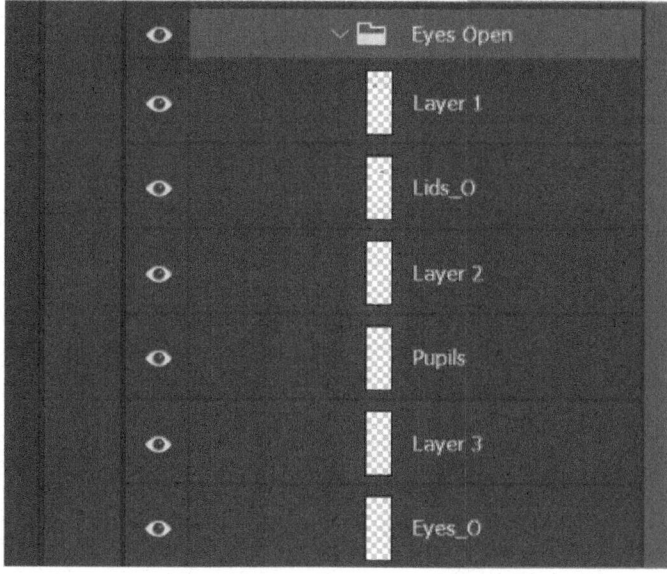

Figure 3.30: Eyes Open containing layers prior to merging

9. Rename these to indicate what belongs to the left and right eyes. Starting at the top, the names should be as follows:

   A. **L Lid**
   B. **R Lid**
   C. **L Pupil**
   D. **R Pupil**
   E. **L White**
   F. **R White**

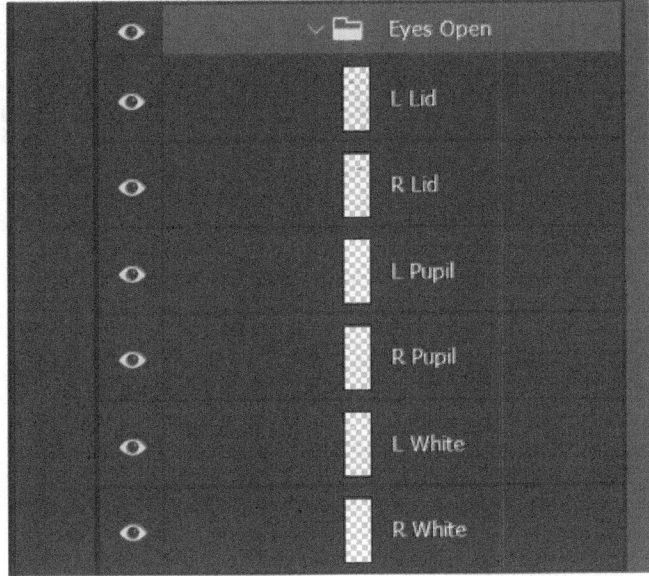

Figure 3.31: Eyes Open layers renamed properly

Luckily, the **Profile** head only shows one eye and doesn't need any separation. With all layers accounted for, we can move on to the final part of this chapter.

Organizing with normal and independent groups

While we can organize and tag to an extent in Character Animator, it's best to do as much work as possible in Photoshop. With that said, we are going to restructure and further refine the layer names. Independent groups are shown with a + symbol before the group name. These groups or layers will act differently in Character Animator, staying separate or independent from the influence of other layers. We will learn more about this in an upcoming chapter.

Creating main groups

To begin, it's best to have your character in its own group, along with the **Head** and **Body** groups housing all the layers underneath. We currently have this setup, which is a good start:

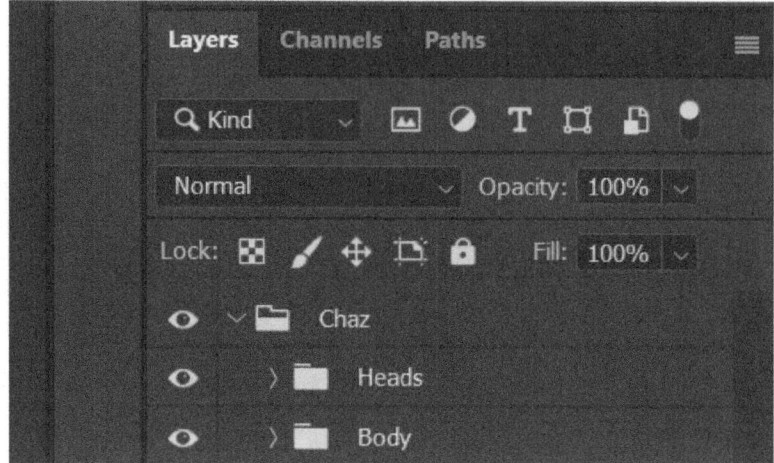

Figure 3.32: Eyes Open layers renamed properly

We will group and label most head items in a specific way:

1. Inside the **Heads** group, expand the first ¾ **Head** group.
2. Inside this group, we're going to add the following groups:
   - **+Right Eyebrow**
   - **+Left Eyebrow**
   - **+Right Eye**
   - **+Left Eye**
   - **Mouths**

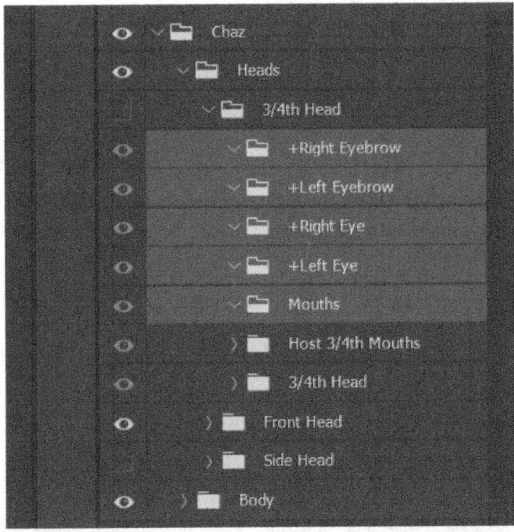

Figure 3.33: New groups added to the layer list

3. Next, expand the **Host 3/4th Mouths** group.
4. Select all the mouth poses in this group and drag them into the new **Mouths** group.
5. Delete the **Host 3/4th Mouths** group.

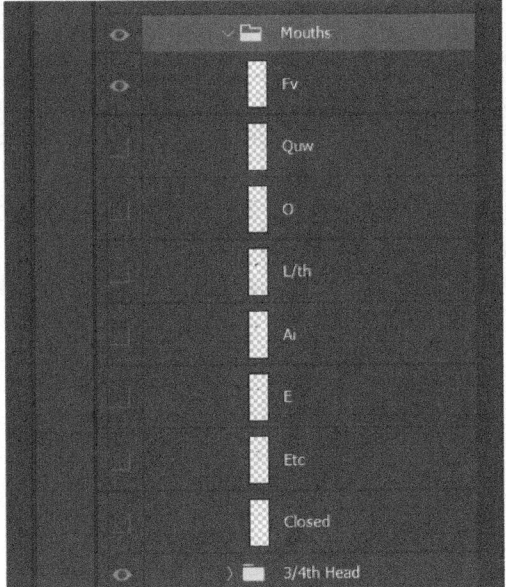

Figure 3.34: Streamlined mouth group for the ¾ view

Now, we can move on to organizing the next groups.

Adding eyebrow phases

The eyebrows can be animated by Character Animator. To achieve this, we need to set three layers for each brow: **Angry**, **Worried**, and **Neutral**:

1. Drag **B EB** into **+Right Eyebrow** and **F EB** into **+Left Eyebrow**.
2. Inside **+Right Eyebrow** and **+Left Eyebrow**, rename **B EB** and **L EB Neutral**.
3. Duplicate each **Neutral** layer twice by selecting the layer, using *Ctrl + C* or *⌘ + C*, and then pasting in place with *Ctrl + Shift + V* or *⌘ + Shift + V* twice.
4. Rename the new layers in each group **Angry** and **Worried**:

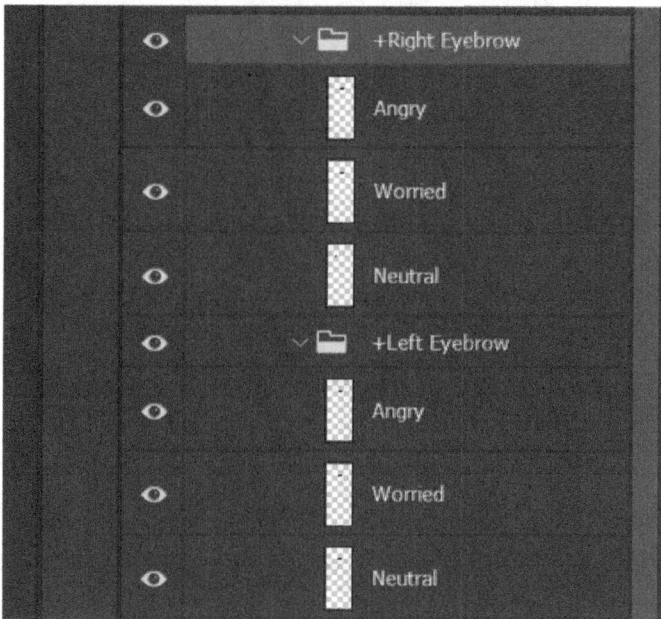

Figure 3.35: Eyebrow phases properly laid out

5. Select the **Angry** layer in **+Right Eyebrow**.
6. Press *Ctrl + T* or *⌘ + T* to engage the **Free Transform Tool** option. A selection area should appear around the canvas
7. Place the cursor on the outside of the selection area and your cursor will change to a half circle, allowing you to rotate.
8. Rotate and move the eyebrow so it's slanted down, sitting on the top of the upper eyelid:

Figure 3.36: Angry and neutral eyebrows

9. Now, select the **Worried** eyebrow and rotate and move it in the opposite direction so that it's raised and its right side is facing up:

Figure 3.37: Worried eyebrow next to the others

10. Repeat these steps for the **+Left Eyebrow** group and ensure **Angry**, **Neutral**, and **Worried** are all represented.

Figure 3.38: Both eyebrows with three phases each

While it may look odd right now, seeing three eyebrows on each eye, the eyebrows are now ready to be animated in Character Animator when the time comes.

Arranging the eye groups

This section will require less work than the previous one. We're just going to rearrange the eye layers and rename them to make them more Character Animator-friendly. Here's what we do:

1. Under the **Eyes Open** folder, select **Front Lid_O**, **F Pupil**, **F Blink**, and **Front Eye_O**.
2. Drag these into **+Left Eye**.
3. Rename the layers to the following:

    A. **Front_ Lid_O** to **Top Lid**
    B. **F Pupil** to **+Left Pupil**
    C. **F Blink** to **Left Blink**
    D. **Front Eye_O** to **Left Eye**

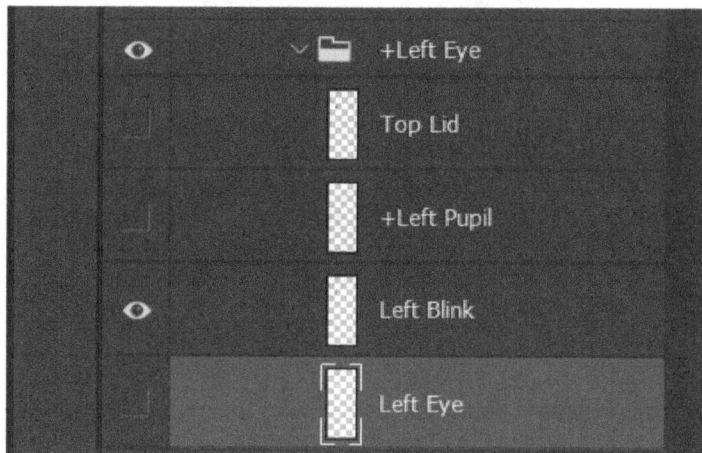

Figure 3.39: The right eye set up properly

4. Now, repeat these steps for the right eye. Drag the remaining **Open Eyes** layers into **+Right Eye** and name the layers the following:

    A. **Back Lid_O** to **Lid**
    B. **B Pupil** to **+Right Pupil**
    C. **B Blink** to **Right Blink**
    D. **Back Eye_O** to **Right Eye**

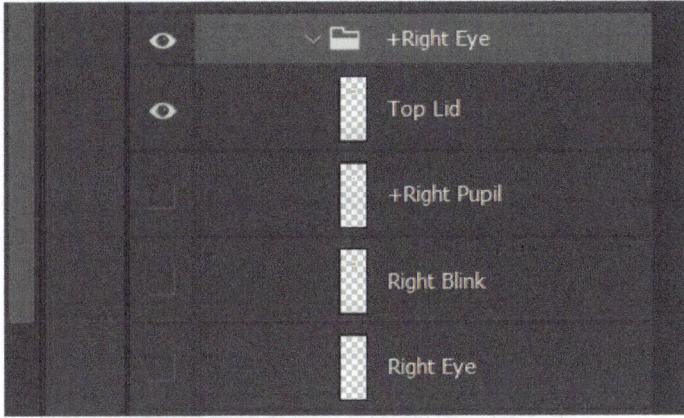

Figure 3.40: The right eye set up properly

5. Now, in the layers, under ¾th Head, let's grab the **Nose** layer and move it above the **+Right Eye** group's list.
6. For the **Head** layer, move it out of the **3/4th Head** group, to the bottom of the group list.
7. Rename the layer **Background**.

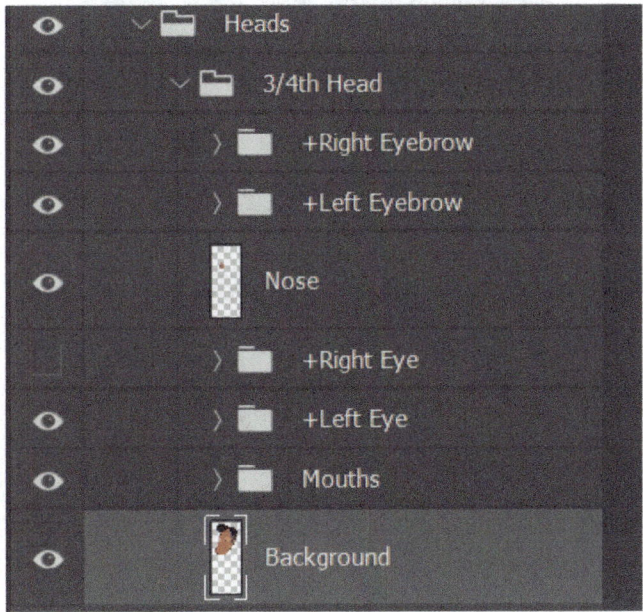

Figure 3.41: The character's head should be labeled Background

From here, you will want to go to the **Profile** and **Front** head groups and repeat the steps in this section. That includes creating three eyebrow phases, ensuring the naming conventions are accurate and all layers are in their proper groups. Look at these images to compare them to your layer list:

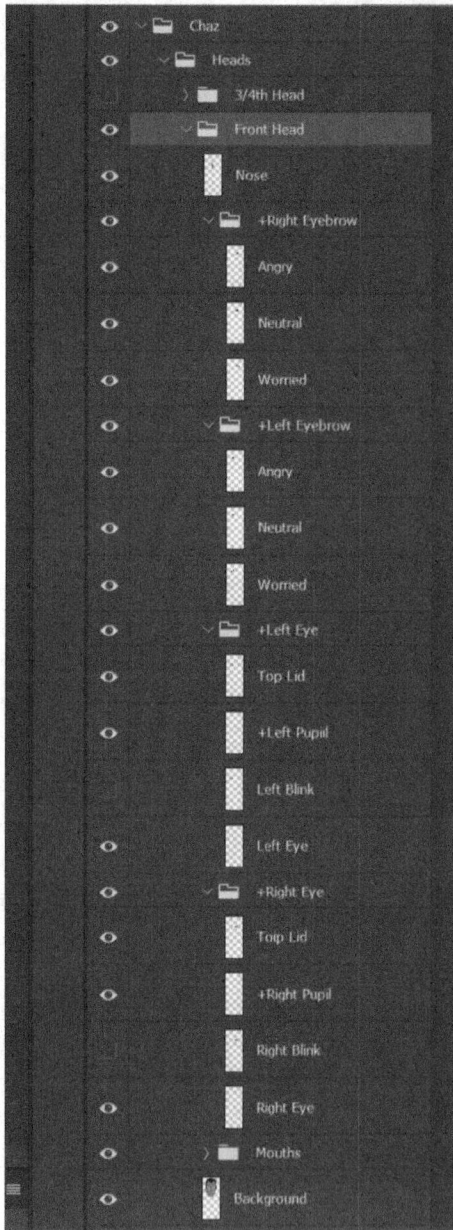

Figure 3.42: The front head's layer list

Organizing with normal and independent groups 65

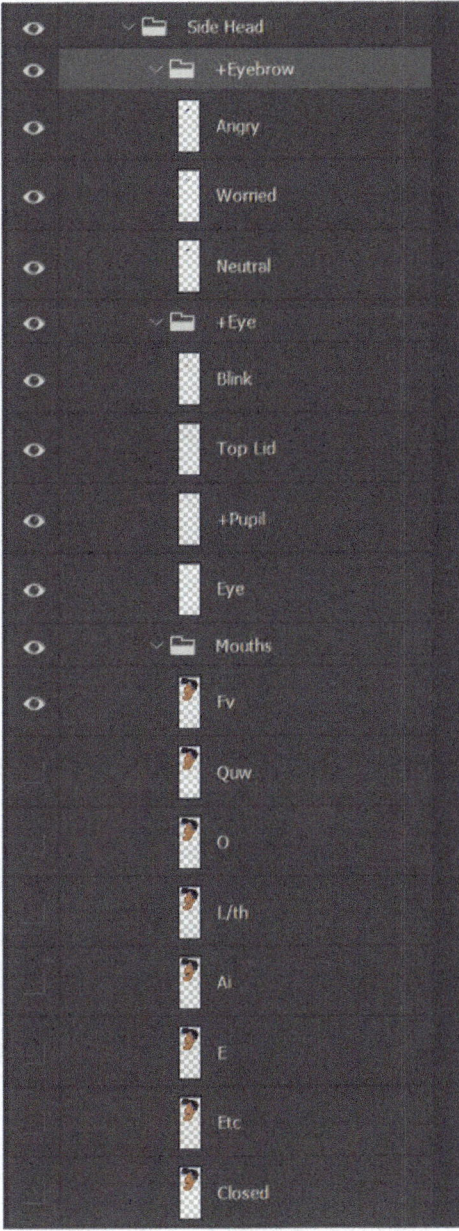

Figure 3.43: The front head set up properly

With the order now established, let's look at the hair and how we should set it up to reflect physics and other interactions in Character Animator.

Separating out the hair

Depending on the complexity of the scene and rig, you may find you want to animate the hair in its own layers, especially as we introduce more behaviors into the mix. This means we will need to go back to the rig and ensure the hair is isolated for the three head phases. To do this, see the following:

1. In Photoshop, start at the top of the layer list. In this case, expand **3/4th Head** and click **Background**.
2. You can select the hair in a variety of different ways. The quickest may be to use the **Magnetic Lasso Tool** option (cycle to it using *L* on the keyboard):

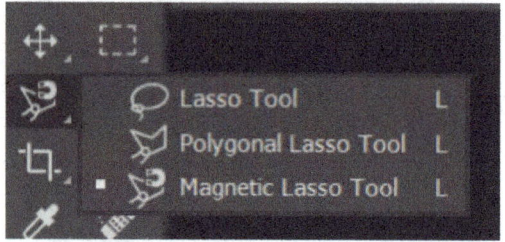

Figure 3.44: Pressing L allows you to cycle through a variety of useful selection tools

3. Click once and drag along the edge of the hair. The magnetic function should snap to the outline. If you need to add a point manually, simply left-click.
4. Keep dragging until you've selected all the hair. If a point gets added by mistake, you can move a step backward with the *Delete* key on your keyboard.

Figure 3.45: If you stay close to the hairline, the tool should easily detect what to select

> **Note**
> If you are having issues selecting the hair or other parts of the rig, you may want to try the other selection tools by pressing *W*. There are three tools to cycle through just as with the **Lasso** tools.

5. Then, cut the hair with *Ctrl + X* or *⌘ + X*.

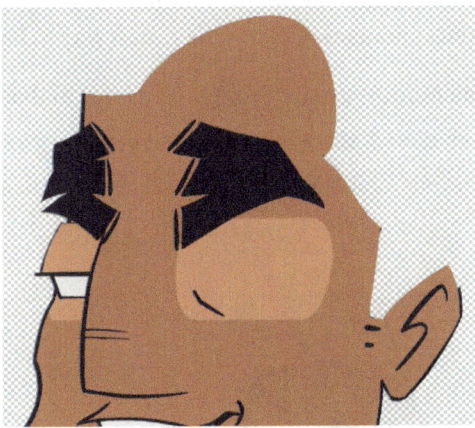

Figure 3.46: When you cut the hair off, your head will look something like this

6. Paste in place with *Ctrl + Shift + V* or *⌘ + Shift + V*.
7. Rename the new layer **Hair** and make sure it's placed above **Background** within the **3/4th Head** group.

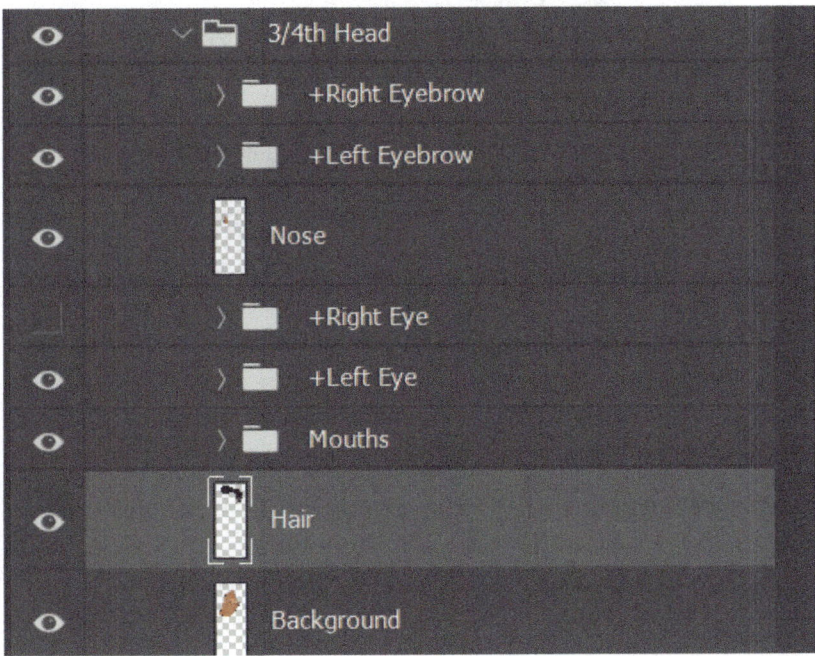

Figure 3.47: Place Hair above Background in the 3/4th Head group

You will need to repeat this process for the other two head phases as well. Isolating the front head hair will be like editing the 3/4th head. However, you will need to account for the hair from each profile phoneme (there are eight profile phonemes). Here's the easiest way to handle this task:

1. Under **Side Head** is the **Mouths** group. Select the **Fv** layer in that group.
2. Select the hair on the layer with the selection tool of choice.
3. Press the *Delete* key on your keyboard. This will remove the hair from **Fv**.

Figure 3.48: Deleting the hair from each phoneme but one

4. Go down to the next phoneme, **Quw**, and your hair should remain selected. Press *Delete*.
5. You will want to repeat this task down to **Etc**.
6. Then, on **Closed**, cut the hair (*Ctrl + X* or *⌘ + X*) and paste it in place (*Ctrl + Shift + V* or *⌘ + Shift + V*).
7. Rename this new layer **Hair** and place it above the **Mouths** group:

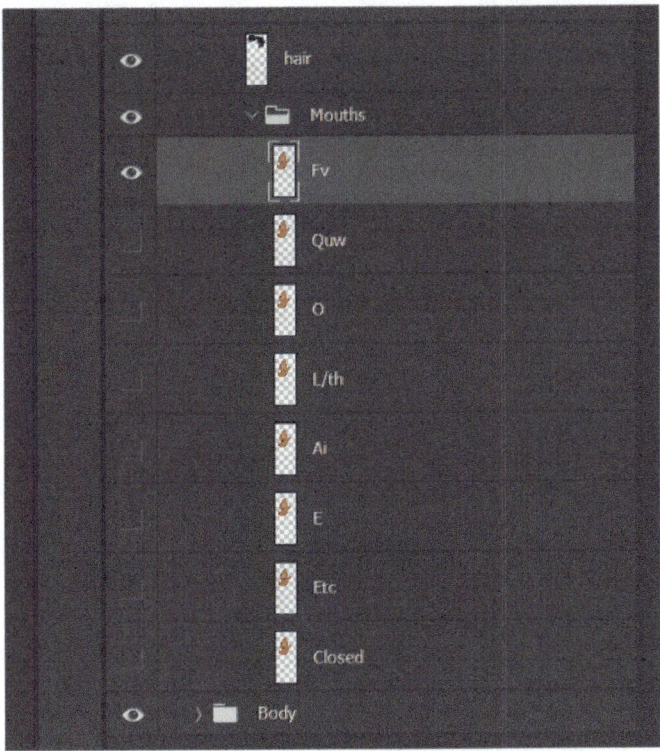

Figure 3.49: Hair will be placed above the head just like the other two phases

8. Save your .psd (*Ctrl* + *S* or ⌘ + *S*) and go back to Character Animator to refresh your rig.

With this step, your hair should now be separated and ready for the next step!

Cleaning up PSD layers

This last step may not apply if the art was drawn in Photoshop itself, but outside apps, such as Procreate, seem to import each layer of the .psd at canvas size as opposed to just what the artwork requires. While in most cases, this will work in Character Animator, some actions, such as moving the pupils and viewing custom controls, may have issues.

To test this, see the following:

1. Locate **Worried** under **+Right Eyebrow** for **3/4th Head**.
2. Select the **Move** tool (*V*).
3. Use *Ctrl* or ⌘ + *A* to select the artwork in the layer.
4. Use *Ctrl* or ⌘ + *T* to activate the **Free Transform Tool** option.

You will see that a selection area forms around the artwork:

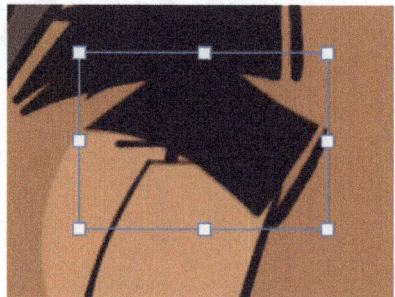

Figure 3.50: The Worried eyebrow is the only artwork being selected

Press *Enter* to deselect the eyebrow. Click on **Neutral** under **+Right Eyebrow** and follow the same steps as before. You should see that the selection area doesn't hug the eyebrow, but rather matches the canvas.

Figure 3.51: The Neutral eyebrow has transparent pixels that cover the entire canvas size, which isn't useable in some cases in Character Animator

We want to have each layer act as **Worried** does and not **Neutral**, so how do we do this? While there are a number of options, all seem to require time and patience, as you will need to review each layer to ensure it's acting appropriately. Here's an easy way:

1. Select the offending layer with *Ctrl* or ⌘ + *A*.
2. Use *Ctrl* or ⌘ + *X* to cut the artwork out of the layer.
3. Use *Ctrl* or ⌘ + *Shift* + *V* to paste it in place.

This should remove the excess pixels while keeping the proportions and locations of all artwork intact. Rinse and repeat until no layer has the issue. Once you are finished with this process, be sure to save your `.psd` file. You can also go to `Chaz_Host_v2.psd` to reference the final result using clean layers, along with all the other work we carried out this chapter.

Summary

Phew – that should be it! Not every rig will require as much work as we covered here. It will all depend on how you or your artist sets up the layers and groups. Everyone has a different way of designing. However, now, at least you know the following:

- Groups must be named and organized for an easier workflow in Character Animator.
- All limbs must be contained in their own group.
- To take full advantage of facial features, be sure to create a blink phase, three emotions for the eyebrows, and a mouth group with phonemes.
- You can always add more layers (such as multiple outfits or hairstyles) to your rig than shown here.
- Rigs also don't have to have everything shown here to function. As an example, you don't have to have three head phases for a character if you don't need the character to turn their head when animating.

If you're unsure about any of these steps, you can always refer to the completed rig for this chapter, `Chaz_Host_v2`. If we missed anything, we can always go back and alter the rig, even when working in Character Animator at the same time.

Be sure to save your file so we can start rigging in the next chapter!

Part 2: Rigging Character Art for Animation

Properly rigging a character for animation in Character Animator requires certain tasks to be completed. We started this process in Photoshop and will continue here as we tag body parts, ground with pins, create mouse controls, and refine animations. From there, we will work with behaviors, triggers, and swap sets, all of which can control and automate lip-syncing, blinking, breathing, and more.

This part includes the following chapters:

- *Chapter 4, Importing and Tagging Your Character*
- *Chapter 5, Creating Control Handles and Behaviors*
- *Chapter 6, Physics, Behaviors, and Meshes*
- *Chapter 7, Assigning Mouths and Props with Triggers and Swap Sets*
- *Chapter 8, Refining Layers and Exploring Optional Rig Features*

4
Importing and Tagging Your Character

With our PSD file streamlined and ready, we can now step over to Character Animator and begin the tagging process. Tagging is the process where we identify layers and points so Character Animator knows what to do with them. Some of the work we did in the previous chapter will help us here, as Character Animator will automatically tag some layers because of the way they're named.

In this chapter, we will learn about the following:

- Adjusting the rig in Character Animator
- Tagging the mouth and head
- Tagging body parts

Technical requirements

We will use both Character Animator and Photoshop in this chapter, so have both apps ready and let's get going!

Adjusting the rig in Character Animator

In the previous chapter, we went into Photoshop and made adjustments to a rig to make it more friendly for Character Animator. While this is the preferred way, you can make minor layer adjustments in Character Animator as well. This can be nice for quick fixes but lacks granular control. You can also change the PSD in Photoshop and the file will update in real time in Character Animator.

To see all this in action, let's import our character first.

Importing Chaz into Character Animator

We imported a .svg file in *Chapter 2*, so we have some knowledge of how to import a character. Here is a refresher:

1. Create a new project by going to **File > New Project** (or by pressing *Ctrl + Alt + N* or ⌘ + ⌥ + *N*). This will allow us to start with a clean slate.
2. Save the project in a safe place and name it Chat_with_Chaz.
3. Import Chaz_Host_v2.psd or the file you worked on in the previous chapter by double-clicking on the **Project** panel or using *Ctrl + I*, or ⌘ + *I*.
4. Rename the imported PSD file to CHAZ by right-clicking and choosing **Rename**.
5. If not already displayed, double-click on **CHAZ** in the **Project** panel to reveal its layers and design.

Once complete, we see the following interface:

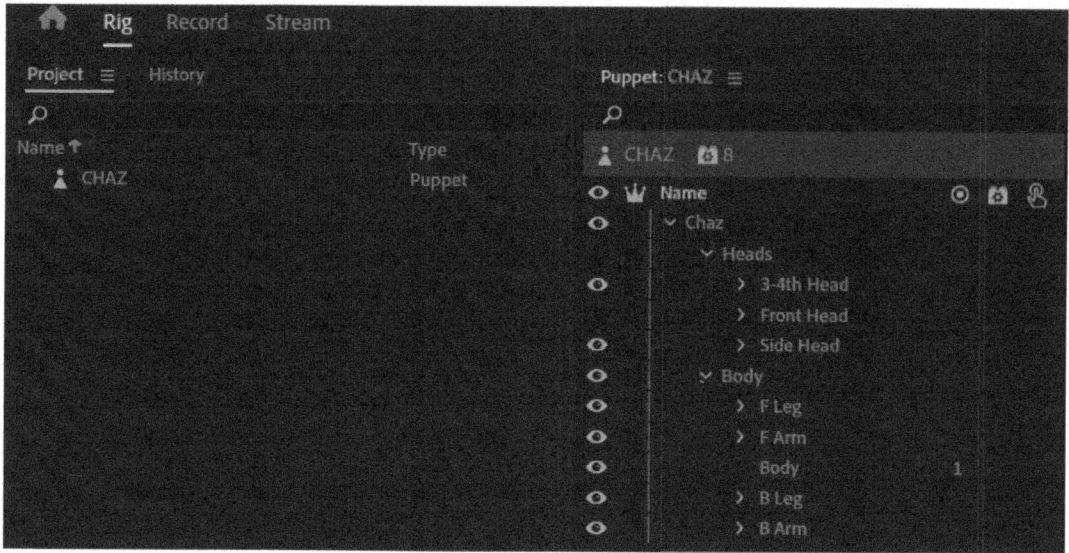

Figure 4.1: Chaz rig's layers revealed in the Rig tab

You will also see the character appear in the Rig tab. The character should look the same as they did in Photoshop.

Adjusting the rig in Character Animator 77

Figure 4.2: Chaz inside of the Rig tab

With the character imported into Character Animator, we can make some modifications.

Making layer changes in Character Animator

With the CHAZ file, we can see the layers. The order and name of these layers should seem familiar, as it's the same list from Photoshop.

You may recall that we created independent groups in the rig using a + sign in the name. These layers act differently and allow them to work without interference from other layers. It's important to know how to identify and change independence in Character Animator. Here's how we can do that:

1. Expand the **Heads** group to reveal the three head subgroups.
2. Expand the **3-4th Head** group. This will reveal **Right Eyebrow**.
3. To the left of **Right Eyebrow**, there should be a crown icon, which shows independence. To toggle independence, just click the crown.

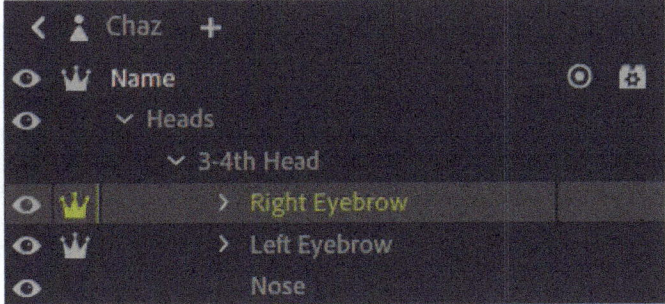

Figure 4.3: When the crown is white (or yellow when selected), the layer is independent

When we toggle independence, it will not reflect this change in the original .psd file. We're essentially overlaying new rules on top of the original.

However, if we go back to the .psd file in Photoshop and make a change, once we hit **Save**, it will instantly reflect the change in Character Animator. To see an example of this, follow these steps:

1. Open `Chaz_Host_v2.psd` in Photoshop. To do this from Character Animator, right-click on **CHAZ** in the **Project** panel and choose **Edit Original** (or press *Ctrl + E* or *⌘ + E*):

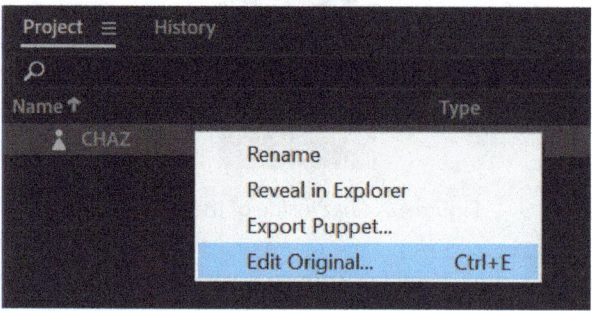

Figure 4.4: Right-clicking on the puppet reveals four useful options

2. Click the eye icon next to the **Front Head** phase to ensure it is visible
3. Now open `Glasses 1.png` in Photoshop as well (the image is also in the book files):

Figure 4.5: A stylish pair of glasses

4. Select **Layer 1** for **Glasses 1.png** and press *Ctrl + C* or *⌘ + C* to copy the layer.
5. Go over to `Chaz_Host_v2.psd`:

Figure 4.6: It's easy to work between two projects in Photoshop with the tabs

6. Paste with *Ctrl + V*, or *⌘ + V*.
7. Rename **Layer 1** to `Glasses`:

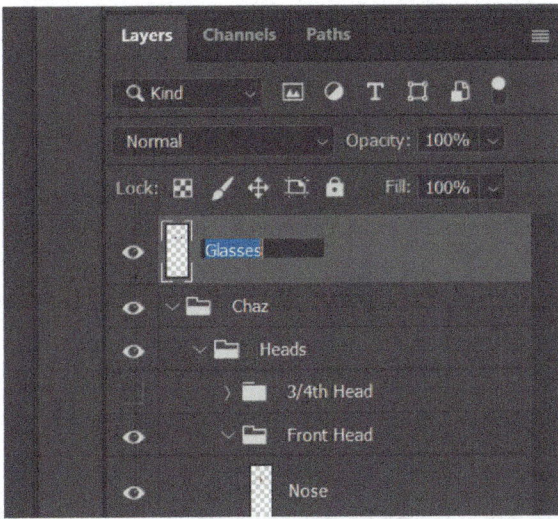

Figure 4.7: Our layer structure will transfer from Photoshop to Character Animator seamlessly

8. Move **Glasses** to the top of the list in the **Front Head** group:

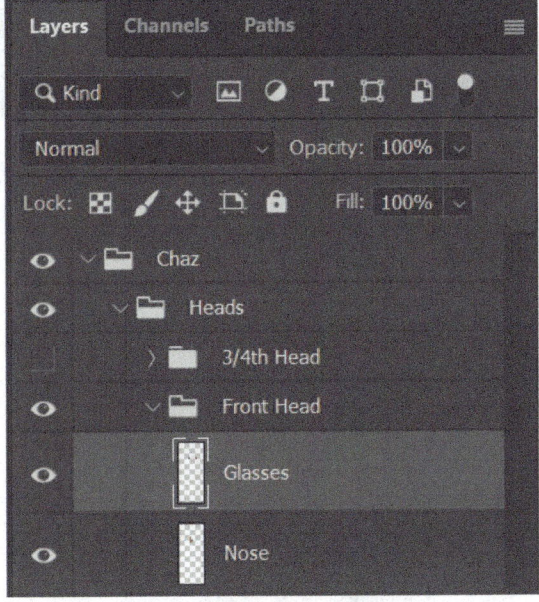

Figure 4.8: Glasses will sit on top of the list under Front Head

9. From here, using the **Free Transform** tool, resize and move the glasses onto Chaz's face in the front view:

Figure 4.9: Glasses placed on the Front Head face

10. Save the file with *Ctrl + S*, or ⌘ + *S*.
11. Go back to Character Animator. You should see the rig refresh, with the new layer present:

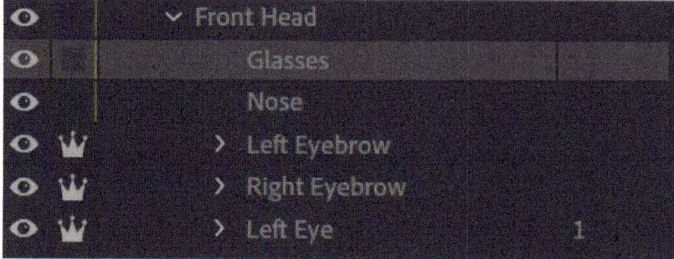

Figure 4.10: Character Animator will refresh the file when changes are made to the .psd file

Not only will the layers update to reflect the current `.psd` version, but the character's appearance will reflect the change, as well.

Figure 4.11: What Chaz looks like in Character Animator. The yellow outline indicates his boundaries when all layers are accounted for

This can be of great use if you need to make additions or minor changes. Just note that if you move ahead with rigging and later decide to make big changes, such as character proportions, you may have to go back to your rig to redo it to accommodate those changes. That's why it's always best to lock down the key components of your design before proceeding to animation.

Creating PSD versions

Let's say when you change your rig, you don't want to override the original. This may be useful if you're unsure of your changes and want to keep the original design as a backup. Here's something we can do:

1. Ensure `Chaz_Host_v2.psd` is open in Photoshop.
2. Use *Ctrl* + *Shift* + *S* or *⌘* + *Shift* + *S* to save a copy of the file.
3. Name the new file `Chaz_Host_v2_with_glasses.psd`:

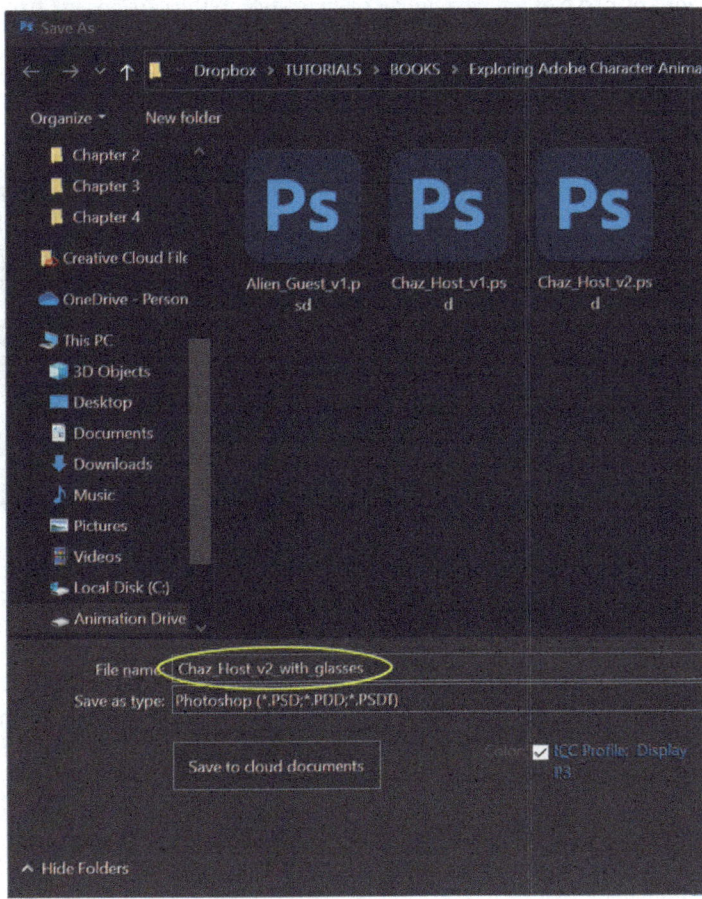

Figure 4.12: Saving a copy of a .psd file

4. When asked about compatibility, just press **OK**.
5. Still in Photoshop, press *Ctrl + O*, or ⌘ + *O* to prompt the **Open File** window.
6. Open `Chaz_Host_v2.psd` again:

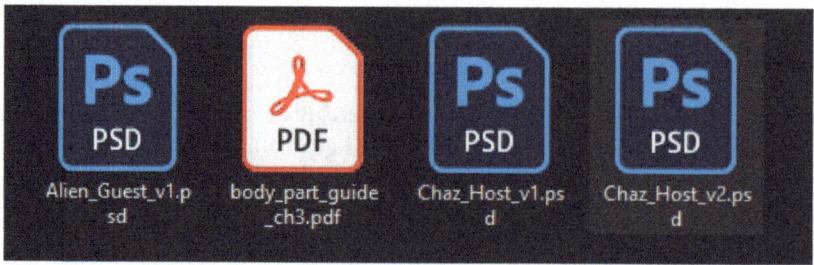

Figure 4.13: Versions of .psd files follow a similar naming style to the versions in Character Animator

7. Click on the **Glasses** layer and press the *Delete* key on the keyboard.
8. Save the new file with *Ctrl + S*, or ⌘ + *S*.

Figure 4.14: You can change the .psd path at anytime by clicking on the file link.

What we've done here is create a new rig *with* glasses while retaining the original *without*. We can swap between these puppets if needed. To do this, follow these steps:

1. Go back to Character Animator. It may take a moment for your rig to refresh and remove the **Glasses** layer.
2. Click once on **CHAZ** in the **Project** panel.
3. In the upper-right, under **Properties**, find the subcategory titled **Puppet**:

Figure 4.15: This links to your source .psd

4. Underneath the Puppet subcategory is a file path, for the `.psd` file that Character Animator is currently reading. Click on that link and choose `Chaz_Host_v2_with_glasses.psd` from the file browser:

Figure 4.16: We will want to bring the rig with glasses in

The puppet will refresh and the glasses should be back in the layer list.

Again, this is useful if you change a rig but don't want to alter the original, as you never know when you may need to reference it again.

We may end up making minor adjustments in Photoshop as we continue to work. That's why it's important to create a breadcrumb trail of files in case you need to step back. Remember, we can create versions of the project in Character Animator as well.

Next, we will prepare the head and mouth of our rig using tags.

Tagging the head and mouth

While some of the naming conventions we used for our layers will help Character Animator identify and implement features, some areas still need a little work from us. Tagging is the practice of adding identifiers to existing layers so that Character Animator can automate more of the animation process. To practice this, we're going to tag the head phases and the mouth.

Switching the tag view

You have two ways of working with tags in Character Animator. We will be taking a look at both of these methods. To tag the head, do the following:

1. Make sure the **Rig** tab is open and the **CHAZ** puppet is visible.
2. Then click on the **Heads** group.

   A diagram will appear on the side labeled **Tags**, representing a character:

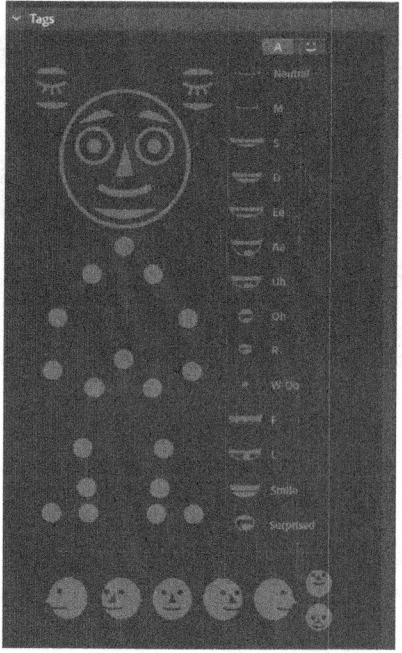

Figure 4.17: The Show Tags as Pictures view

3. At the top right of this panel are two buttons. The **Smile** button is the current view we're on:

   A. The **Smile** button represents the **Show Tags as Pictures** option
   B. The **A** button represents the **Show Tags as Text** option

Smile is the current view we're on, so click on the **A** to change the tag view:

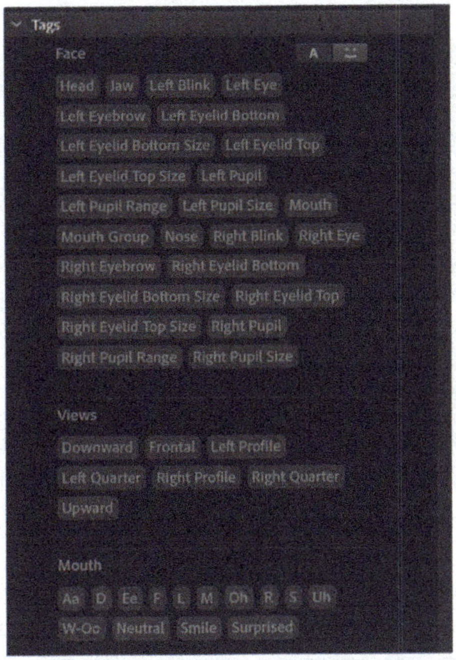

Figure 4.18: The Show Tags as Text option

The list view is harder to decipher, especially for newcomers. We will use **Show Tags as Pictures** moving forward, but you can use **Show Tags as Text** if you wish.

Understanding left and right tags

With Character Animator, when we tag something as left or right, we are referring to the character's left or right, which means that what's left on our screen is actually right for the character.

As an example, under **3-4th Head**, click on **Right Eye**.

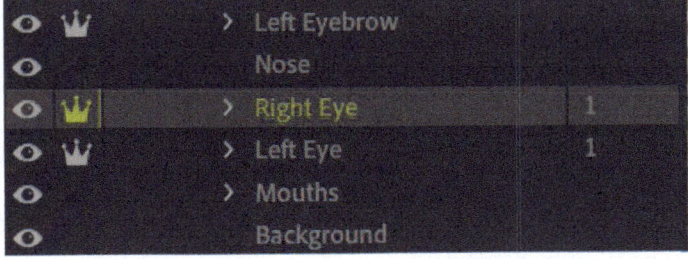

Figure 4.19: The screen's left is the character's right

You'll see that the selected eye is on the left of the screen (be assured, this isn't an error in the naming convention; this is correct):

Figure 4.20: Note how the character's right eye, outlined in yellow, sits on our left

What about Side Head? We will dig into this more when creating a head turn, but Side Head has the character looking to the right. That means the eye and eyebrow visible are on his left:

Figure 4.20: Luckily, we only need to deal with one eye and brow with the side view

So, when the time comes to tag that view, we know what direction we need to account for.

Tagging head layers

Next, we will tag the main Heads group and the three phases:

1. Under the **Puppet**'s layers, click on the **Heads** group:

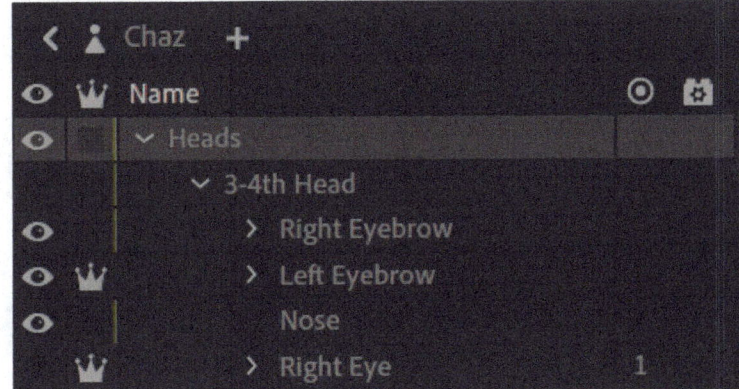

Figure 4.22: Simply click on the Heads group

2. Click on the head outline in the **Tags** panel:

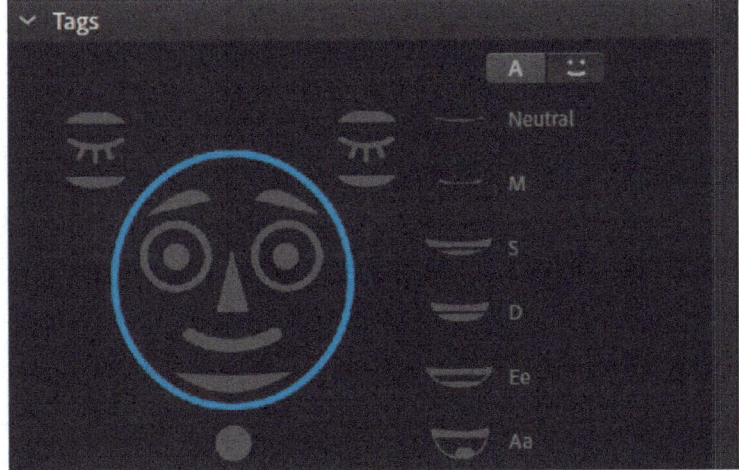

Figure 4.23: Click the head outline to properly tag the head

3. Then click on **3-4th Head** and click on the head outline in the **Tags** panel again.

Now, we're going to focus on the layers that make up **3-4th Head**.

4. You should ensure that the **Left Eyebrow** and **Right Eyebrow** are situated properly. You can double-check this by clicking on the eyebrow groups and seeing whether the correct eyebrow highlights in the **Tags** diagram. If not, click the unassigned layers for each eyebrow to tag them properly.
5. To set the **Nose** layer, click on the nose in the **Tags** diagram.
6. The **Right Eye** and **Left Eye**, like the eyebrows, should automatically be tagged. If not, click on an eye and choose the correct position in the diagram:

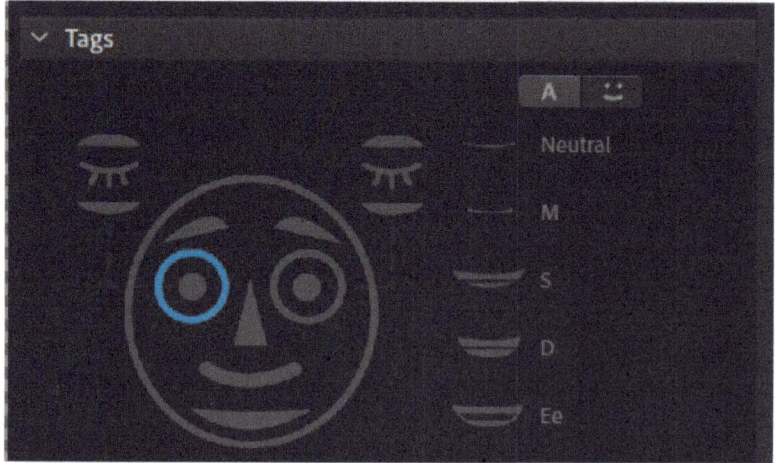

Figure 4.24: Clicking the eye outlines to tag each eye

7. Under the **Eye** groups, **Blinks**, **Eyes**, and **Pupils** should all tag automatically. If not, go through each layer and click on the appropriate icon in the **Tags** panel:

Figure 4.25: Blinks and eyelids appear above the head in the diagram

However, you will need to click on **Top Lid** as it may not automatically tag:

Figure 4.26: We only have the top lid to work with. You don't need to include every layer the diagram shows

8. The **Mouths** group will need to be tagged. Click on it, then click on the mouth in the diagram. We will need to also tag the individual mouth poses, but we will cover that in the next subsection.
9. The **Background** layer will not be tagged. So, we can leave it alone.
10. At this point, you will want to go back through all groups under **Side Head** and **Front Head** to ensure that the following are tagged in each group, just like the **3-4th Head**:

    A. That each head group is tagged to the head

    B. That the **Front Head** eyes and eyebrows are properly tagged for left and right

    C. That for **Side Head**, the **Eye** and **Eyebrow** are assigned as **Left**

We now need to tell Character Animator how to work with the pupils:

1. To ensure the pupils mask properly, click on the **Eye** layer under **Left Eye**.
2. In the **Tags** panel, click on the **A** icon to go into the list view for your behaviors:

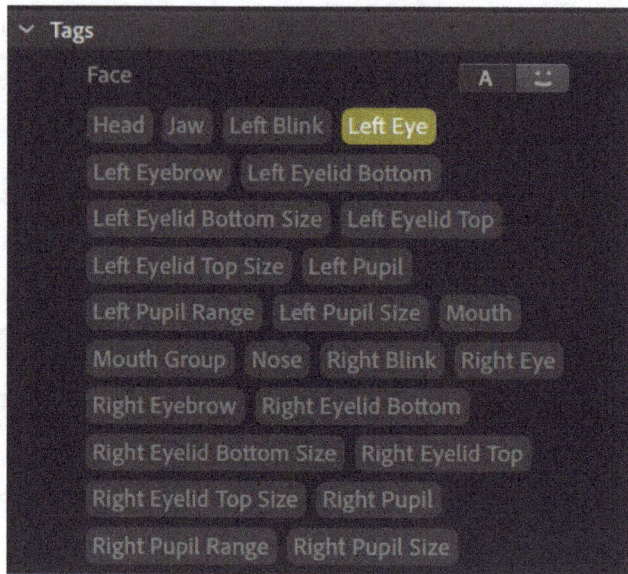

Figure 4.27: Clicking on the A button will reveal more tags than shown in the diagram

3. New behaviors will now be visible, one of which is labeled **Left Pupil Range**. Click on it to enable it as a tag.

4. Now, tag the right eye with **Right Pupil Range** to ensure proper tracking for both eyes.

   If you test the eye gaze now, the eyeball acts as a mask or boundary, but also moves based on the position of your pupils:

Figure 4.28: The pupils should now be using the eyeballs as a border and mask

You can adjust the strength of the behavior, as well as other behavior attributes, when recording, but for now, we should be okay with the default choices.

With that, you now have an idea of what to look out for if rig issues crop up in the future. While it's best to correct these issues early on, sometimes things are missed or changes are made that affect the outcome. But, if you take a moment and backtrack, the issue can be corrected. Hopefully, this gives some idea of how such a process could play out.

Tagging mouth layers

To tag the mouth poses, follow these steps:

1. With the **3-4th Head** layer, locate and expand the **Mouths** layer.
2. With the eight mouth poses revealed, click on **Fv**:

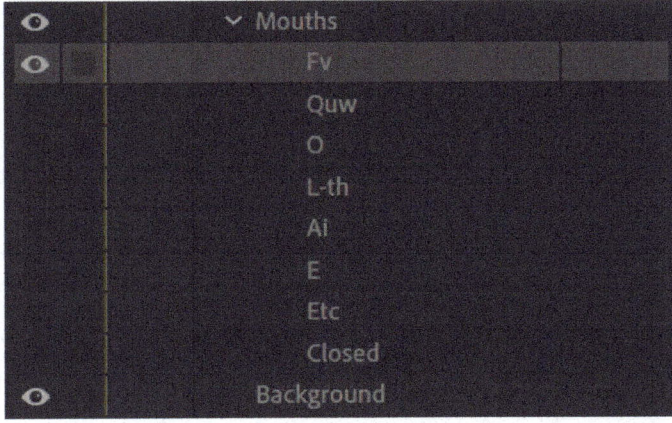

Figure 4.29: The eight phonemes, or mouth poses, we will be tagging

3. In **Tags**, next to the puppet diagram, there is a list of mouth poses. Click on **F**:

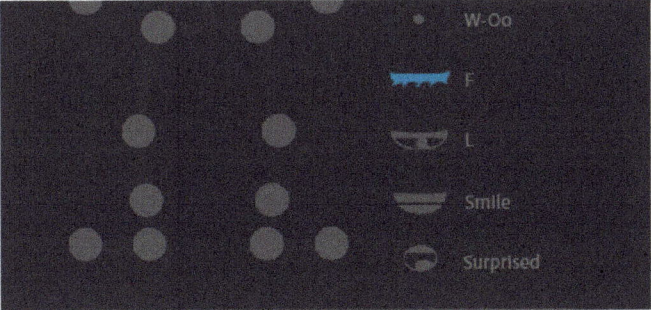

Figure 4.30: Selected items in the diagram will always highlight in blue

4. Now, whenever our character makes an *F* or *V* sound, Character Animator will switch the mouth to this pose.

5. Next, you're going to tag the following seven poses like so:

   A. **Quw** tagged with **W-Oo**
   B. **O** tagged with **Oh**
   C. **L-th** tagged with **L**
   D. **Ai** tagged with **Aa** and **Uh**
   E. **E** tagged with **Ee**
   F. **Etc** tagged with **S**, **D**, and **Smile**
   G. **Closed** tagged with **Neutral** and **M**

6. Once you complete tagging the **3-4th Head** mouth, move down the list and make sure to tag the phonemes for **Front Head** and **Profile Head** in the same way.

Now, with the head and mouth layers tagged, we can move on to the body layers.

Tagging the body layers

Like the head and mouth, we need to tag the body properly. Tagging the body parts works a little differently – we will need to add puppet handles and then tag them so the software knows how to react.

A **puppet handle** is essentially a control point we put on the rig, which can behave in various ways. Right now, we need to decide which parts of the rig need handles. Luckily, the Tags diagram makes it easy to keep track of which points go where on a character. Let's get going:

1. Collapse the main **Heads** group.
2. Expand the **Body** group so we can see all the body layers:

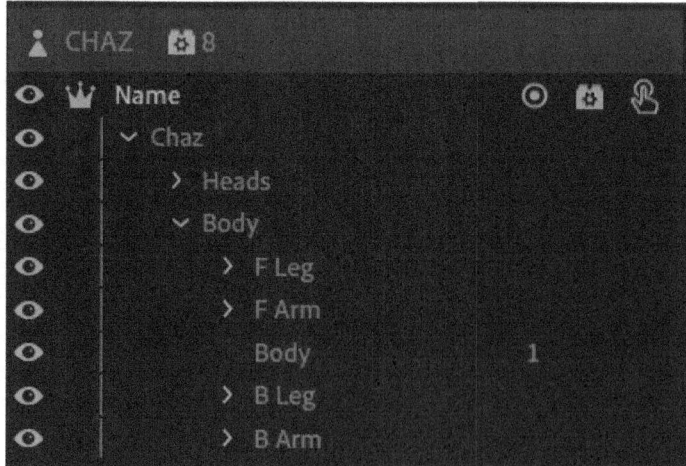

Figure 4.31: The body layers

3. Start by clicking on the **F Leg** group.

4. Click on the **Handle** tool located at the bottom of the screen (*L* on the keyboard):

Figure 4.32: The circle with the dot in the middle is the Handle tool

5. Add two handles to the leg: one for the knee and one for the ankle. These handles will tell Character Animator how each point of the leg should bend and react.

6. A tag labeled **F Leg** will appear near the middle of the rig. Click and drag this toward the top of the leg:

Figure 4.33: The three tags will represent the left hip, knee, and ankle

7. With the top handle still selected, click on the **Left Hip** handle in the figure to tag the handle as the left hip. You can also click on the plus icon next to the tag and choose the **Left Hip** tag through that menu:

Figure 4.34: Click on the handle on your rig then select the point on the diagram

8. Click on the middle handle and choose **Left Knee** in the **Tags** panel.
9. Tag the bottom handle as **Left Ankle**:

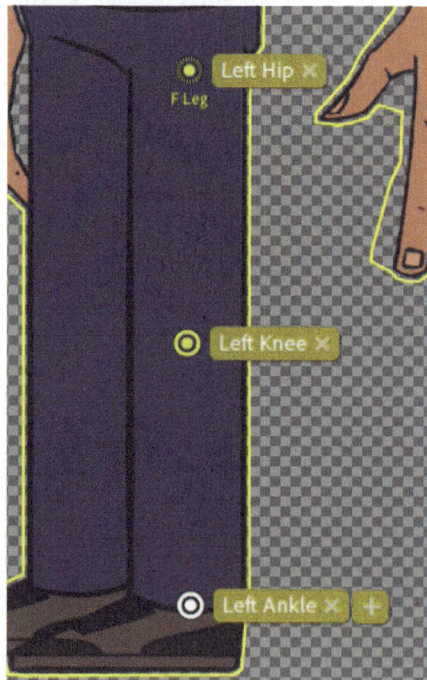

Figure 4.35: Tags will also be visible so you can identify them at a glance

10. Now, add two points to the left foot: one for the heel and the other for the toes.

11. Using the **Tags** diagram, assign the appropriate tags for the foot:

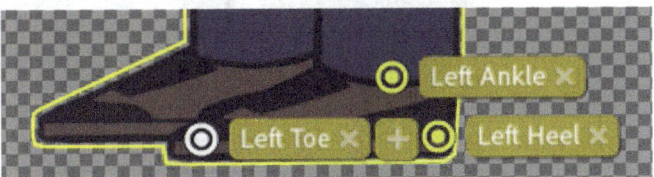

Figure 4.36: Two tags for the feet – toes and heels

12. Move over to **B Leg** and add handles in the same spots as the left. This time though, you're going to tag them as **Right Hip**, **Right Knee**, **Right Ankle**, **Right Heel**, and **Right Toe**:

Figure 4.37: The back leg will be considered the right leg

13. For the arms, you will follow a similar pattern to the legs, except you will use **Shoulder**, **Elbow**, and **Wrist** for the tags:

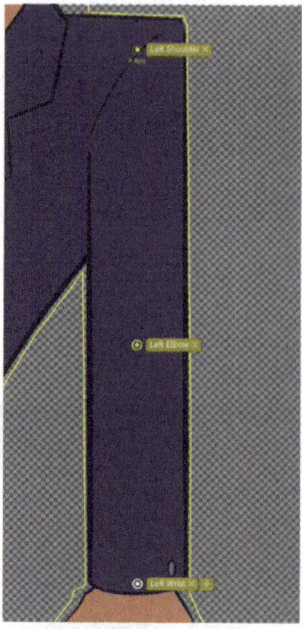

Figure 4.38: Tagging the front arm

Tagging the back or right arm will follow a similar process. Just be sure to use the **Right** tags:

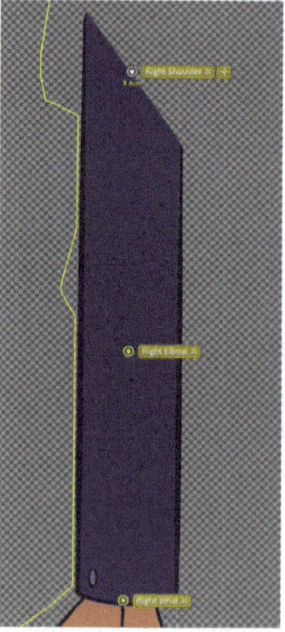

Figure 4.39: Tagging the back arm

14. Finally, for the **Body** layer, you will need to tag **Neck** and **Waist**. Try to match the positions to the following figure:

Figure 4.40: Tagging the body

With the body tagged, everything should be laid out for us to start testing and refining the rig. We may come back and make some minor modifications if certain things don't line up. But for now, this is looking good!

Summary

As you can see, setting up a rig in Character Animator can be a bit time-consuming. However, it's important that we take the time to get it right. That way, when we animate, we can focus on the production and not have to work around defects of the rig. The good thing is you can retag, rename, and rearrange your layers as you see fit, and you can choose whether you want to make select modifications in Character Animator or Photoshop.

You can find the completed product of our work in this chapter by accessing Version 1 of the rig inside the book's project file history.

Up next, we're going to go further with the rig, test out some animation, and add even more functionality to the handles with various behaviors.

5
Creating Control Handles and Behaviors

In the previous chapter, we went through our character's layers and added tags. These tags, at the moment, don't really have much influence on the rig. We can change that though by assigning different controls and behaviors to our tags. These behaviors and controls can be universal, affecting the whole rig, or we can target layers for our behaviors. In this chapter, we will work with the following:

- Adding modifiers for mouse control
- Linking **Independent** groups
- Refining limbs with the stick tool
- Adjusting limb rotation

By the time we have finished this chapter, you will have a functional rig you can control using your mouse. This will also open up more options for us in future chapters. Let's get going!

Technical requirements

Be sure to have your tagged character open in Character Animator, or you can access `Chat_with_Chaz.chproj` and load **Version 1** under the **History** panel if you wish to work with the book's example. Let's get going!

> **Note**
> You may find when loading a Character Animator project version the .psd file for the puppet may appear to be missing. This can be fixed by relocating the file through the Properties panel or disabling than re-enabling Auto Sync Artwork.

Adding modifiers for mouse control

Modifiers are essentially controls or behaviors we can add to the rig. This can involve the ability to drag that part of the rig, anchor it to the ground, dangle things, and much more.

100   Creating Control Handles and Behaviors

Let's move over to the **Record** tab for a moment. If your scene is blank and you don't see the rig, see the following:

1. Drag and drop the **CHAZ** puppet from the **Project** panel into the middle of the screen.
2. Chaz should appear on the **Scene** panel. He will probably be larger than the scene dimensions. If this is the case, let's shrink him down.

    A. Click once on **CHAZ** on the **Timeline panel** (located at the bottom of the screen).

    B. On the right-hand side, see **Properties** and change **Scale** to 30%.

You should now be able to see Chaz fully.

As it stands, right now, the rig doesn't react in any way when we click or drag around on the canvas. The only other thing that may react is the character's face if you have your camera and microphone enabled. It's recommended you turn those options off for now so we can focus on the draggers without distraction:

Figure 5.1: Scaling the puppet allows us to make sure he's in the workspace

Let's click on the **Rig** tab, bringing us back to the setup phase for the character.

Adjusting the layer and mesh properties

When you select any layer or group on the **Puppet** panel, **Properties** on the right will display for the given **Layer**. This means you can resize, rotate, and more with the options here. This may be useful if we missed something in Photoshop. Making modifications is easier to make in real time to test **Attach Styles** and such as well. We may need to refer to this panel from time to time, but we can leave everything as is for now:

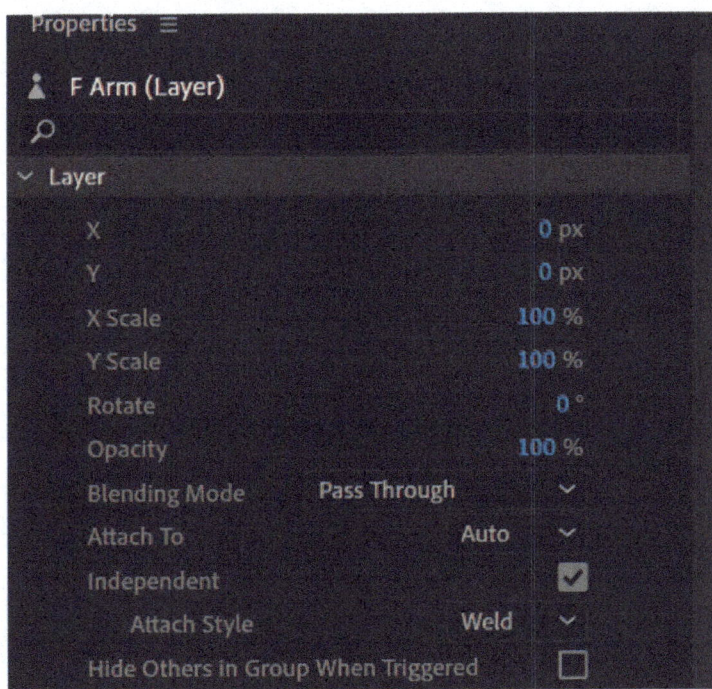

Figure 5.2: The Layer panel analyzing the F Arm group

Your **Layer Mesh** options are available below the **Layer** options. By default, we can see the following:

- **Mesh Shape** is set to **Contour**
- **Mesh Island Connection Width** is set to 1
- **Connect Each Island to** is set to **Nearest**
- **Mesh Expansion** is at 0

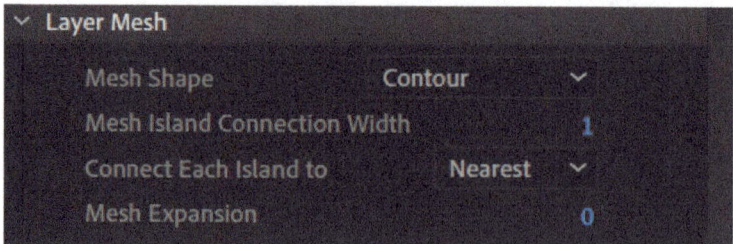

Figure 5.3: You can adjust aspects of each layer's mesh if further refinement is needed

These settings are optional and are only needed if the mesh isn't fitting around the rig correctly, so if you see a piece of the rig sticking outside of the mesh, these options can help correct that. However, for now, we can leave these options alone.

Now that you know where to access **Layer Properties**, let's add some controls so we can move a hand!

Adding draggers and fixed modifiers

To add dragger controls to Chaz's hands, see the following:

1. Click on **F Arm**, which is under the **Body** group for the Chaz puppet.
2. Select the bottom tag, which is **Left Wrist**.

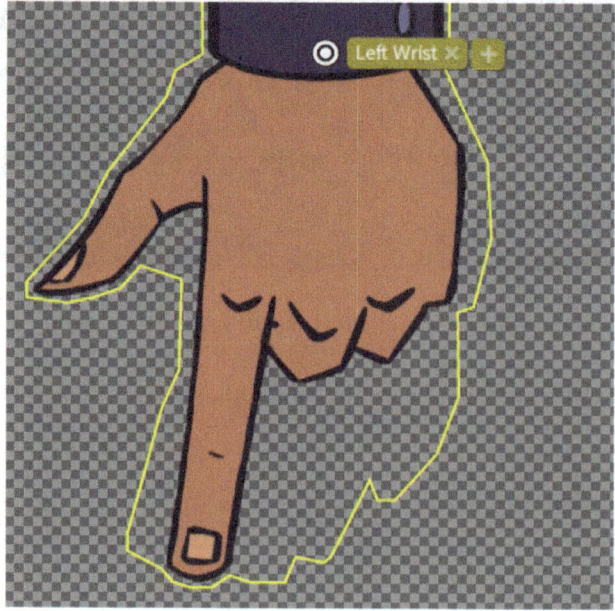

Figure 5.4: The selected tag will highlight in white

Adding modifiers for mouse control

> **Note**
> To properly select a tag, you will need to click on the tag icon (the circle highlighted with a box in *Figure 5.4*) itself, not the label. You will know when it's selected when the tag turns white. Clicking on the **X** sign on the label will remove the tag. If you do this accidentally, don't worry! You can easily click the modifier on the **Tag** panel to re-enable it.

In the **Tags** panel, which is on the right-hand side of the screen, locate **Modifiers** near the bottom.

Click **Draggable**, the first option under **Modifiers**.

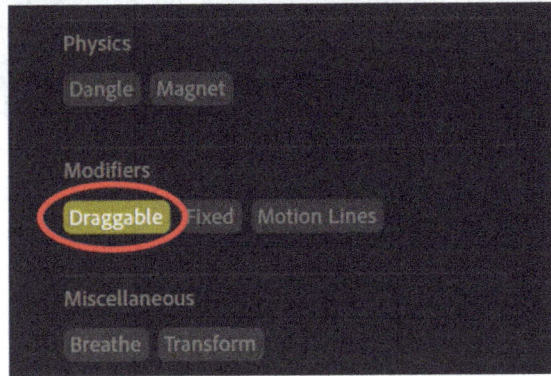

Figure 5.5: Modifiers, Physics, and Miscellaneous are all categories we can play with

Click on the **Record** button and click and drag the front hand to see the result.

As you'll see, the entire rig, not just the arm, moves around the screen when we click and drag. Why is this? Well, with no other **Modifiers** to work with this **Draggable** wrist, the entire puppet will move. Here's how we can fix this:

1. Go back to the **Rig** tab.
2. Click on the **F Leg** layer.
3. Click the bottom tag labeled **Left Heel**.

Figure 5.6: Properly tagging the front or left foot

4. Under **Modifiers** in the right-hand **Tags** panel, click **Fixed**.

Figure 5.7: Fixed will lock the heel in place

5. Now, go to the **Record** tab.
6. Try moving the hand after the scene loads.
7. The arm should move with the left or front foot anchoring the character down.

Figure 5.8: We can easily pull the arm back if we want

As you can see, adding the **Fixed** modifier allows us to anchor tags on the rig. This not only helps with the current situation but also allows for more realistic or grounded animation. This is a good start, but you may notice it's difficult to point the arm where we want it.

Figure 5.9: Trying to point the finger forward, however, is more difficult

That's because we have more modifiers and parameters to add. So, let's continue:

1. Go back to the **Rig** tab.
2. Click on the **B Leg** layer.
3. Go down to **Right Ankle** and click on the tag. By tagging everything properly, we can create flexible feet that we can pin down on the heel or toe.
4. Under **Modifiers**, enable **Fixed**.

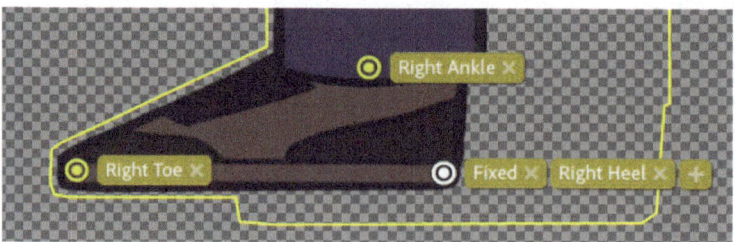

Figure 5.10: Fixing the back heel as well

5. Click **B Arm** on the **Layers** panel.
6. Select the bottom tag, **Right Wrist**.
7. Enable **Draggable** under **Modifiers**.

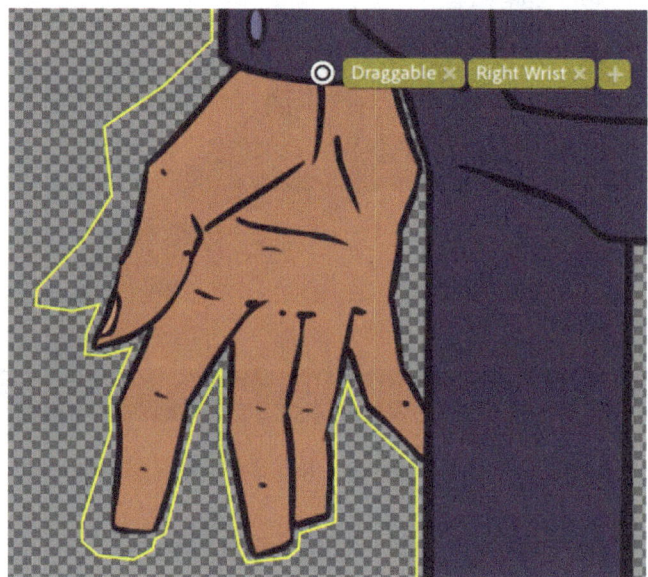

Figure 5.11: Make the back hand draggable

8. Go back to the **Record** tab and test the rig by dragging the hands.

The back hand should move and the back foot should be fixed, but something isn't quite right when moving either hand.

Adding modifiers for mouse control 107

Figure 5.12: Pointing backward looks a little better with both feet fixed

Figure 5.13: The back hand is stuck to the back leg

Now that the back hand is draggable, we now have an additional issue: the back hand sticks to the back leg of the rig. Remember in *Chapter 3* when we talked about making layers and groups independent when setting up our character? This is where that becomes important. Let's talk more about it.

Linking Independent groups

By default, your rig will act as one piece when animating. The best example of this is the back hand being stuck to the back leg. Since we tagged none of the body layers as **Independent**, Character Animator thinks we want this all to act as one piece. The reason we don't have the same issue with the front arm is because of the front hand is not touching the rig, unlike the back hand.

Luckily, we can easily assign new **Independent** layers without having to go back to Photoshop. From there, we will need to weld some pieces together to ensure the rig will properly animate.

Assigning layers as Independent

Let's inspect how Character Animator is currently viewing the connection of our body layers. Go back to the **Rig** tab. Do you see the yellow outline surrounding the character? This is the boundary of the mesh. The mesh allows Character Animator to interpret the way the layers connect. Since we labeled no body parts as **Independent**, Character Animator works with just one mesh, which explains why the back hand sticks to the back leg.

Figure 5.14: The yellow outline indicates one mesh is making up the entire body

This is where independence comes in handy. Here's what we can do to make this work in our favor:

1. Select the **B Arm** group.
2. Click to the right of the layer visibility icon (the eye) to enable independence (indicated by a crown).

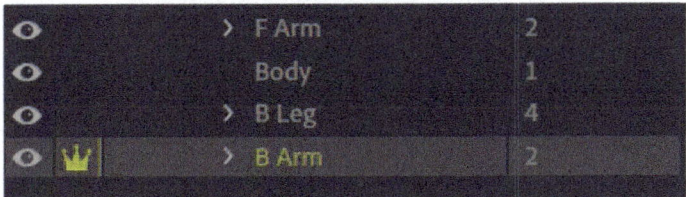

Figure 5.15: The crown is essentially the same as adding a "+" to the name in Photoshop

3. You may be seeing a change already. If you click on **Body**, the back arm is no longer included in the main **Body** mesh.

Figure 5.16: The back arm is no longer included in the main mesh

4. Enable independence for **B Leg**, **F Arm**, and **F Leg**, and note how the yellow mesh outline appears now when clicking on **Body** again. Just the head and torso are now outlined.

Figure 5.17: All limbs now appear separated from the main mesh

With the body parts now set as **Independent**, we can tell Character Animator how to connect all of these pieces.

Welding Independent groups to the body

To ensure everything is connected properly, let's test out the front arm first. To do this, see the following:

1. Click on **F Arm** under the **CHAZ Puppet** panel.
2. Click on the top tag, **Left Shoulder**, and drag it a pixel or two. Note how the body and head turn green:

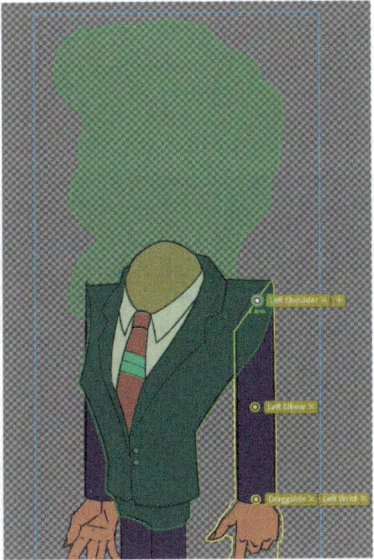

Figure 5.18: The green highlight means the Independent layer is welded to the main mesh

The green highlight is telling us this **Independent** group is properly welded to the main body.

3. To test this further, grab the same tag and move it away from the body. Note the change to a yellow highlight.

Figure 5.19: Yellow means the current layer is not welded to the main mesh

This is telling us the layer is not connected and will act on its own. This can be useful in some cases, but for standard character animation, we want the arm to connect to the body. So, move the tag back to its original spot, reinstating the green highlight.

Now, let's go through and weld each limb to the body (if it isn't already):

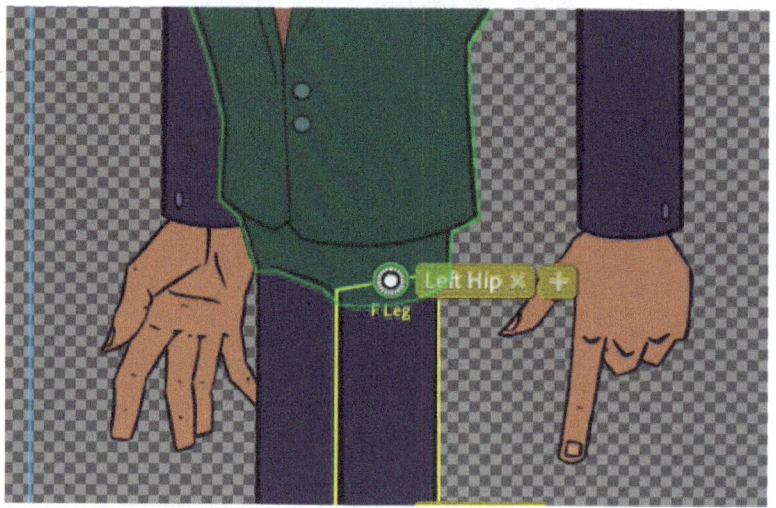

Figure 5.20: Connecting Left Hip to the bottom of the main mesh

With **Left Hip** connected to the torso, we can do the same for **Right Hip**:

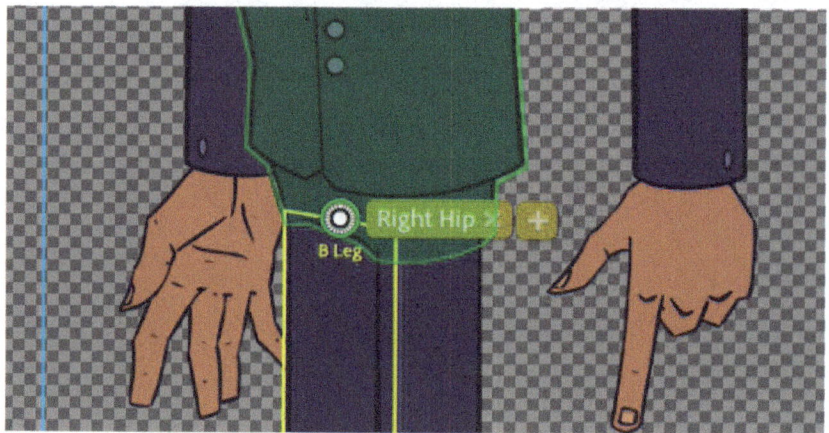

Figure 5.21: Connecting Right Hip to the bottom of the main mesh

Let's not forget the back arm! Click and drag to ensure the arm is attached to the torso:

Linking Independent groups 113

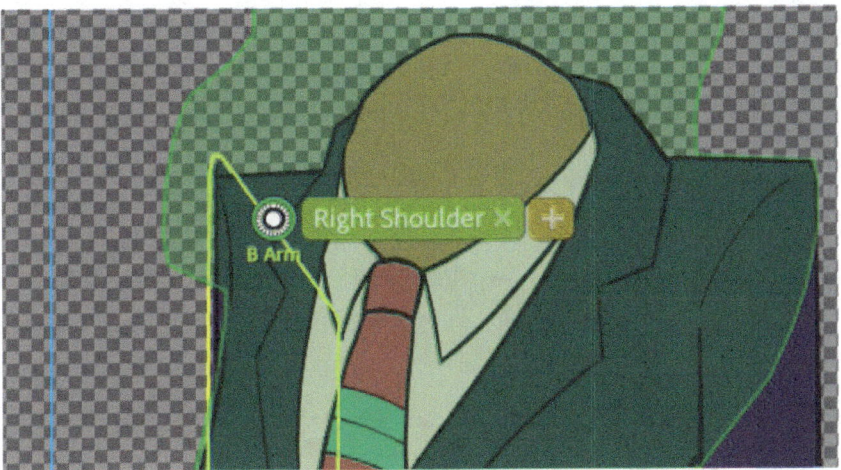

Figure 5.22: Connecting Right Shoulder to the top left on the main mesh

Once you have finished welding the tags, jump over to the **Record** tab and try moving the arms. You should now see the arms move independently while remaining attached to the body.

Figure 5.23: Properly setting the limbs as Independent fixes the stuck back hand

With our limbs properly linked with the body, we can move on to refining the movements a bit more.

Refining limbs with the stick tool

As you have seen by now, by default, Character Animator does its best to set up the limbs based on tags alone. While this can work sometimes, further refinement is required.

Figure 5.24: While the arms bend, the effect isn't pleasing

Let's check out the stick tool. This will allow us to refine the bends, creating more pleasing movement:

1. Go back to the **Rig** tab.
2. Click on **F Arm**.
3. Select the stick tool from the bottom toolbar (*S* on the keyboard is the shortcut). The icon is a line with a circle in the middle:

Figure 5.25: The stick tool lies to the right of the handle tool

4. Starting right below **Left Shoulder**, click and drag down to the elbow to create a stick.
5. Below **Left Elbow**, click and drag again down to the wrist. We have now created two sticks:

Linking Independent groups 115

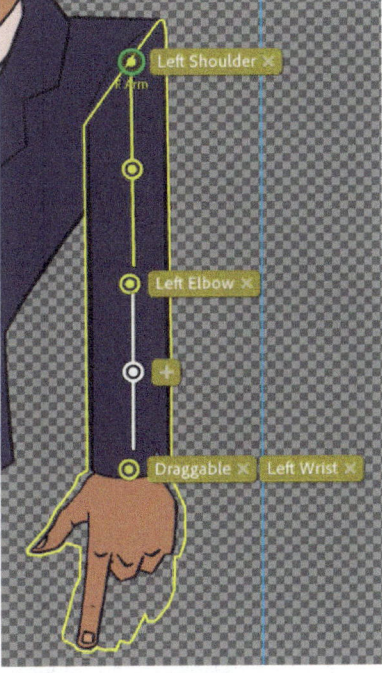

Figure 5.26: Two sticks to refine the arm bend

6. Go to the **Record** tab, grab the front hand, and drag around. The bend should be less rounded and squished and more defined.

Figure 5.27: Testing the bend reveals a cleaner result

7. Repeat this step for the three other limbs, drawing two sticks for each. Once you're finished, you can test out the second arm to ensure the bends are more refined.

Figure 5.28: The back arm also looks more refined

8. If you'd like to test the legs, set the heels and toes to **Draggable**, go to the **Record** tab, and move the feet. You should be able to see enough to make out the bends.

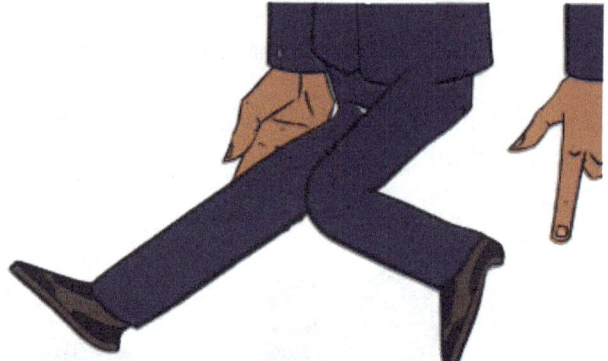

Figure 5.29: Draggers can be added to any handle, including fixed feet

And with that, we have a more functional rig that's ready for further refinement. There is one more thing we can look at when it comes to working with limbs.

Adjusting limb rotation

When working with your rig, you may find that the arms and legs bend in an undesirable way. As an example, you may decide you want the rig's front arm to point forward, not back.

Linking Independent groups 117

Figure 5.30: Right now, when moving the front arm, it will bend back

This can easily be modified by adjusting the rig's pins. Let's take a look at an example:

1. Go back to the **Rig** tab. Note how the pins are in the middle of the arm.

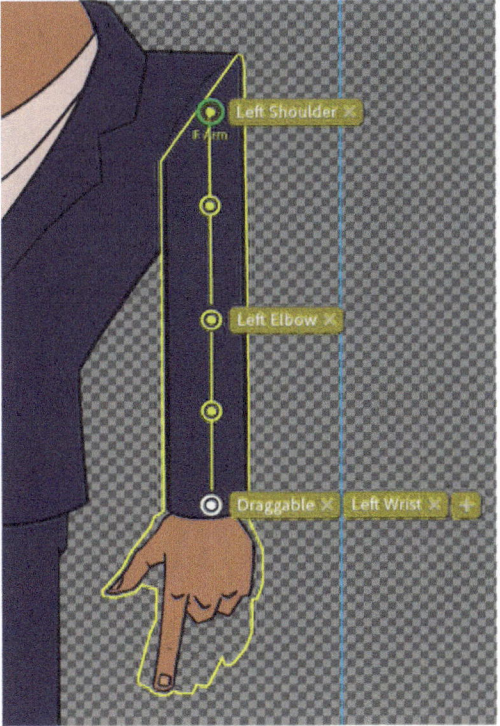

Figure 5.31: Note how the pins are laid out

2. Let's grab the wrist pin and move it to the left.

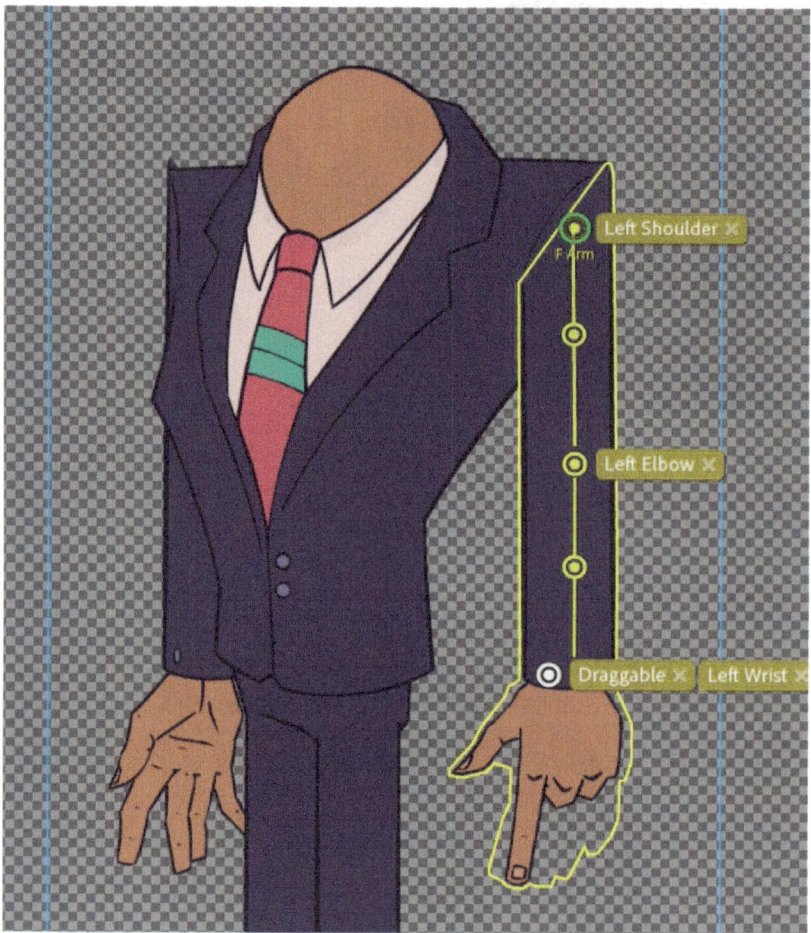

Figure 5.32: The wrist pin is aligned to the left

3. Go to the **Record** tab and try moving the arm. You should find the arm now points forward.

Figure 5.33: The arm now points forward

You can use this method for any rig you need to adjust the limb bends for. Be sure to keep this in mind as you rig new characters!

And with that, we have a more functional rig that's ready for further refinement. For now, we will save a new version of this rig in the **History** panel. It will be labeled **Version 2** for your reference.

Summary

We have set up the rig for basic movements and refinement. There is a lot more to cover and many more ways to interact with the rig, but it's always best to start with the basics and work up from there. Just remember the following:

- Tagging your handles appropriately is important to the entire setup
- Sometimes, you need layers to act on their own, which is where **Independent** groups come in handy
- We can only weld **Independent** layers to non-independent layers
- **Fixed** and **Draggable** are just two functions you can assign to handles
- Using the stick tool will shore up any glitches that may occur in the limb bends
- Adjusting the location of pins can alter the way a limb bends

In the next chapter, we are going to go even further by setting up swappable assets with props and changing the rig with more behaviors.

6
Physics, Behaviors, and Meshes

With a workable rig now in place, we can now dive further into Character Animator's strengths. We can set up a rig to not only interact with movement or other entities, but layer-specific and universal behaviors can add more interactivity and realism. We will also look at meshes and how they can help change the rig further.

More specifically, we will cover the following topics:

- Adding physics and danglers
- Modifying universal behaviors
- Creating layer-specific behaviors
- Refining animation with meshes

By the time we finish this chapter, you will have an enhanced rig that reacts to different environmental effects – a great way to create subtle animations without having to do it by hand.

Technical requirements

Be sure to have your tagged character open in Character Animator. Or, you can access `Chat_with_Chaz.chproj` and load **Version 2** under the **History** panel if you wish to work with the book's example.

Version 2 will also be referencing `Chaz_Host_v3.psd` in the event you need to access that file.

Adding physics and danglers

Being able to add physics to your rig is a great way to create automatic movement based on various factors. As an example, we can have hair bounce in reaction to what action the rig is taking. We can adjust gravity strength and direction. We can even enable wind and have hair or clothes flowing.

With our hair now ready for physics, we will need to add new handles to the rig. Given we learned about handles in the previous chapter, this process should be straightforward.

These handles will tag what we want to add physics to. Here, we will use Chaz's hair as our point of reference. To begin this process, we need to perform the following steps:

1. With **Version 2** ready to go, click on the **Rig** tab.
2. If **Heads** is not visible, toggle it on and make sure **3-4th Head** is visible.
3. Under the **Chaz** puppet, locate **Hair** in the **3-4th Head** group.
4. Select the **crown** icon for the layer to enable independence.

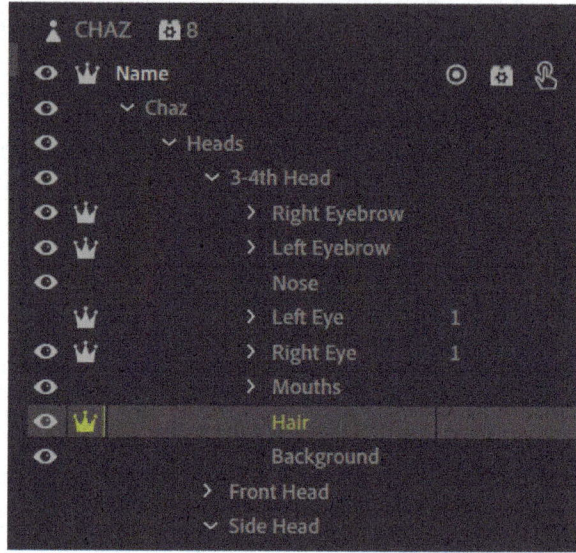

Figure 6.1: Hair will be set as independent (indicated by the crown icon)

5. Select the now visible origin point for **Hair** and move it over Chaz's sideburn.

Figure 6.2: Set the origin point near the bottom right of the Hair layer

Next, we want to add a handle to coordinate the physics. To do this, follow these steps:

1. Select the **Handle Tool** (by pressing *L* on the keyboard).
2. Click the top of the hair to add the handle.
3. With the new handle selected, in the **Tags** panel, under **Physics**, enable **Dangle**.

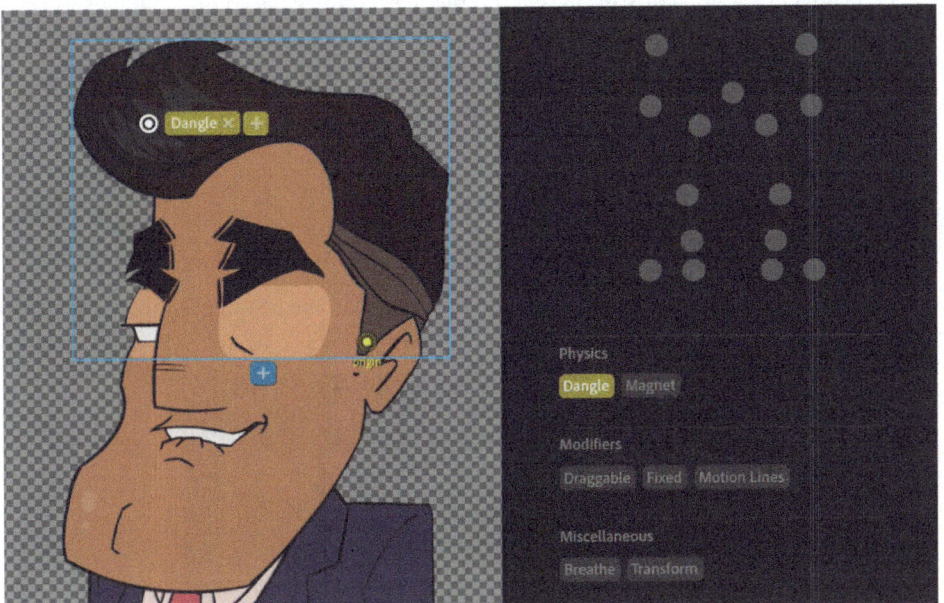

Figure 6.3: Dangle will be assigned to the new handle on the hair

Now, click the **Record** tab to see the result. There isn't much going on with this handle. You can see the hair is hanging down, so physics is applied, but that's our only sign.

Figure 6.4: Gravity is affecting the handle we applied

But without moving the character, or adding behaviors, we can't really see this in action yet. So, let's add some behaviors next!

Modifying universal behaviors

Universal behaviors are actions or stimuli that interact with our rig based on what tags were applied. Using the previous example, we have a handle set to interact with physics. We can adjust the physics so that every handle marked **Physics** will react, and this applies to other tags and behaviors as well.

Another nice thing is we can change universal behaviors in real time while recording, which allows us to refine and tweak the effect to our liking. Let's look at this now:

1. Click on the **Record** tab.
2. Click once on the **CHAZ** rig, which is located at the bottom of the timeline.
3. On the right, you will see the **Properties** panel. Under that, the heading **Puppet Track Behaviors** is listed.

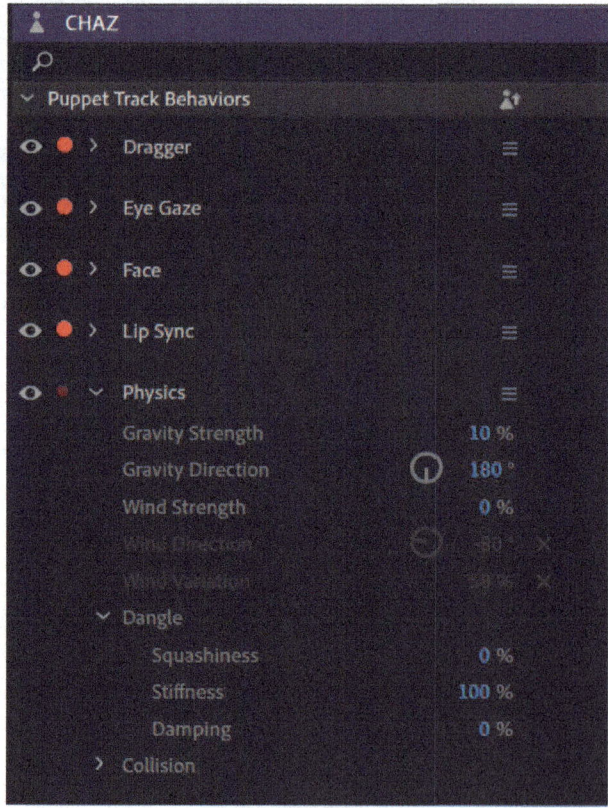

Figure 6.5: The Puppet Track Behaviors panel allows for adjustment to universal behaviors

Physics is a subcategory under this panel. Click the arrow next to the heading to expand and see the options. There are many options you can adjust here, and each project will have its own unique requirements.

4. Let's try adjusting **Wind Direction** to -80. The hair should be bouncing now, with the origin point keeping the back end of the hair locked down.

Figure 6.6: The hair is revealing the head underneath (this is something we can go back to and fix if the issue persists)

Go ahead and play around with the other **Physics** parameters if you wish.

Let's play with some more behaviors:

1. Go back to the **Rig** tab.
2. Click on the character's **Left Hand** handle.
3. Enable the **Dangle** physics through the **Tags** panel.
4. Go back to **Record** and witness what happens. You should see the left hand flapping in the breeze along with the hair. Play around with the wind direction to see the result.

Figure 6.7: The wrist is now susceptible to the wind physics

You may also notice we have other universal behaviors to enable and adjust. Here is a brief description of each:

- **Dragger**: Enables or disables the ability to grab and drag points. You can also adjust the range and whether the dragger stays in place after being moved.
- **Eye Gaze**: Used to toggle whether the camera, mouse, or keyboard is used to control the eyes. These settings are also nice if the movement is too extreme and needs to be dialed back.
- **Face**: Covers a wide range of options: from disabling the camera for face control to the strength of eyes, brows, and your character's mouth.
- **Lip Sync**: Enables or disables mouth movement by using a microphone.
- **Physics**: As discussed above, allows us to adjust gravity, wind, and more.
- **Transform**: Moves, scales, and aligns the rig to your specifications.
- **Triggers**: Enables or disables trigger control.

We can set each of these to record (indicated by the red circle to the left of the behavior name). When we do this, whenever we go the **Record** tab to animate, any behavior with a red record icon will animate and add keyframes to the timeline. This means you can focus on as many behaviors as you want each time you record, making the process more managable.

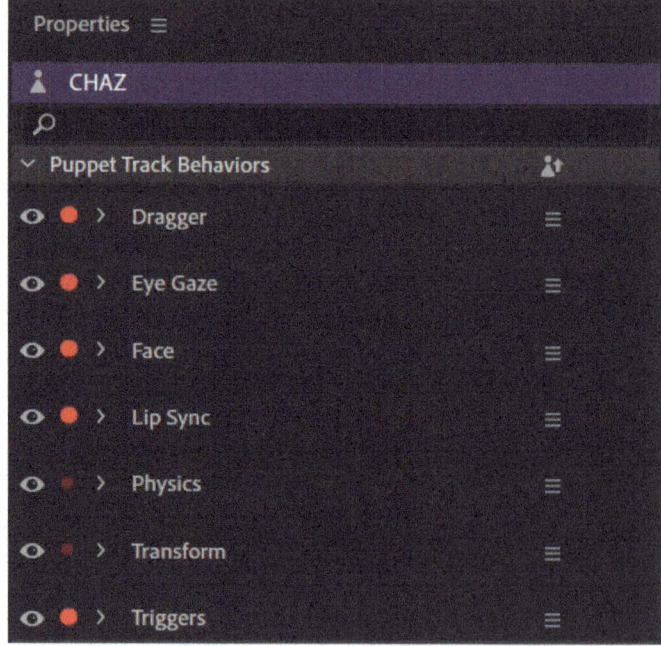

Figure 6.8: The list of behaviors for the currently selected puppet

So, what if you have multiple physics-based handles but want different wind controls for each? That's where layer-specific behaviors come in.

Creating layer-specific behaviors

Let's control the wind strength for two dangle-based handles. We already have these set up for the wrist and hair, so it's just a matter of applying these specific parameters. To illustrate this, take the following steps:

1. Click on the **Rig** tab.
2. Click the **Hair** layer under **3-4th Head**.
3. On the right side of the screen, direct your attention to the bottom. Look for **Behaviors**.
4. Click the + button next to **Behaviors** and choose **Physics** from the list.

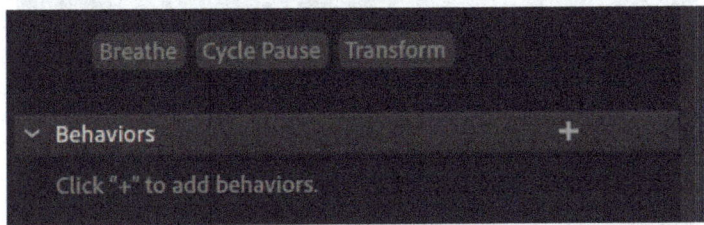

Figure 6.9: You can add new behaviors by clicking the + button

5. A new set of options will appear. Click **Physics**.
6. New **Physics** options will now appear under **Behaviors**. These options should be identical to the ones we set when on the **Record** tab.
7. Now set **Wind Strength** to 73% and **Wind Direction** to 1.
8. Go back to **Record**. Notice how the hair is blowing up as we set it. But the hand is still being blown to the right, based on the universal physics behavior.

Figure 6.10: Note how the hand and hair are blowing in different directions

You will also note the **Puppet Track Behaviors** panel listed the hair physics behavior among the universal behaviors (labeled **Physics [Hair]**). This means we can adjust universal and layer-based behaviors in real time as we animate. It also gives much more control to the rig, as we can target any layer to set this process up.

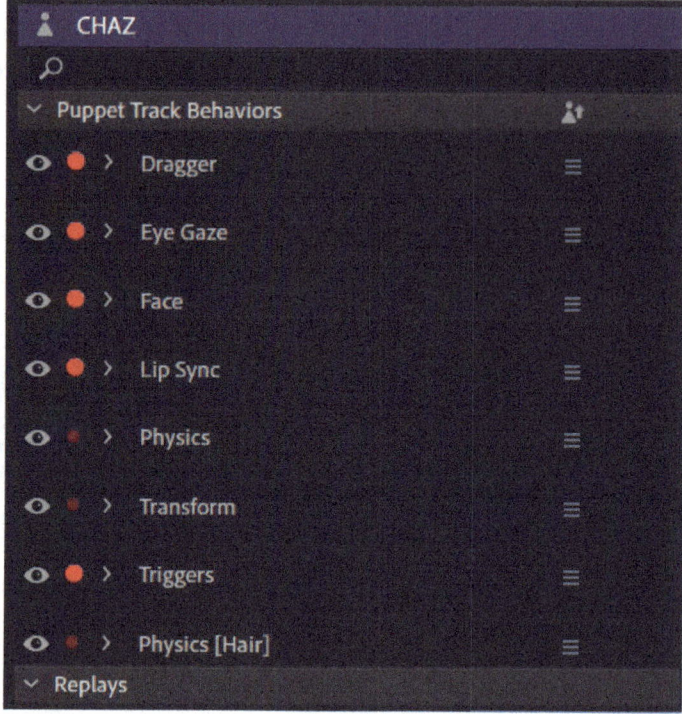

Figure 6.11: Layer-specific behaviors will be added to the panel

We will work with both types of behaviors as we continue to progress through the book. For now, it's important to know the difference in how they function.

Refining animation with meshes

As we continue to add handles to create behaviors, we are actually altering a mesh that was automatically created when we imported the .psd file. While we can't do much to alter this mesh beyond this, it allows us to see how Character Animator is interpreting the bends and flexibility of the layers. To see this, follow these steps:

1. Go to the **Rig** tab.
2. To view the mesh, locate the **Mesh** buttons under the rig. They are to the right of the **Show Rigging Issues** button, which is the triangular icon with an exclamation point.

Figure 6.12: The right mesh button will show an outline, while the left will reveal the entire mesh

3. Click on the left mesh button (labeled **Show Mesh**). This will show us every part of the mesh on the rig.
4. Now click on the **Front Arm** layer. You should see the mesh being more defined by the handles, especially since we added sticks in the previous chapter.

Figure 6.13: The mesh is tighter around the bends due to the sticks we added

If we remove the sticks, we get a mesh that looks like the following screenshot:

Figure 6.14: Removing the Sticks makes the mesh more relaxed

Again, this is mostly used as a reference if you're having issues getting meshes to look or function a certain way. Leave the mesh view on if you find it to be useful.

You will find a new version, **Version 3**, in the **History** panel if you need to view the final result for this chapter.

Summary

Setting behaviors is a big part of the animation process and allows us to create rig or layer-based changes in real time. Danglers are great for adding physics to any layer you wish; they can be subtle or extreme, it's completely up to you! If you're having issues with getting things to link properly, viewing the mesh may give some insights. Being able to control all these elements will allow for a smooth recording process.

In the next chapter, we will focus on triggers, which allow for lip-syncing, swappable props, and more. Before you know it, we will animate a scene with your first fully functional rig!

7
Assigning Mouths and Props with Triggers and Swap Sets

As you continue to develop your characters and build scenes, you may find you need more flexibility with your rigs. Let's say you want a character to hold a prop but later need that hand free. Or perhaps you have multiple props, or phases – for example, for a hand – that you want to change when the production calls for it. Triggers and swap sets can handle these functions, and each function has different uses.

In this chapter, we will look at the following topics:

- Creating triggers for props
- Creating swap sets for mouths and hands
- Further exploring triggers and swap sets

Once this chapter is complete, you will know how to add even more interactivity and flexibility to your Character Animator productions. With that said, let's get going!

Technical requirements

We will be using Character Animator along with the `Chat with Chaz` project file. Be sure to load up **Version 3** from the **History** panel so you can follow along.

Creating triggers for props

Props can mean many things, depending on your background and design philosophy. For this book, a prop will mean whatever item a character can hold or interact with.

Creating triggers for props is useful, as it allows us to evoke or trigger a prop into view when needed. We will use the keyboard, as it's the most common device to control triggers.

Importing props

First, in order to create a trigger, we will need to add at least one prop to our current rig. We can do this in one of two ways: editing the .psd in Photoshop or importing the props directly to the Character Animator file. Since we've edited the PSD already in previous chapters, let's import a prop into the project. To do this, follow these steps:

1. Make sure you're on the **Rig** panel.
2. Open the **Import** window by going to **File | Import** or using the *Ctrl + I* or *Command + I* keyboard shortcut.
3. Inside this chapter's exercise files, double-click coffee cup.png.
4. Open the **Project** panel. The **coffee cup** image should now appear in the list.

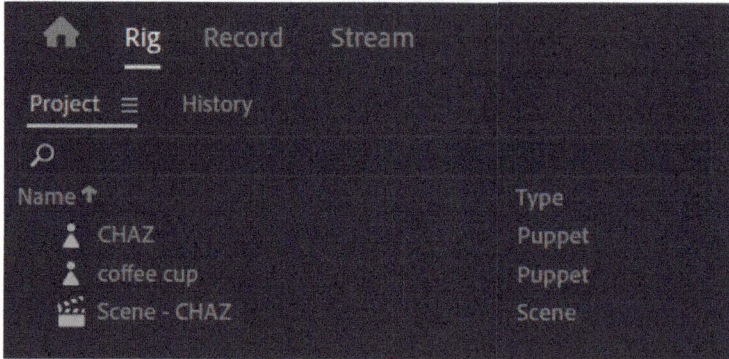

Figure 7.1: The current state of the Project panel

5. Drag the coffee cup into the **F Arm** group and below **F Hands** (the cup will appear large on the screen).

Figure 7.2: The mug is imported but not in the right spot

Also note that we have a puppet, with the coffee cup image placed inside it.

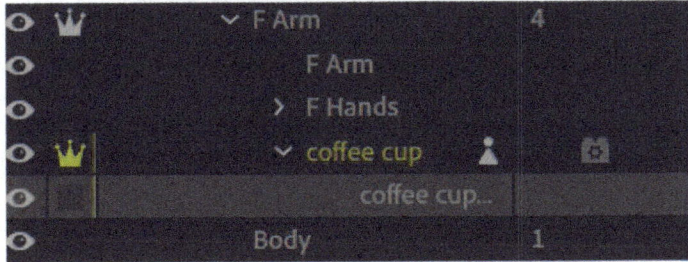

Figure 7.3: The imported image automatically converts to a puppet with one layer, which is the image itself

6. Click on the giant mug in the workspace. This will select the coffee cup puppet.
7. Using the **Properties** panel, we can adjust the position, size, and rotation of the mug to fit into Chaz's front hand:

- **X** = -19.8 px
- **Y** = 1,272.4px
- **X Scale** = 29%
- **Y Scale** = 29%
- **Rotate** = -90°

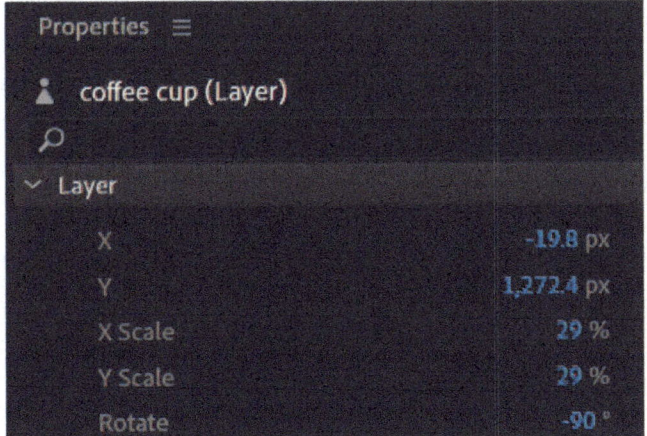

Figure 7.4: We can adjust any layer during the design or animation process with the Layer Properties panel

As you make adjustments on the **Properties** panel, you will see the changes in real time on the **Puppet** panel:

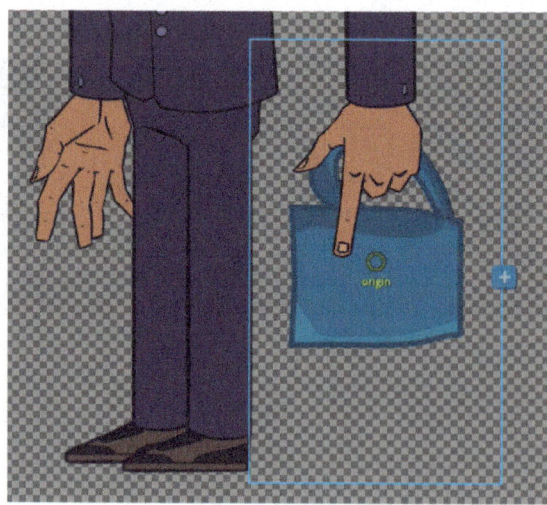

Figure 7.5: Move and resize the mug to fit the front hand

8. Click and drag the origin point to the knuckles of the hand. This will allow us to rotate or create physics that allow the mug to bob and move as if it's being held by a moving person:

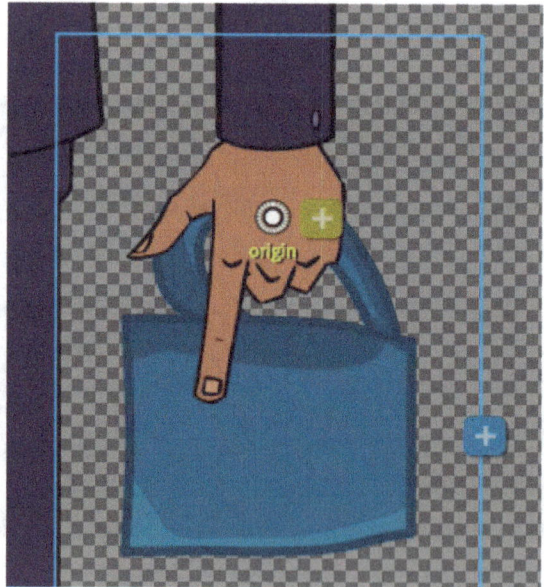

Figure 7.6: Setting the origin point toward the hand will allow us to add different behaviors properly later on if we wish

With our prop properly placed in the rig, we can now set up a trigger.

Creating triggers

In order to create a trigger, follow these steps:

1. Go to **Window | Triggers** to reveal the **Triggers** panel if it's not visible. It'll appear on the bottom left of the screen.

Figure 7.7: The Triggers panel is currently blank

2. Locate the only image, **coffee cup.png**, in the layers list of the rig.

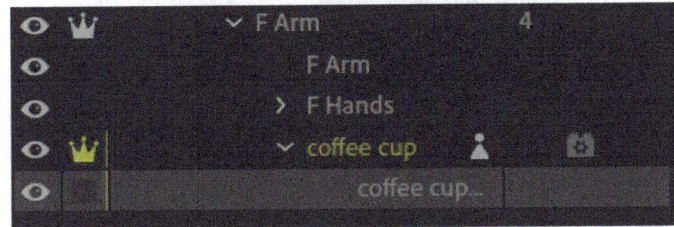

Figure 7.8: Clicking the coffee cup layer will allow us to focus on this layer's triggers only

3. Right-click on **coffee cup** and choose **Create Trigger in "coffee cup"**.

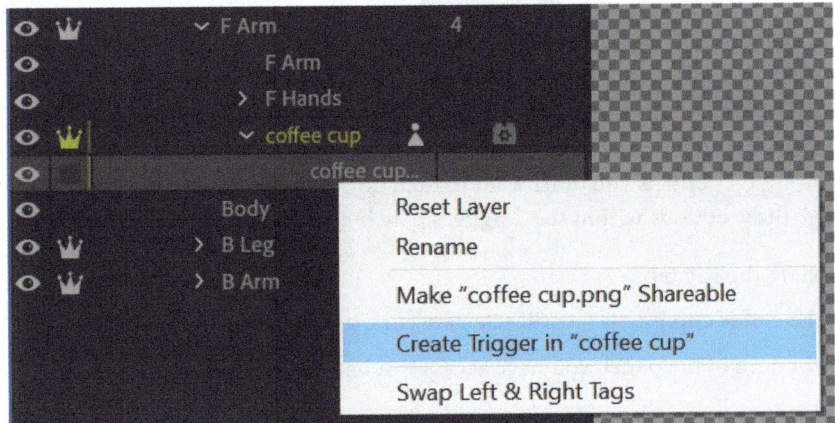

Figure 7.9: Right-clicking a layer reveals some useful options

4. In the **Triggers** panel, **coffee cup.png** will appear with an open field next to it. Here, you can click the field and press any key on your keyboard to set this trigger. For this example, we will use the *C* key, which will be reflected in the panel.

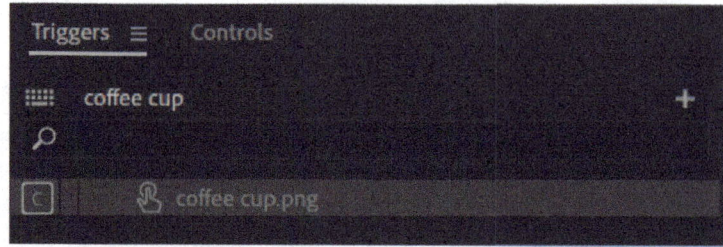

Figure 7.10: The coffee cup layer now shows up in the Triggers panel

With the trigger set, we can test it out by going to the **Record** tab and pressing the *C* key. Note how pressing the key toggles the visibility of the cup.

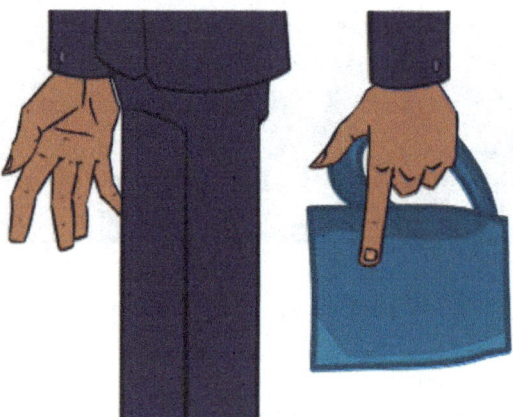

Figure 7.11: Pressing C will reveal the mug

As it's set up right now, we hid the mug until we press the *C* key. But what if you want to have the mug visible right away? Or perhaps you don't want to hold down the *C* key to keep the mug on the screen. We can change these options within the **Triggers** panel:

1. Go back to the **Rig** tab.
2. With the **coffee cup.png** layer still selected, click the **coffee cup.png** trigger.
3. At the bottom of the panel, you have access to a handful of options:

    - **Midi Note** allows you to set a key to trigger the action, assuming you have the device to use it.
    - **Latch** allows you to toggle the trigger rather than having to hold the key down.

- **Default for Swap Sets**, which we will use, allows us to set which pose displays with no key presses.
- **Layers and Replays** will show layers tied to the trigger. Right now, we only affect the coffee cup with the *C* key.

Figure 7.12: The current state of our Project panel

So, what are swap sets and how do they compare to triggers? Let's take a look at that next.

Creating swap sets for hands

Triggers are binary, allowing for the layer assigned to be turned on or off. Swap sets allow us to switch or swap out different layers as we record. For this book's project, we will set up a swap set to change our hand poses.

Since we grouped our hands when laying out the rig in Photoshop, we can set this up pretty easily:

1. Make sure you're on the **Rig** tab.
2. Locate **F Hands**, found under **F Arm**.
3. Right-click on **F Hands** and choose **Create Swap Set**.

Figure 7.13: Choosing Create Swap Set will automatically make the group layers swappable

The **Triggers** panel should now show **F Hands** with the three hand poses we organized below it.

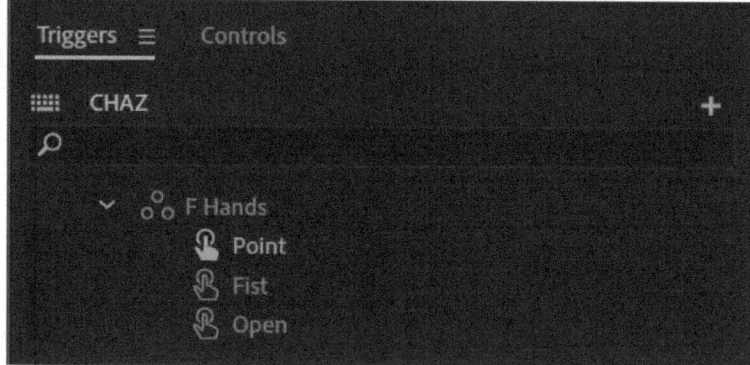

Figure 7.14: A swap set lays out each asset in the group, allowing you to customize your keys

Don't worry – the cup trigger is still present. We can access it again by clicking the **coffee cup.png** layer from the list. But for now, we are fine focusing on the swap set.

Swap sets allow us to set multiple triggers. In this case, let's set the swap to the following:

- *P* for **Point**
- *F* for **Fist**
- *O* for **Open**

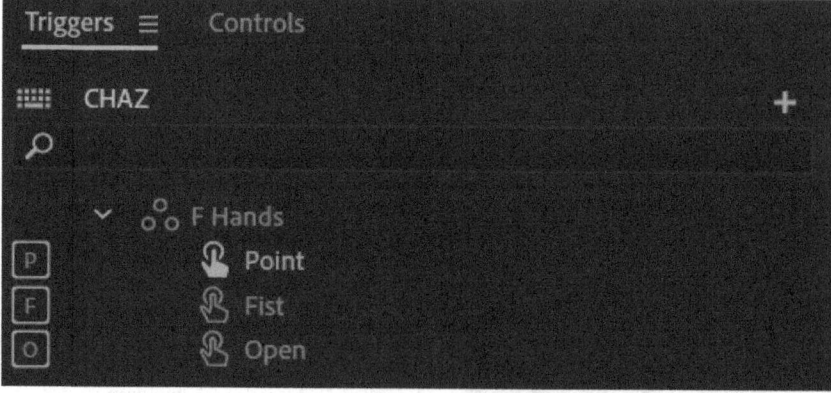

Figure 7.15: A swap set lays out each asset in the group, allowing you to customize your keys

Before we go to the **Record** tab, let's decide which hand pose we want to appear first.

4. Click **Open** and choose **Default** from the bottom options.
5. Right-click on any of the poses and choose **Select Label Group**. This will select all poses for the hands.

Creating swap sets for hands 139

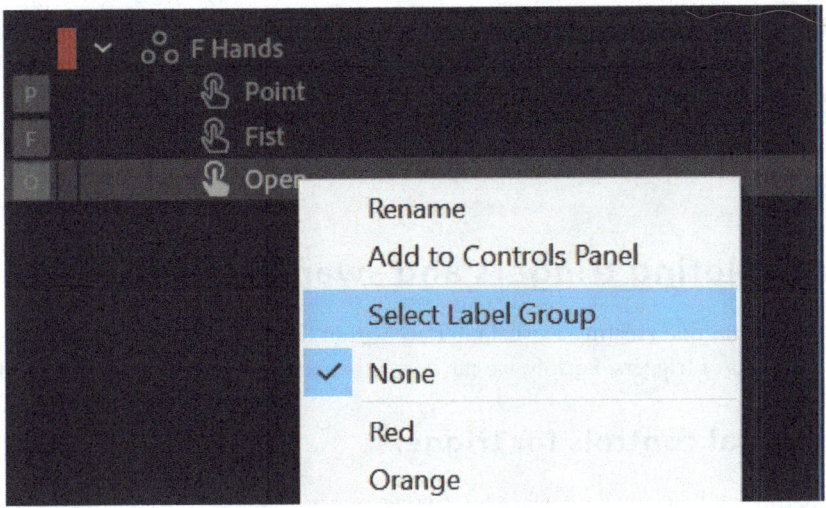

Figure 7.16: You can also assign colors for your swap sets for easier organization

6. Click **Latch** on the bottom of the panel so that we don't have to hold down keys to keep poses on the screen.
7. Now, go to the **Record** tab. Note how the front hand starts with the open pose.
8. Press *P* or *O*. The hand pose should change. Pressing the key again will switch the hand back to the default open pose.
9. Switch the hand to the fist pose and then press *C* to bring in the cup. As you can see, such actions will allow us to drop and pick up the cup when needed.

Figure 7.17: Combining triggers and swap sets can allow for some nice animation tricks

10. Finally, make sure to make **B Hand** a swap set (right-click the group and choose **Create Swap Set**). Ensure no triggers for the back hand are the same as the front, or else they will both swap at the same time when pressing the key.

Now that we have some understanding of triggers and swap sets, let's talk about some other uses for these two features.

Further exploring triggers and swap sets

In some cases, you may find creating a visual interface within Character Animator to be more beneficial when using swap sets or triggers. Luckily, we can trigger actions beyond using the keyboard, if desired.

Creating visual controls for triggers

Here's how we can set up a visual interface for our swap sets:

1. In the **Triggers** panel, right-click on **F Hands** and choose **Add to Controls Panel**.

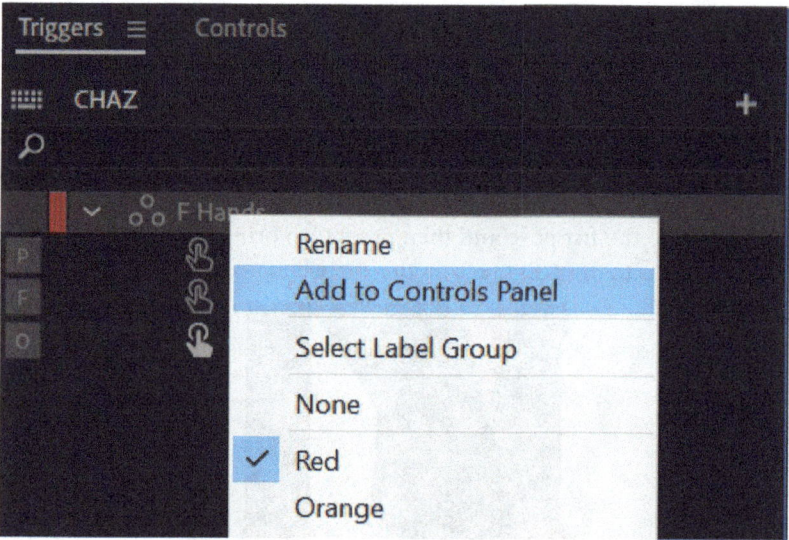

Figure 7.18: We can easily generate controls with Add to Controls Panel

2. Click the **coffee cup.png** layer in the **Puppet** panel while on the **Rig** tab.
3. In the **Triggers** panel, right-click on the **coffee cup.png** trigger and choose **Add to Controls Panel**.

Further exploring triggers and swap sets   141

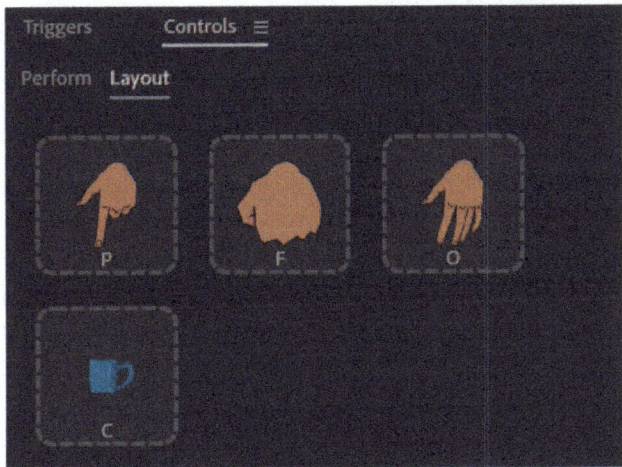

Figure 7.21: The Layout tab under Controls allows for a visual representation of your current triggers and swap sets

4. The **Layout** view allows you to organize the keys. If you have a certain preference for how the controls are laid out, simply drag and drop where you want them to go.

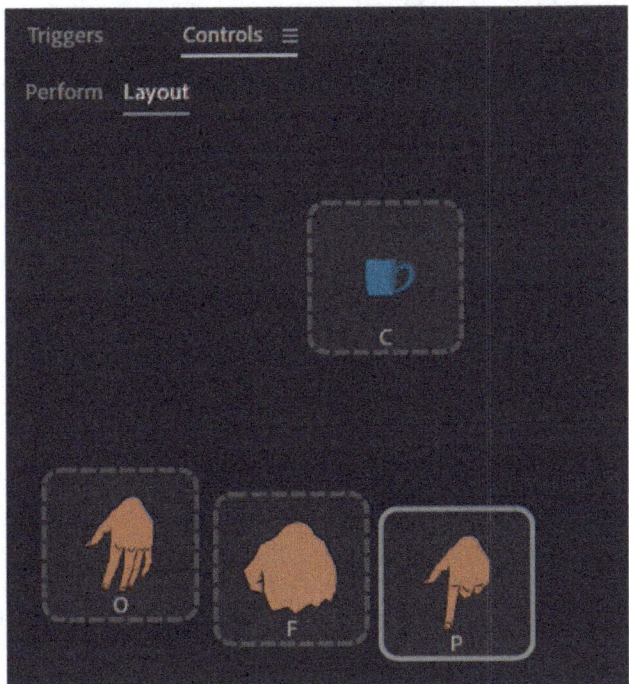

Figure 7.22: You can set up the Controls panel however you see fit

Press any of the keys on the keyboard. Doing so will light up the linked control, showing the connection.

5. Go to the **Record** tab, if you are not there already.
6. Under **Controls**, go to **Perform**.
7. Now, click on any of the controls. Note how you can interact with these triggers in the same way you used your keys.

Again, this is simply an optional extension to triggers. If you want to use just hardware, such as your keyboard, that's fine. However, you may find a touch interface or other peripherals benefit from the **Layout** and **Perform** interface.

Other tips for using triggers and swap sets

You can set up triggers and swap sets for any item in your Character Animator project. It's impossible to cover every scenario that requires or benefits from these tools, and we will be using triggers and swap sets when we animate our little production. So, here is a list of ideas:

- You can use triggers to turn props off that may be in the scenery. A good example of this would be having the coffee cup placed outside of the rig on a table. A second cup, rigged with a trigger, will be in the hand of the puppet. This cup will be invisible at first. When we animate the rig to grab the cup, we can trigger the scenery cup to disappear and the rig cup to appear. This quick switch will make it look like the character has grabbed the cup and lifted it up. You can set one key to trigger multiple layers. Let's say you want both hands to open at the same time. Placing *O* as the open phase for both hands will allow this simultaneous animation.
- Swap sets could be used for changing clothing, hairstyles, or any other design choice that would benefit from being changed on the fly.
- While Character Animator relies heavily on a camera and microphone to track emotion, eyes, the mouth, and more, you could use a swap set to evoke these actions manually if desired.

There are several other uses, but hopefully, these will give you some ideas, especially as we start to build our animated scene in this book.

Summary

Triggers and swap sets are great for turning assets on and off or swapping the state of one asset for another. They are mostly used for simple switches, such as hands, but other more advanced uses can be integrated. Also, be sure to take advantage of the **Control** panel if the keyboard controls are not working out for you.

Next, we will build on the concept of triggers by working with more facial features, as well as integrating head turns for even more control and immersion.

8
Refining Layers and Exploring Optional Rig Features

With everything we've worked on, your rig should be close to ready to be put into an animated scene. All we need to do is fix and polish a few things and refine the behavior strengths, and we should be ready to go. However, there are also additional features we can take advantage of. Some of these are style choices, while others can enhance any rig you're using. To achieve this, we will cover the following topics in the chapter:

- Animating eyelids
- Animating breathing and jaw animations
- Designing a character for head turns

After this, you will have more options for animating your character, opening up style possibilities and enhanced control. With that said, let's get going!

Technical requirements

Make sure to have Character Animator open with **Version 4** loaded under the `Chat_With_Chaz` project file. Additionally, we will be referencing the PSD files labeled `Chaz_Host_v5_fixed_eyes` and `Chaz_Host_v6_eyelids`.

Animating eyelids

With the rig set up as it is, we cannot take advantage of animating eyelids. The reason for this is the blink layers we have inserted into the eye groups cancel this feature out, even if we properly label and set the rig up for it. Simply disabling the visibility of the blink layers won't work either. We also only have one eyelid for each eye. To do this, we will require two.

To test the current layer switch for the blink, go to the **Record** tab and try blinking. While it may be hard to tell (since you're closing your eyes and can't see the screen) the blink layers come in and replace the eye for that moment. You can try winking with one eye or create a small recording to test this as well. We can animate the lids in real time, like the pupils, head, or mouth, for a more fluid motion.

Is it better to track eyelids or simply have the layer switch over? It really comes down to your rig layout and aesthetic preferences. Let's see what our character looks like with animated lids.

Importing a character with eyelids

To test a character with eyelids that can be animated, let's bring in a version of Chaz equipped with bottom eyelids:

1. Make sure you're on the **Rig** tab.
2. Click on **CHAZ** on the **Puppet** panel.
3. In the **Puppet** section on the **Properties** panel, click the file link to change the file path:

Figure 8.1: Clicking on the file path to select a new .psd file

4. In your exercise files, double-click on `Chaz_Host_v6_eyelids.psd` to replace the rig.

Figure 8.2: Choosing Chaz_Host_v6_eyelids.psd to test how we can animate eyelids

5. When the file comes in, the head may be hidden. Simply click the eye icon next to the head if this is the case. You should now have a new version of Chaz. This time, he's missing two blink layers but has gained two bottom eyelids.

Figure 8.3: Chaz looks a bit odd with eyelids, but don't worry, this is just a temporary test

Since the artist didn't name the eyelids to be Character Animator-friendly, we will need to add some tags so the lids will properly track movement. You may also want to hide the **Angry** and **Worried** eyebrow layers again for a cleaner work area.

Tagging the eyelids

Tagging the eyelids is just like tagging any other body part. Here's what we need to do:

1. Go back to the **Rig** tab.
2. On the **Puppet** panel, expand the **Left Eye** group to reveal its layers:

Figure 8.4: The Left Eye's layers for 3/4th Head

3. Click on the **Bottom Lid** layer and then click on the bottom-left eyelid on the **Tags** tab to tag it:

Figure 8.5: The diagram displays both the bottom and top lids for each eye

The tag, in this case, Left Eyelid Bottom, will also display on the Puppet panel.

Figure 8.6: Once the eyelid is tagged, you will see the label update on the rig

4. Click on the **Top Lid** layer and then click on the top left eyelid on the **Tags** diagram.
5. Expand **Right Eye** and repeat the steps for the right top and bottom eyelids.
6. Make sure the crown is turned on for each layer – that way, they can be animated freely from the head.

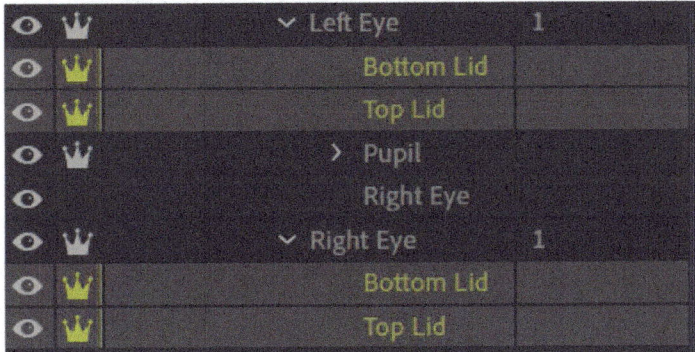

Figure 8.7: If you leave the lids dependent, it will affect the scale of the face when animating

7. Finally, make sure the origin points are moved over the assets they represent:

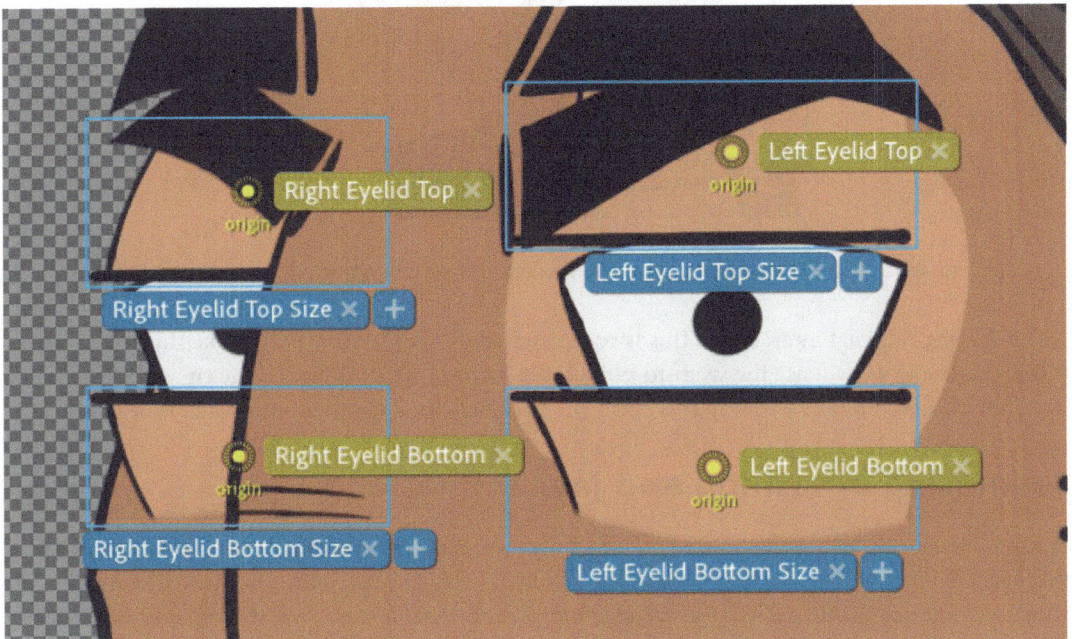

Figure 8.8: It's always best to make sure your tags and origin points match the artwork

With the new eyelids properly tagged and origin points set, we can test out those eyelids:

1. Click on the **Record** tab.

   Note how the eyelids track your eye movements.

2. You can adjust the strength of the eyelids with the **Eyelid Strength** dial in the **Behaviors** panel. Around `88%` should allow the eyelids to touch when the eyes close:

Figure 8.9: The lids should separate and come together when tracking the actor's blinks

Again, having lids that interact like this is completely optional. Leave your rig like this if you prefer it. For this book, we will use the swap-to-blink layer method, as we designed the rig with that choice in mind. However, before we swap the `.psd` file back, let's look at other optional handles.

Animating breathing and jaw animations

While Character Animator can lip-sync by switching mouth poses based on phonemes, we can enhance this effect even further by adding a **Nutcrack Jaw** behavior. This will allow the jaw to drop based on what the mouth is doing. As with the eyelids, this is an optional feature. We will also add a **Breathing** behavior for further exploration:

1. Click on **Mouths** inside of **3/4th Head**.
2. Using the handle tool, click and add a handle below the mouth:

Animating breathing and jaw animations | 149

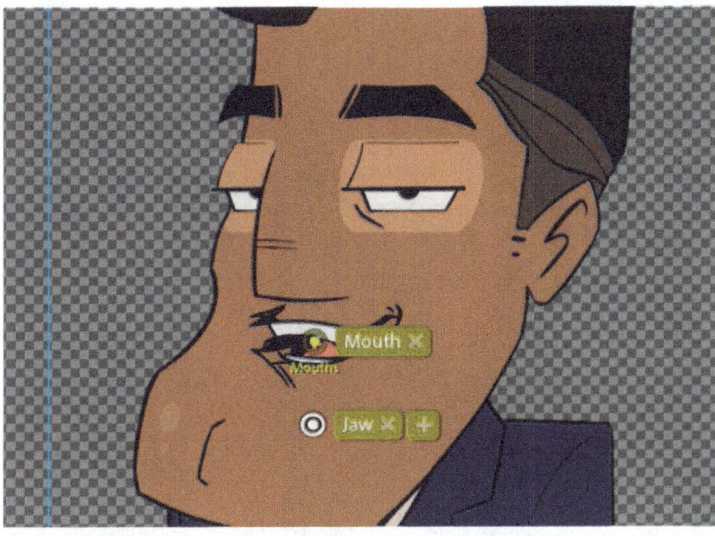

Figure 8.10: The new handle can be placed below the mouth

3. On the **Tags** panel, click on the jaw icon to define the layer.
4. At the bottom of the **Tags** panel is a plus sign next to **Behaviors**. Click on the plus sign and choose **Nutcracker Jaw** from the list:

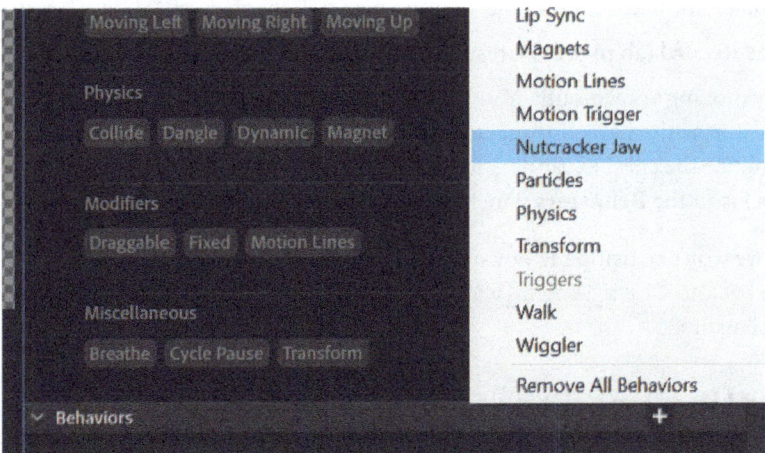

Figure 8.11: Adding the Nutcracker Jaw behavior to the mouth will allow us to control the parameters when recording

5. Next, click on the **Body** layer and add a handle in the middle of the tie.
6. Tag it as **Breathe**, which is located under **Miscellaneous** in the tag panel.

Figure 8.12: The Breathe handle will be the focal point of the transformation effect

7. While still on the body, click on the + button next to **Behaviors** and choose **Breathe** from the list.
8. Go to the **Record** tab to see the results.
9. Now, try moving your mouth. You should notice the jaw for the character moves as well. You can adjust how the behavior reacts on the right. The same goes for the **Breathe** panel. You should notice the chest expanding and compressing. You can adjust how fast and how extreme this effect is in the **Behaviors** panel.

For this book, we won't be using the **Jaw** or **Breathe** behaviors. It really comes down to a style choice and we will go back to `Chaz_Host_v5_Fixed_Eyes.psd` and remove the **Jaw** and **Breathe** handles and behaviors.

Implementing head turns

With a rig set up properly, it can react to the actor turning their head on camera, and as with most behaviors, it can be modified and controlled using a keyboard and mouse if desired. All it takes is setting the proper tags, duplicating layers, and adjusting some values.

Tagging the head phases

As you have seen, our Chaz rig comes with various layers to create a head turn. The three main poses are left ¾, left profile, and front. We went through and refined the rig structure. Now, we just need to tell Character Animator how to react.

Let's tag the phases and set up the behavior:

1. On the **Rig** tab, click on the **Heads** layer.
2. On the bottom right should be the **Behavior** panel. Click on the + icon and choose **Head & Body Turner** from the list. This will tell Character Animator that this is where the sub-groups are for the head phases:

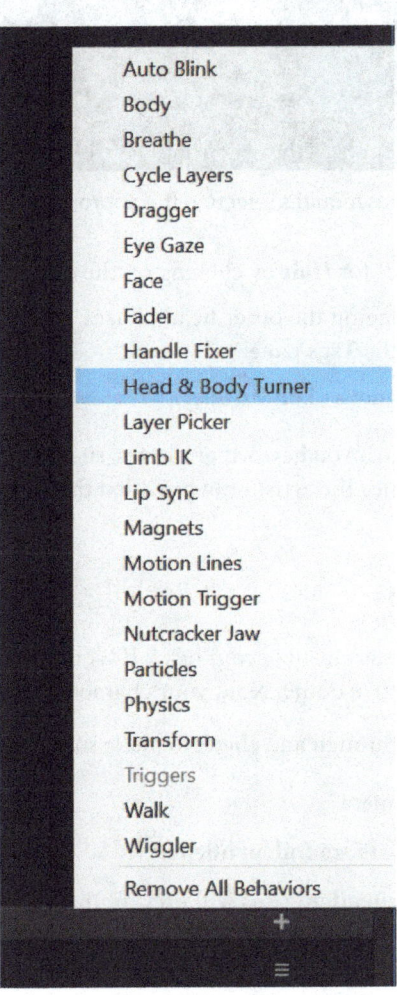

Figure 8.13: The Head & Body Turner behavior enables us to animate head turns

3. With this behavior enabled, it will now listen for the phase changes.
4. Click once on the **3/4th Head** layer.
5. Under the **Tags** diagram, you will find head phases. Since we are on **3/4th Head** and it's looking to the left, we will want to choose **Left Quarter**.

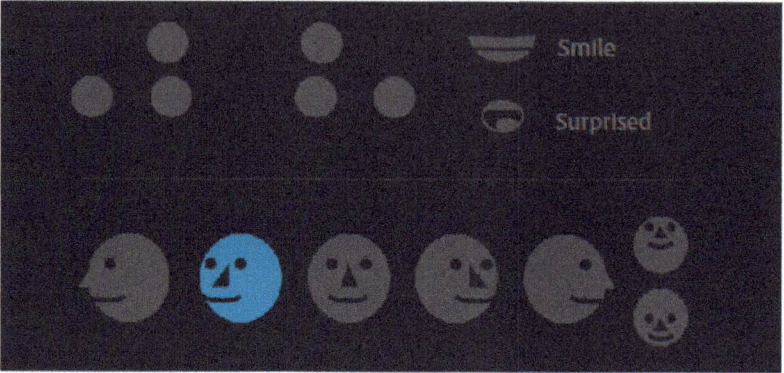

Figure 8.14: Tagging the head turns requires selecting the appropriate phase for the layer you're tagging

6. Let's disable independence for **Hair** by clicking on the crown to turn it off.
7. Now, we can continue tagging the other head phases. Click on **Front Head** and choose the **Frontal** head view from the **Tags** panel
8. Click on **Side Head** and choose **Left Profile**.

As you can see from the diagram, if you have other phases, such as right facing or tilting up or down, we can include those as well. Since the artist only provided three head phases, we will just focus on the left views.

Testing the head turns

Jump into the **Record** panel and start turning your head. If set up correctly, the character's head phases will switch according to what you're doing. Now, your character has more movement than before!

If you're having issues, go back through and check to make sure the following applies:

- You've calibrated your camera
- Your eyebrow and eye layers are **Independent**
- Your head layers are **Independent** (this will prevent the brows from morphing the forehead)
- The rig itself is set to **Independent**
- Everything on the face is tagged appropriately

One little adjustment or setting can throw the whole rig off. It's not uncommon to have to test things a few times to get everything right. This is especially true for more advanced rigs. You can also refer to **Version 5** in the Character Animator project file to see the completed result.

Summary

After some refining and polishing, our rig is now closer than ever to being ready for animation. Sometimes, going back to the PSD file multiple times is required if additions are needed or errors need correcting. Depending on your needs, you can choose to animate eyelids or jaws. Head turns add yet another dimension to your project.

Up next, we will look at how to use preset animation to help speed up the production workflow of your project.

Part 3: Animating and Refining Your Scene

With the rig set up and ready, we can now focus our attention on recording and exporting a scene using the character we've been working with. Animating can be a mix of real-time and post- actions. Using our face, voice, mouse, keyboard, external image sequences, and a properly assembled rig, we can record keyframes on the timeline, creating simple or complex scenes. More ambitious projects usually involve other software, such as Premiere or After Effects. We can do this for multiple characters and props. We can even transmit it live through a stream if desired.

This part includes the following chapters:

- *Chapter 9, Working with Preset Actions*
- *Chapter 10, Animating a Simple Sequence*
- *Chapter 11, Rearranging, Polishing, and Enhancing Our Sequence*
- *Chapter 12, Exporting, Editing, and Sharing Your Character Animator Sequence*
- *Chapter 13, Additional Character Animator Tools and Features*

9
Working with Preset Actions

While you can make all of your character animations from scratch, preset actions are included to help you get your character moving. Walk cycles, running animations, and more can easily be added with a click of a button. Furthermore, you can refine these actions to make them more customized to the character in the scene.

In addition, we can add more than one action at a time to create a more complicated or dynamic animated sequence. Once we have looked at this, we will polish up the rig and correct any final errors that may pop up.

More specifically, we will cover the following topics:

- Creating a walk cycle
- Modifying a walk cycle
- Mixing actions on the timeline

With that said, it's time to open up Character Animator and get going!

Technical requirements

Make sure that you have Character Animator open with **Version 6** loaded under the `Chat_With_Chaz` project file. We will be working with the `CHAZ WALK` rig for this chapter.

Creating a walk cycle

Walk cycles are a big part of the animation process. If you can learn the fundamentals of this animation, then anything else you choose to animate will come more naturally.

However, Character Animator is unique compared to other animation software. While it is possible to move limbs, create keyframes, and time everything appropriately to animate a walk, it proves to be a bit more difficult.

Fortunately, Character Animator has a built-in walk cycle animation that can be applied and tweaked for any rig that's been appropriately tagged and set up. And that's what we will learn here.

For this example, we will use a modified version of the original Chaz rig. The only difference is that this rig has not been set up for head turns.

To start adding a walk cycle, follow these steps:

1. Make sure you're on the **Rig** tab.
2. If the body or head is hidden, reveal the layers so that the whole character is visible:

Figure 9.1: Making the rig fully visible will help with the animation process

3. To make viewing the layers easier, expand the **HEAD** and **BODY** groups while keeping the subgroup or layers compressed:

Creating a walk cycle   159

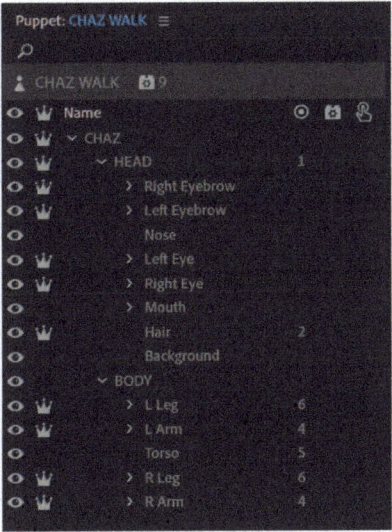

Figure 9.2: The layers are close to the rig we worked with before. Now, we only have one HEAD phase

4. Next to **CHAZ WALK** is the **Behavior** icon. Remember, this is where our universal behaviors for the puppet are. Click the + button next to this and choose **Walk** from this list:

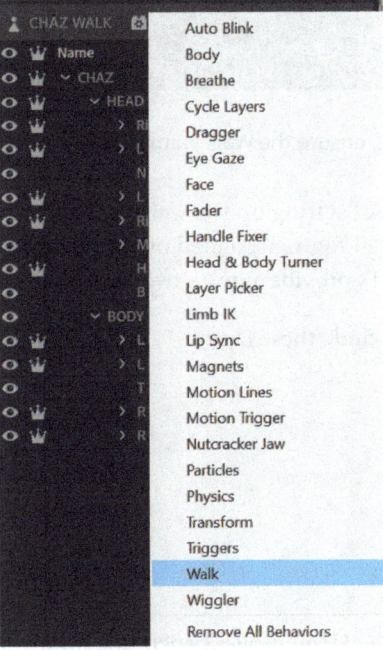

Figure 9.3: Choosing to add Walk to the CHAZ WALK puppet

The new **Walk** behavior will appear on the bottom right **Behaviors** panel. Here, we have several options to choose from. For now, we will leave the adjustments alone and direct our attention to the bottom, where the **Handles** section lies:

Figure 9.4: For the best results, ensure the Walk animation is detecting all the handles listed here

This is the most important part of setting up the walk cycle. For the best results, you will want to ensure each tag listed is accounted for, represented by a **1** to the right of the listing. While we have done some work with tagging, let's provide a quick overview of the tags on the rig:

- The **Torso** layer should include these tags:
    - **Right Hip**
    - **Left Hip**
    - **Right Shoulder**
    - **Left Shoulder**
    - **Waist**
    - **Neck** (can also lay on the **Head** group, depending on the design):

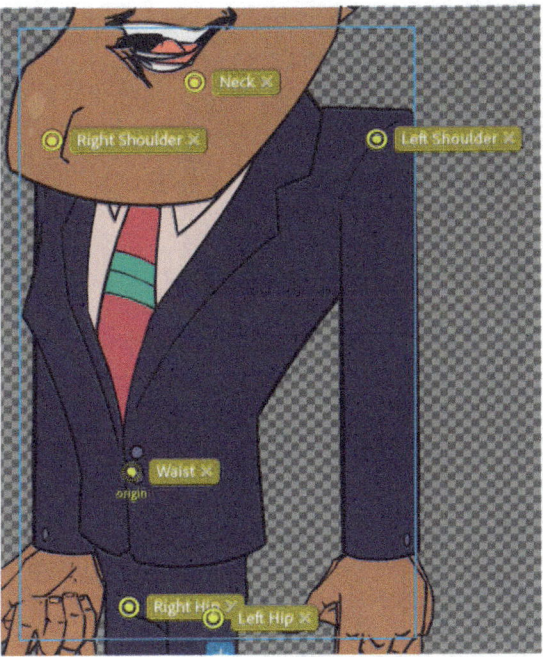

Figure 9.5: Be sure these are added to the torso or body graphic layer, not the Body group

- For the legs, you will want to tag the following:

    - For **Right Leg**:

        - **Right Knee**
        - **Right Ankle**
        - **Right Toe**
        - **Right Heel**

    - For **Left Leg**:

        - **Left Knee**
        - **Left Ankle**
        - **Left Toe**
        - **Left Heel**:

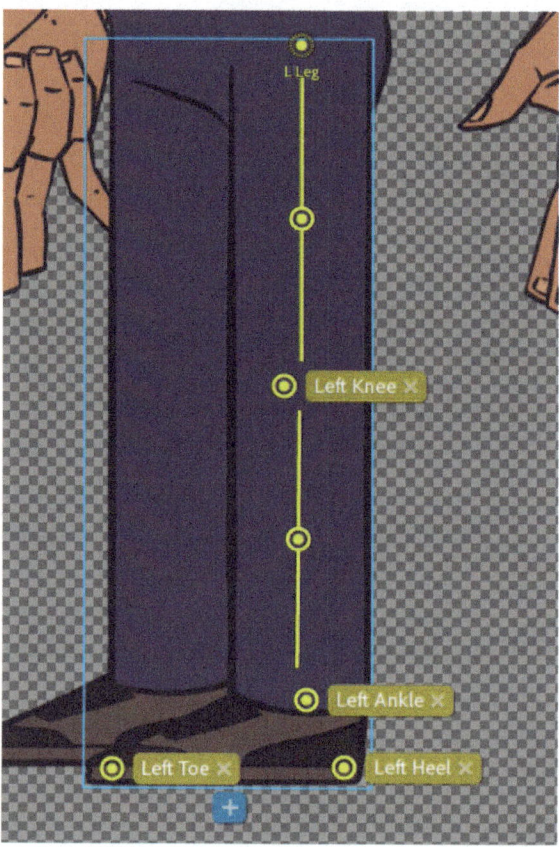

Figure 9.6: Each leg should be tagged with its appropriate direction

- For the hands, you will want to tag the following:
    - For **Right Arm**:
        - **Right Elbow**
        - **Right Wrist**
    - For **Left Arm**:
        - **Left Elbow**
        - **Left Wrist**:

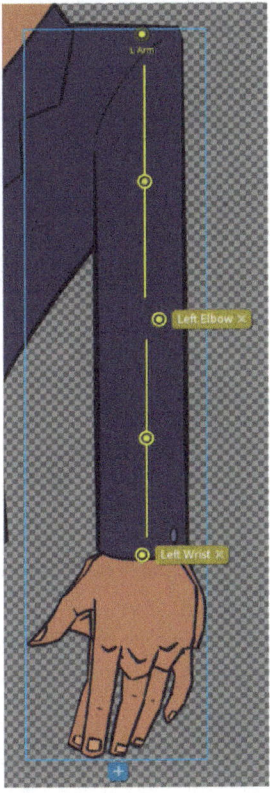

Figure 9.7: Like the legs, ensure the arm groups have their elbows and wrists tagged

Finally, **HEAD** is set to **Independent**, along with the hair, pupils, blinks, and eyebrows:

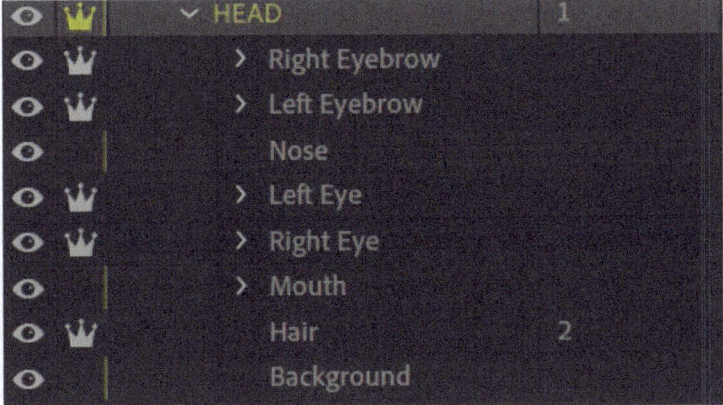

Figure 9.8: To ensure you can control the eyes and eyebrows, keep their layers independent

To test the animation, go to the **Record** tab. You should see Chaz walking in place:

Figure 9.9: Chaz's default walk

If you have any issues, such as the body or head morphing, or perhaps another visual anomaly is prevalent, go back to **Rig** and ensure everything has been tagged appropriately, along with your limbs and head being set to **Independent**.

With the walk now animating, we can adjust how the walk functions. Let's take a look at that now.

Modifying a walk cycle

Once you tag the character appropriately for a walk, the hard part is over. Now, it's time to personalize the animation. Luckily, you have several options to accomplish this.

Let's click on the **Record** tab and start adjusting the parameters. Here are a few of the main ones:

- **Mode**: This allows you to adjust how the rig walks. You can loop the animation, control it with the arrow keys, or use a position-based parameter to move the rig. This provides several ways to record the animation. Try switching the modes and trying it for yourself:

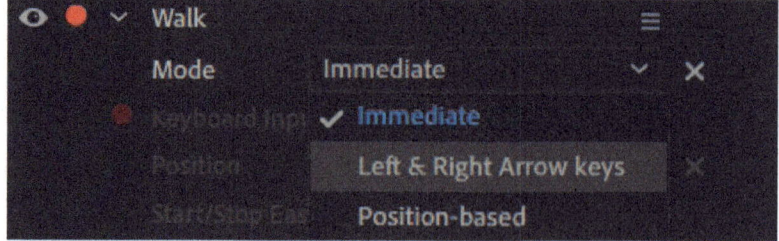

Figure 9.10: You can control the walk with three different functions

- **Style**: This allows you to change how the animation looks. Walking, running, strutting, and slumping are just some of the presets you can implement, providing a base for you to customize and personalize:

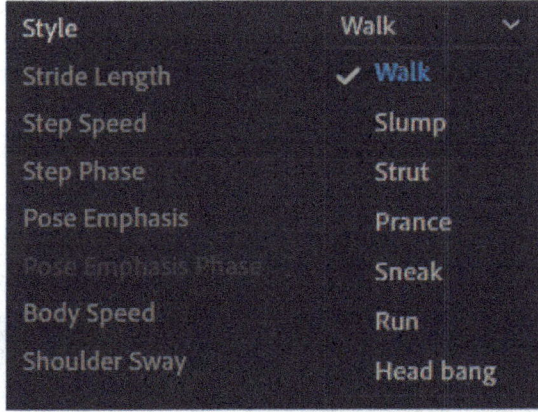

Figure 9.11: Each style can be adjusted for maximum customization

- **Style**: Below the **Style** drop-down are options that allow you to hone and adjust how you want the animation to look. If you want the character to take shorter strides, adjust how the arms move, or modify hip movement, you can do so here:

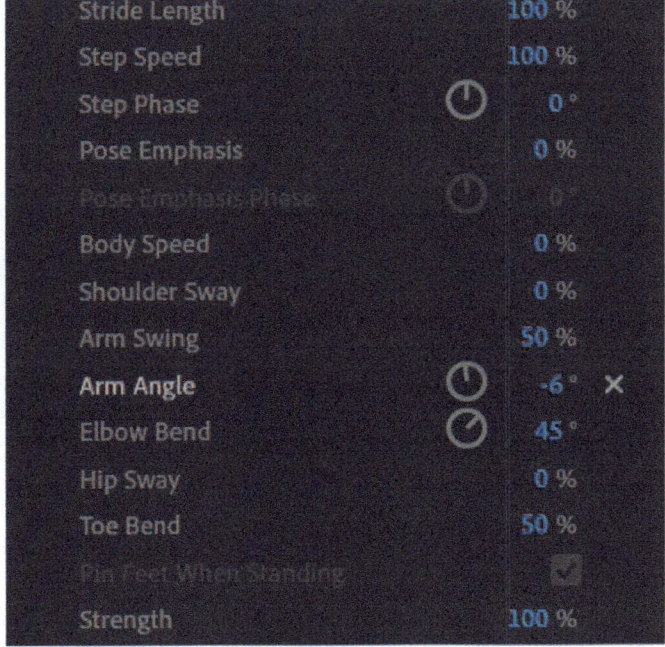

Figure 9.12: There are many parameters you can adjust to customize to your liking

Now that we know how to easily add preset animations to our characters, let's jump over to the **Record** tab and create a simple sequence so that we can get a better handle on the timeline and how keyframes work.

Mixing actions on the timeline

So, we have our walk animation set up the way we want. But how do we record it on the timeline? Can we mix other actions while doing this? Well, let's take a look at trying to record some basic animation. To do this, follow these steps:

1. Make sure you're on the **Record** tab.
2. For the **Walk** behavior, switch the **Mode** option to **Left & Right Arrow Keys**:

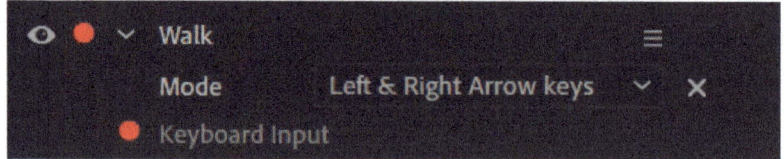

Figure 9.13: We will use the arrow keys for this test

3. Press the **Record** button above the timeline.
4. Once the countdown completes, the timeline will scroll and anything you do will record. In this case, move the character with the left and right arrow keys.
5. After about 10 seconds, press the **Stop** button.
6. You should now see, below the puppet, your recorded frames for the walking animation:

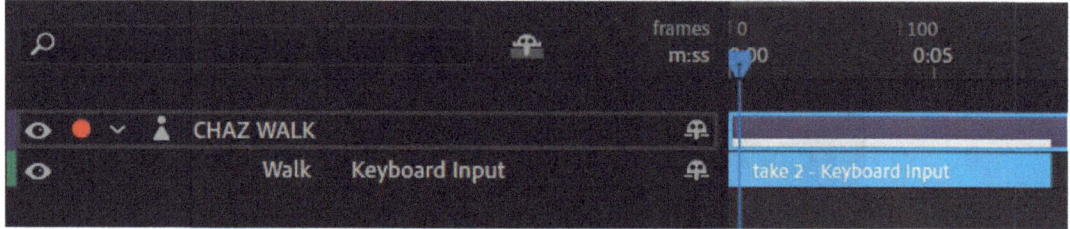

Figure 9.14: The keyframe input is shown on the timeline

So, what happens if we want to, in the middle of the animation, raise Chaz's left arm? We can do that. Here are the steps:

1. Go back to **Rig**.
2. On the **L Arm** group, click the **Left Wrist** tag and choose **Draggable** on the right.

3. Go back to **Record**.
4. Play the animation.
5. Halfway through the walk cycle, grab the left arm and drag it up.
6. Once the walk animation has finished, press **Stop**. New keyframes should form above the **Keyboard Input** area:

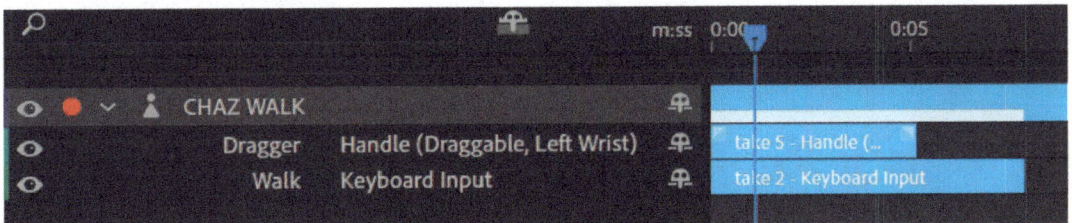

Figure 9.15: You can stack and mix actions to create detailed animations

Play the animation back – you should see the walk cycle, along with the new arm animation, coupled together as the play head moves along. Using this method allows us to layer animations on top of each other. Not only that, but they can modify each other, creating more complex sequences.

In the next chapter, when we start to work on our animated scene, we will be layering multiple keyframed actions. The flexibility of this system will allow us to create detailed animations with multiple puppets and props.

Summary

When it comes to creating walk cycles, Character Animator makes the process simple, so long as you have your rig properly tagged. If your rig appears to not function correctly during the cycle, be sure to double-check check all the tags have been accounted for. It's also important to keep the limbs independent from the body. Finally, remember that once you have set up the cycle, you can customize it in several ways to fit the personality of the character. Mixing animations with preset cycles is also easy to do and edit once in the **Record** phase. You will find that working with these cycles can save you a lot of time!

In the next chapter, we will start the process of animating our sequence by using Chaz, another puppet, props, and a set or scene for our characters to interact in.

10
Animating a Simple Sequence

Up to this point, we have learned all about rigging a character for animation. Now, we will put that character into a scene and have them move around, talk, and interact with a second character. We will be splitting this task over this chapter and the next – here we will start with some of the more simple tasks, and work up to creating a more cohesive scene in the next chapter.

So, in this chapter, we will be laying down key moments and actions to plug into the scene. We will record dialogue using our camera and mic, as well as using the external audio lip-sync feature. With these actions in place, we can then arrange and polish what we have created in the next chapter.

More specifically, we will be covering the following:

- Assembling the set
- Positioning the characters in the scene
- Recording dialogue

Technical requirements

For this chapter, we will reference **Version 7** in the `Chat_With_Chaz` Character Animator project file. We will also reference `Alien_Guest_v2.psd`, which is a rig that is set up similarly to Chaz, but there are some minor differences. You may find exploring the rig layout to be useful, but it's not required. An audio file labeled `alien_line.wav` will be referenced. Also, we will use the following images to build our set:

- `BG.png`
- `CAMERA.png`
- `GUEST CHAIR.png`

- `HOST CHAIR.png`
- `STUDIO LIGHT.png`
- `TABLE.png`

With that said, let's start by building our set and laying out the first frame.

Assembling the set

When you load **Version 7**, `Alien_Guest_v2.psd` will already be in your project panel, rigged and ready. But what about a background or set? Setting our characters on a white background may be a bit boring. Let's import some images and assemble a set for our characters to interact in.

Importing the background assets

To start this process, we will need to import the background assets:

1. Make sure you're on the **Rig** tab.
2. Double-click the **Project** panel.
3. Browse your book files and choose the six background assets we listed in the *Technical requirements* section.

Figure 10.1: List of images that make up the scene

You may find the **Project** panel is becoming cluttered and hard to navigate. Let's take a moment and organize it. Let's create three groups, `bg assets`, `rigs`, and `scenes`, and group our files accordingly. You can use the following screenshot as a visual example:

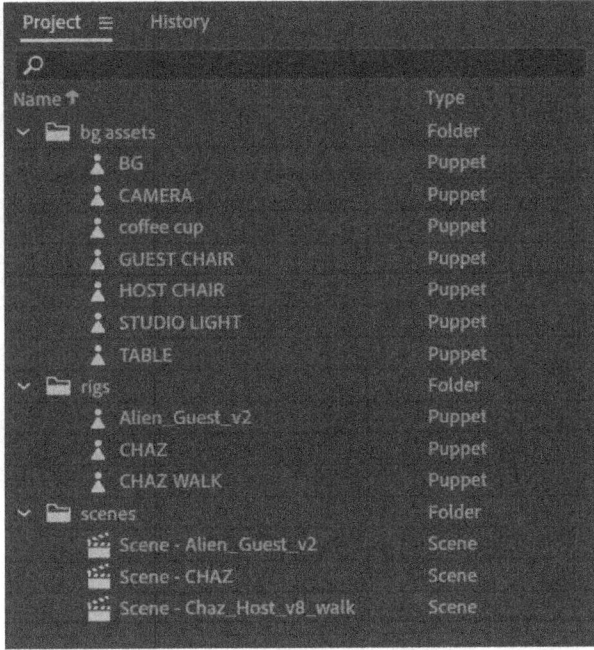

Figure 10.2: The Project panel rearranged with groups

Getting started with building the set

Now, with the assets in our project, we can create a new scene and start building the set:

1. Click **BG** in the **Project** panel.
2. Click the **Scene** button at the bottom of the panel to create a new scene with this image.
3. Rename the new scene to MAIN and drop it into the **scenes** folder in the **Project** panel.
4. In this new scene, while on the **Record** panel, drag and drop the remaining images from the **bg assets** folder onto the scene.
5. Finally, rearrange the images on the timeline so that they appear in this order:

    - **STUDIO LIGHT**
    - **CAMERA**
    - **TABLE**
    - **GUEST CHAIR**
    - **HOST CHAIR**
    - **BG**

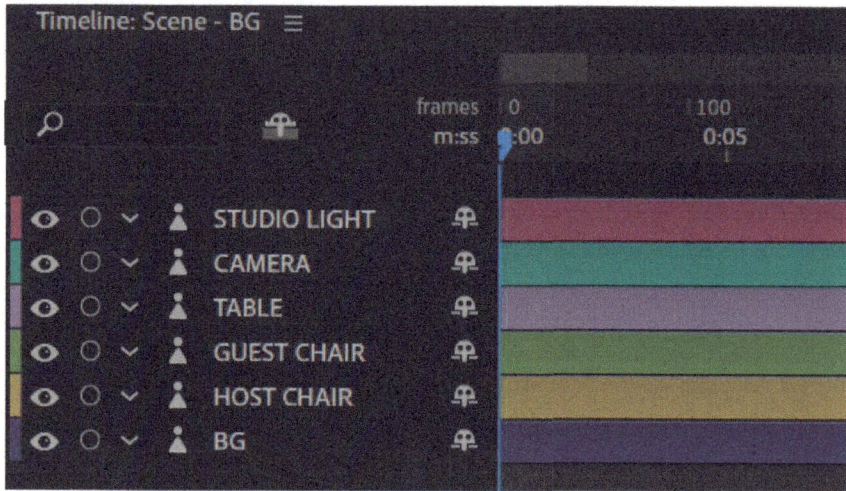

Figure 10.3: The proper layer order for the timeline

With the images in place, your set should now look as in the following screenshot:

Figure 10.4: The set assembled in the scene panel

With the set arranged with the proper layer order, we can move on to positioning our characters on the set to create the start point.

Positioning the characters in the scene

With the assets for our background and foreground in place, it's time to bring in our rigs, set up the first frame for our sequence, and start adding Chaz into the scene.

Importing and positioning Chaz

To import Chaz into the scene, take the following steps:

1. Go into the **rigs** group on the **Project** panel.
2. Click and drag **CHAZ** onto the scene.
3. On the **Behavior** panel, resize the layer to `31%` using **Scale**.
4. Rearrange the layers so Chaz is behind his desk, but in front of his chair.

Figure 10.5: We can move the rig around to properly set the scene

Move Chaz down and move the feet up to hide them behind the table. This will make it look like he's sitting in the chair.

Figure 10.6: Moving the rig down and hiding the feet gives the appearance he's sitting in the chair

You may also find **CHAZ**'s whole body tilts when moving your head to control the rig with your webcam. While some tilting is fine and adds life, having too much can be distracting. You can adjust this by reducing **Head Tilt Strength** to 28% under the **Face** behaviors.

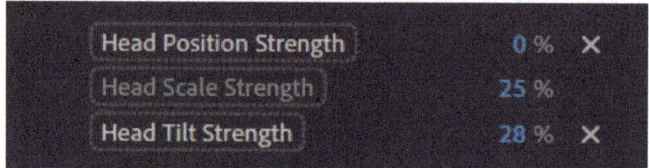

Figure 10.7: Head Position and Head Tilt parameters for Chaz

With Chaz positioned behind his desk, we will want to create a keyframe and record this frame on the timeline. Right now, if we were to move back to the **Rig** panel or focus on something else, we would lose the position we just set.

To record the action, take the following steps:

1. Make sure **CHAZ** is still selected on the timeline.
2. To ensure we don't record any unnecessary actions, let's disable the record action for all behaviors except for **Dragger**. To do this, click the red button next to each unwanted action.

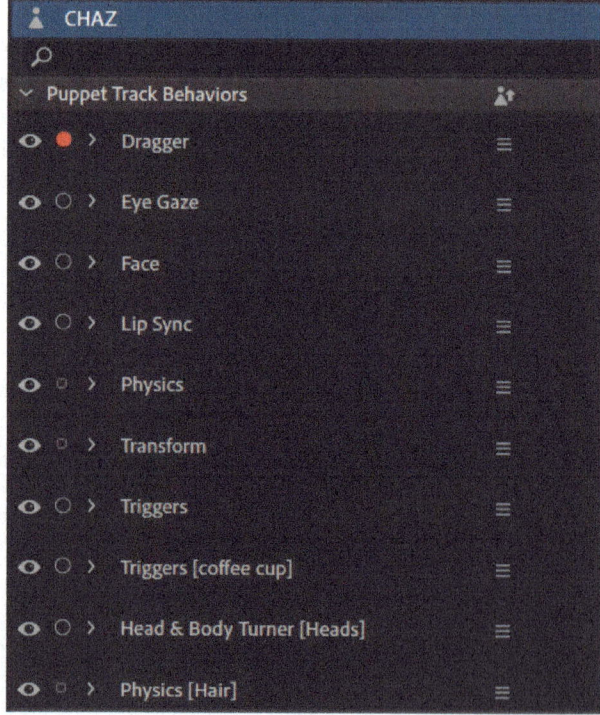

Figure 10.8: All behaviors are disabled from tracking except for Dragger

3. Click the record button above the timeline to begin recording.

   The recording countdown will launch.

4. After about a second has been recorded, press **Stop**. You should now have the **Dragger** action recorded for **CHAZ** on the timeline.

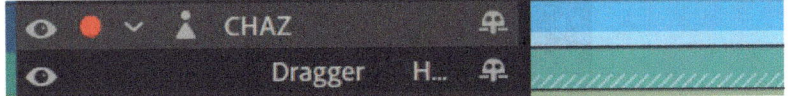

Figure 10.9: The Dragger keyframe on the timeline for CHAZ

Chaz is now set and ready for the scene! Let's move over to the alien guest and get him ready next.

Importing and positioning the alien guest

To import the alien guest, we will follow a similar procedure as we did for Chaz. But we will add a little body language to his performance as well. Here's what we need to do:

1. While still on **Record**, drag the **Alien_Guest_v2** rig onto the scene.
2. Resize the character to `32%` using **Scale** under **Transform** on the **Behavior** panel.
3. For **Scale X**, set the number to `-100`. This will cause the character to face right.

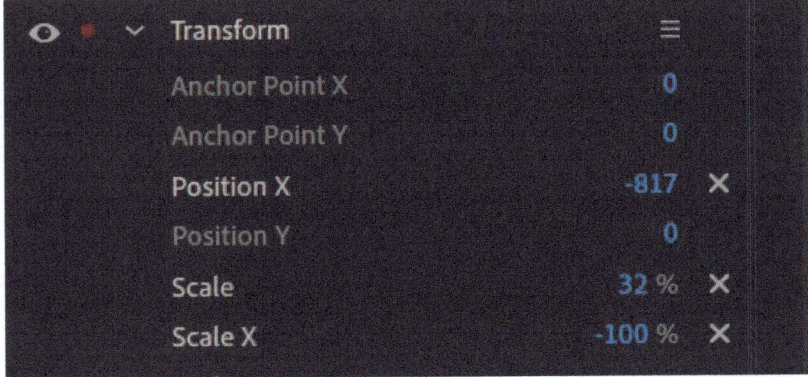

Figure 10.10: The Transform behavior properties of the alien

4. Position the alien over the chair using the **Position X** and **Position Y** settings under **Transform**.

Figure 10.11: Using a negative scale, we can flip the character horizontally or vertically

5. Now, following a similar pattern as we did for Chaz, let's reposition our character using the draggers to make it look like he's sitting in the chair; there are many positions we could choose, so choose the one you'd like!

Figure 10.12: By using draggers, we can sit the alien comfortably in the chair

Like with Chaz, you will want to record the **Dragger** behavior for a few seconds to set the pose. With the characters now set, we can focus on adding dialogue to the scene!

Recording dialogue

There are a couple of ways we can add dialogue to a scene. First, we can use a mic in the **Record** panel to capture audio in real time and have the rig track the mouth poses. We can also import external audio and have Character Animator calculate it for the poses. Both methods are viable and depend on your setup and how you want to go about the production.

To show both methods, we will record in real time with Chaz and use a .wav file for the alien.

Using a screenplay or outline

When recording your dialogue and setting up scenes, you will want to have a script, or at least an idea, ready to go so you know what to say and how to act. The same especially applies if you plan to use outside actors. You will want to convey the feeling and emotion of the scene so the actors have a blueprint. With this book, we will keep it simple. Here is the scene outline we will follow:

We will start with a zoom-in on the stage as the audience cheers.

Chaz laughs and welcomes the audience back from the commercial break:

"Welcome back to Chatting with Chaz! I am, of course, your adoring host, Chaz, and today we have a special guest!"

Cut to show alien.

"An alien from outer space! How are you doing, sir?"

The alien replies: "Oh, you know, just sort of hanging out, planning to take over Earth, that sort of thing."

"Well, that's great, I... wait, what?"

Suddenly, three more aliens transport onto the set!

This is a very simple script but should be effective for this example.

Recording Chaz's dialogue in real time

To record Chaz's dialogue, or any character, in Character Animator, you will need to be in the **Record** panel. Make sure your mic and webcam are on and calibrated.

Figure 10.13: Be sure to calibrate your webcam and enable the microphone

Since we only have one voice actor, we are going to break the dialogue up and edit it at the end of the chapter to match what Chaz and the alien are saying. Let's record all of Chaz's lines first:

1. Click the **CHAZ** layer.
2. Turn the behaviors we turned off for **CHAZ** back on, except for **Dragger**, so we don't record over the position we set previously.

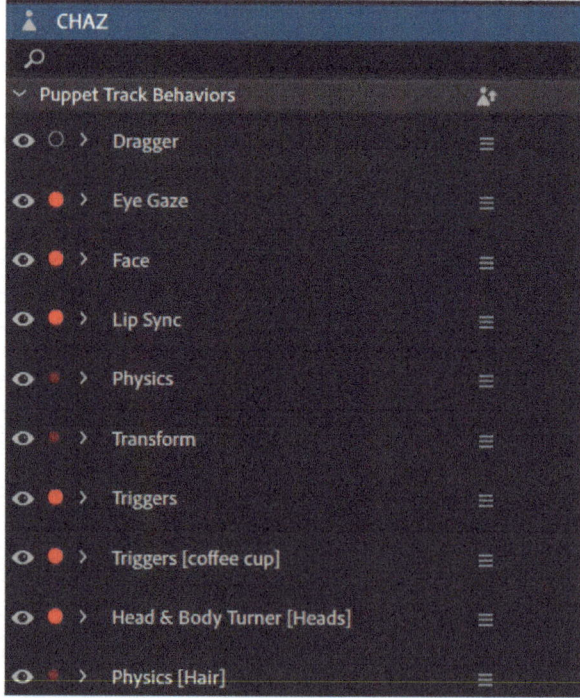

Figure 10.14: Enable all behaviors to track except for Dragger

3. Place your script in front of you, or memorize the lines.
4. Press **Record** and start speaking after the countdown.
5. As you recite the script, watch the character's mouth react accordingly. You will also see the head turn, eyes blink, pupils move, and body tilt as you act out the scene. If you mess up, don't worry! Just press stop, then undo the action or delete the keyframes that appear and try again.
6. Once finished, press **Stop** and you should now see new keyframes for all the behaviors we were tracking.

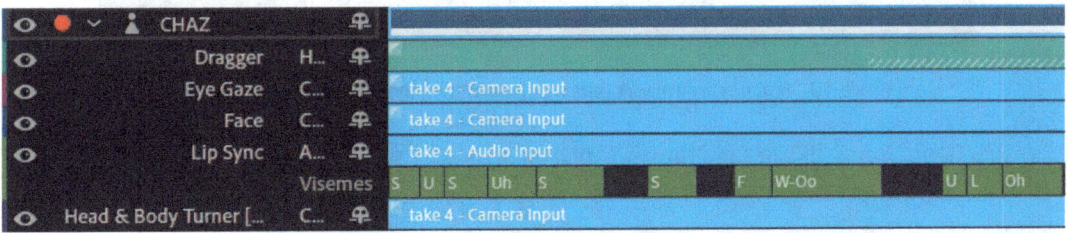

Figure 10.15: Any behavior marked for record will appear on the timeline once you complete a record session

Play back the animation. Depending on your setup, you may find the results to be a bit lacking. Perhaps the head turn is too sensitive. Or maybe the eyes didn't track, or a mouth pose doesn't match a word. Don't worry, we will come back to this in the next chapter as we make the scene more robust and add polish. For now, having the base animation down with audio recorded is what we need.

Now, let's add the alien's dialogue. We're going to tackle this a bit differently to show another way you can lip-sync, especially if you have little desire to use the webcam for animation.

Importing and lip-syncing the alien's dialogue

As stated, we are going to use a different tool to lip-sync the alien. We are going to import audio and have the software read the waveform and generate visemes for us. This is useful if you have actors who are sending you audio files and can't record directly in Character Animator. Or maybe you want to edit the audio, such as adding a filter, which can't be done live. Perhaps you just want to use the lip-sync feature and forgo using a webcam or microphone to animate. These are just a few examples of how this could be useful.

So, here's how we do this:

1. While still on **Record**, use the **Import** command to bring the `alienline.wav` audio file into the project.

180 Animating a Simple Sequence

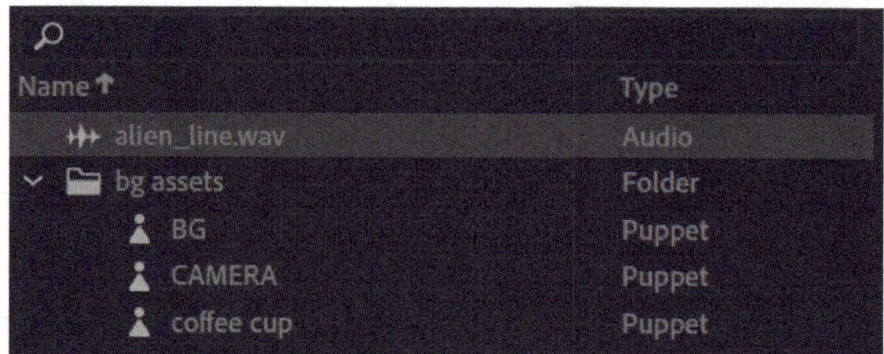

Figure 10.16: You can import external audio files into Character Animator

2. Drag the audio file onto the timeline. Placing it above Chaz's audio is a good practice to keep the audio organized.

Figure 10.17: Both audio files on the timeline

3. Click the **Alien_Guest_v2** layer on the timeline.
4. Hold the *Ctrl* or ⌘ key and click **alienline.wav** on the timeline so both layers are selected.

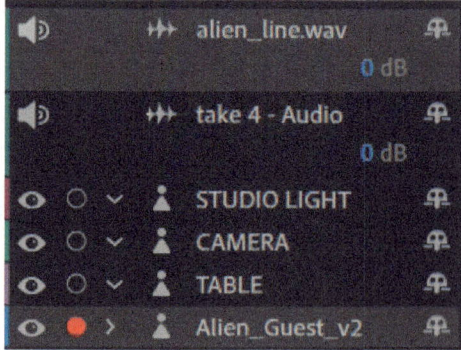

Figure 10.18: Both the rig and audio files must be selected

5. Go up to **Timeline > Compute Lip Sync Take from Scene Audio**.

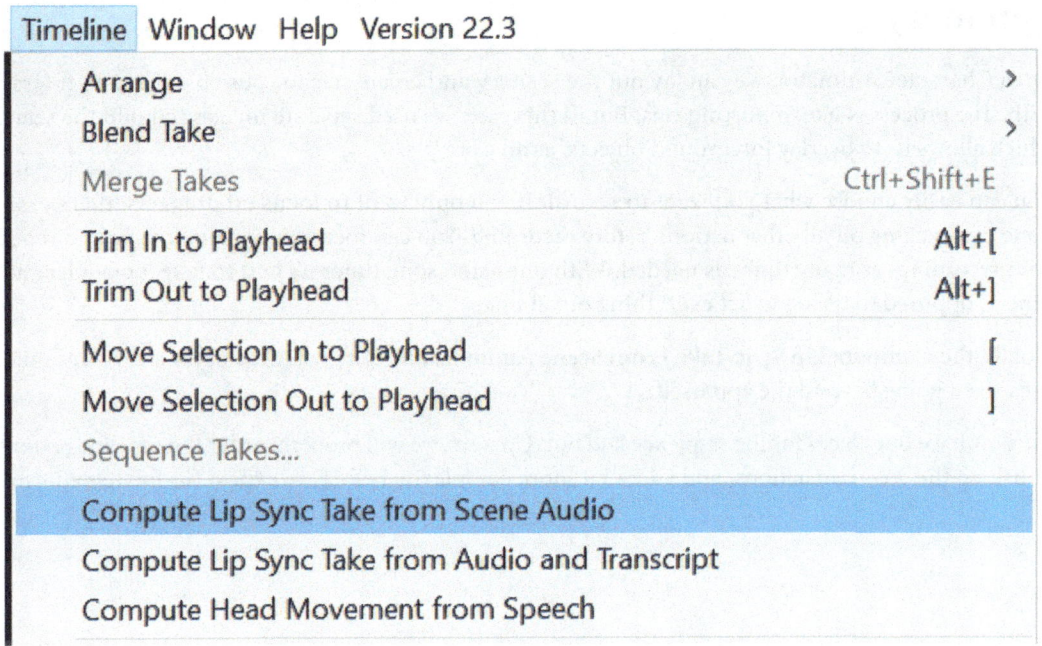

Figure 10.19: The Project panel rearranged with groups

The app will render the take.

6. Once complete, you will see a new action, **Lip Sync**, with visemes visible under the **Alien_Guest_v2** layer.

Figure 10.20: The alien's visemes

Play the scene. You should find the audio matches well with the mouth. If not, we will show how to make viseme corrections, plus more, as we finish the animation for this sequence in the next chapter. But this is a significant feature that can literally save hours, compared to traditional lip-syncing.

This auto lip-sync feature can go beyond Character Animator, if desired. As an example, you might want to animate a mouth automatically using this method, export out a synced mouth as a sequence, and bring it into another animation software you may be using. That goes beyond the scope of this book. But we wanted to mention it, just so you're aware of how robust this system can be.

Summary

With Character Animator, we can lay out the scenery and create sets for our characters to interact with. The process is like importing rigs. But in this case, we used separate images to build the scene, which allows us to overlay foreground objects, as an example.

You can easily choose what you want to record. If you only want to focus on draggers, that's easily done by checking off all other actions before recording. You can focus on certain actions and repeat your recordings as many times as needed. With one actor, sometimes it's best to take it one piece at a time as opposed to trying to act everything out at once.

Finally, the **Compute Lip Sync Take From Scene Audio** feature is a great time-saver and has multiple uses, even going beyond the app itself.

We now have our pieces for the sequence laid out. Up next, we will properly order the timeline actions, polish up the recorded actions, and add a bit more complexity before we export for further editing.

11
Rearranging, Polishing, and Enhancing Our Sequence

In the previous chapter, we laid down animation for both of our fully rigged characters. Now, we are going to arrange the actions to create a linear scene, as well as looking at any other areas that could use some improvement. This will set us up to export the scene as a video so we can do some editing in **After Effects** and **Premiere**, which will come in the next chapter.

But for now, we will cover the following:

- Using PNG sequences for external animations
- Adding more character actions
- Arranging character actions in sequence
- Correcting flaws and enhancing animations

By the time we are done, you will have a coherent sequence you can view in Character Animator and export out for further editing or sharing. This will also give you an opportunity to further understand how the timeline works. So, with that said, let's get going!

Technical requirements

In this chapter, we will reference **Version 8** in the `Chat_With_Chaz` Character Animator project file. We will also reference the `AudienceAnimation.png` sequence, which comprises 60 images in a folder. We will combine these images to take advantage of the **Cycle Layers** behavior.

Using PNG sequences for external animations

While Character Animator is great for quick character animation, there may be some tasks best left to other apps. In these cases, we have choices of how to implement external animations. These PNG sequences can be implemented during editing once you export them from Character Animator, or you can import sequences to Character Animator and integrate them into the set. In this chapter, we will do the latter.

Importing PNGs for the sequence

Like importing PSDs or other files, we will import the sequence of images onto our **Project** panel. This animation comprises 60 individual images and we can link behavior to allow a cycle effect.

To import the image sequence, take the following steps:

1. Make sure you're on the **Rig** tab.
2. Double-click a blank area on the **Project** panel to bring up the import prompt.
3. Browse to the `AudienceAnimation` folder, which is in the book project files.

Figure 11.1: You will find 60 images inside the AudienceAnimation folder

4. Inside the folder will be 60 images. Select these (*Ctrl +A* or ⌘ + *A*) and select import.
5. Once the images are on the **Project** panel, create a new folder labeled `audience animation` and drag the images into it to keep the panel organized.

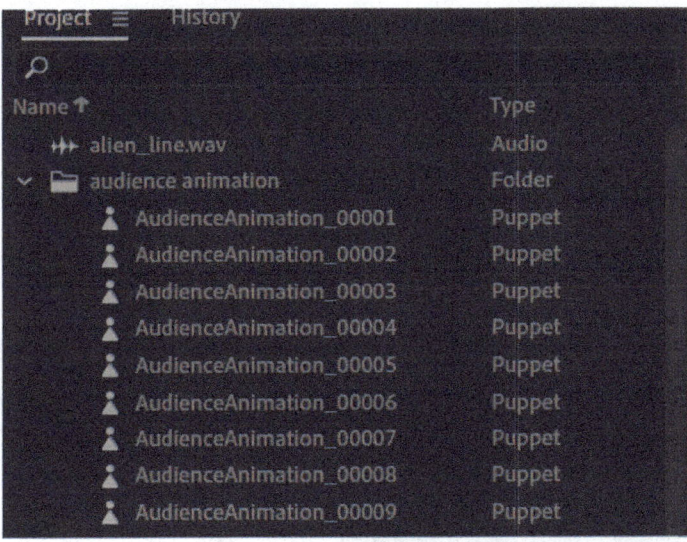

Figure 11.2: The audience images on the Project panel

6. Right-click on **AudienceAnimation_00001** and rename the layer to `Audience Animation Main`.
7. Double-click the newly renamed **Audience Animation Main** to jump into the **Puppet** panel.
8. Select **AudienceAnimation_00002** to **AudienceAnimation_00060** on the **Project** panel and drag them into the **Puppet** panel.

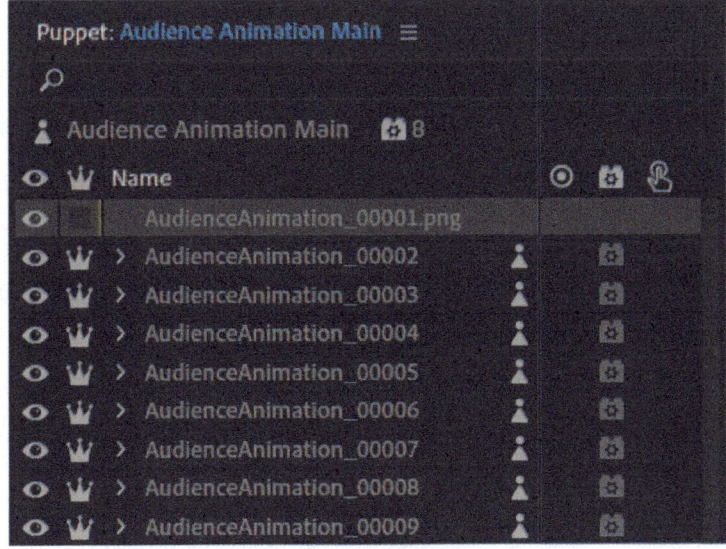

Figure 11.3: You will find 60 images inside the AudienceAnimation folder. You can see the first nine in this image

Right now, this will not do much other than overlap 60 images over one another. We will need to add behavior to tell Character Animator to cycle through the images.

Adding Cycle Layers behavior

We will add a behavior to this sequence just like we added behaviors to our Chaz rig:

1. While in the **Puppet** panel, locate the **Behaviors** button for **Audience Animation Main**.
2. Click the **Behaviors** button and choose **Cycle Layers** from the list.

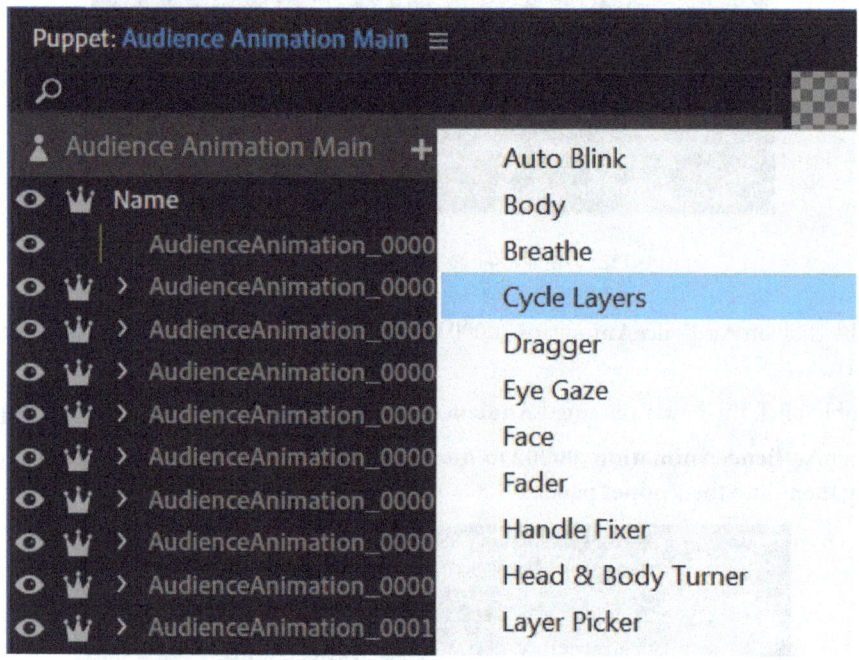

Figure 11.4: Clicking the + icon next to Audience Animation Main will allow you to add behaviors

3. Once you set this behavior, a new panel will appear with Cycle options. There are a few ways you can control the sequence. For our purposes, we want the animation to play once when we hit the **Play** or **Record** button.

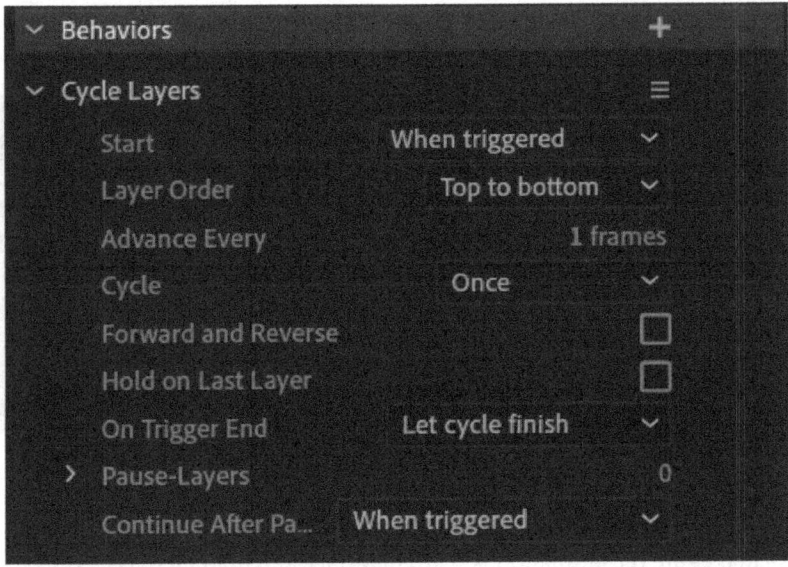

Figure 11.5: The Cycle Layers behavior provides many options for your .png images

By default, you will see the animation won't start unless enabled by a trigger. But what about the other options? Here is a quick rundown of them:

- **Start**: Choose to start the cycle automatically or by trigger.

- **Layer Order**: This will dictate the animation order. Since we have our images labeled 1–60, with 1 being at the top, **Top to bottom** is the option we want to choose here.

- **Advance Every**: Dictates the speed of the animation. If set to **1**, the cycle will play on every frame based on Project's established frames per second. If set to a higher value, the animation will play slower based on the framerate.

- **Cycle**: You can choose whether you want the animation to play once or loop continuously.

- **Forward and Reverse**: Choose to reverse the animation as it's currently displayed.

- **Hold on Last Layer**: When enabled, will freeze on the last image in your sequence once the cycle is complete.

- **On Trigger End**: If you have a trigger set to stop the animation in this cycle, you can choose whether you want the animation to play all its frames before stopping or stop right when the user presses the trigger.

- **Pause-Layers**: Choose layers you'd like to pause on during the animation.

- **Continue After Pause**: Choose whether to continue right when the key is pressed down or when it's released.

4. With a better understanding of how we can work with cycling layers, let's begin by changing **Start** to **Immediately**, so that way the audience will animate with no intervention on our end.

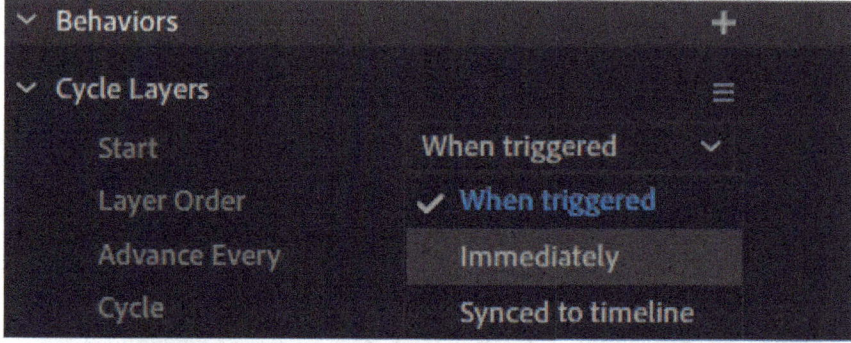

Figure 11.6: You have three options for how you want to trigger the animation

5. Let's also make sure the animation is set to play once and hold on to the last layer. This will let the audience cheer for 3 seconds and then freeze on the last frame.

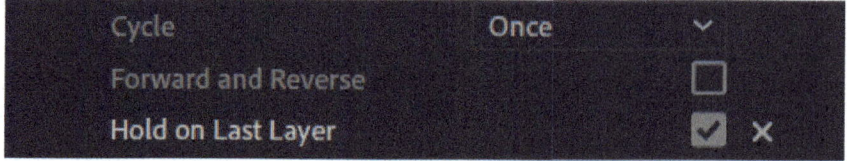

Figure 11.7: Hold on Last Layer will prevent the .png sequence from disappearing on completion

Now we can move on to placing the audience appropriately in the scene.

Adjusting the audience in the scene

We will need to add the audience animation to the scene and make the adjustments. To do this, take the following steps:

1. Make sure you're on the **Record** tab.
2. Drag **Audience Animation Main** above **STUDIO LIGHT**.

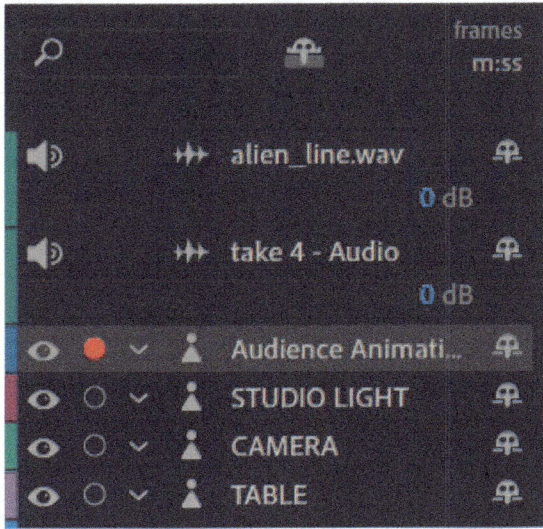

Figure 11.8: The audience will overlay all other layers

3. The audience will appear offset. Go to the **Transform** panel with the audience still selected and set **Position Y** to 544%. This should place the audience properly within the set.

Figure 11.9: You will find 60 images inside the AudienceAnimation folder

With the audience now on set, we have all major sequences ready to be polished and reordered. Up next, we will focus on arranging the layers so that everything runs in a nice linear and logical fashion. Luckily, we can edit our keys on the timeline. Let's rearrange, tweak, and even add some more actions through triggers.

Adding more character actions

While we added some basic face and head animations to Chaz using the webcam, the alien is only currently being lip-synced. With the alien's gaze, emotion, and body language being static, the animation is less engaging. Luckily, we can go back in and add some actions, breathing more life into the conversation.

Adjusting the alien's gaze

Setting the alien's pupils to look at Chaz will give the character and the scene a bit more depth:

1. Go back to the **Rig** tab and double-click **Alien_Guest_v2** in the **Project** panel.
2. Click once on the **3-4th Head** layer.
3. Using the + icon on the bottom right, add a new **Eye Gaze** behavior.

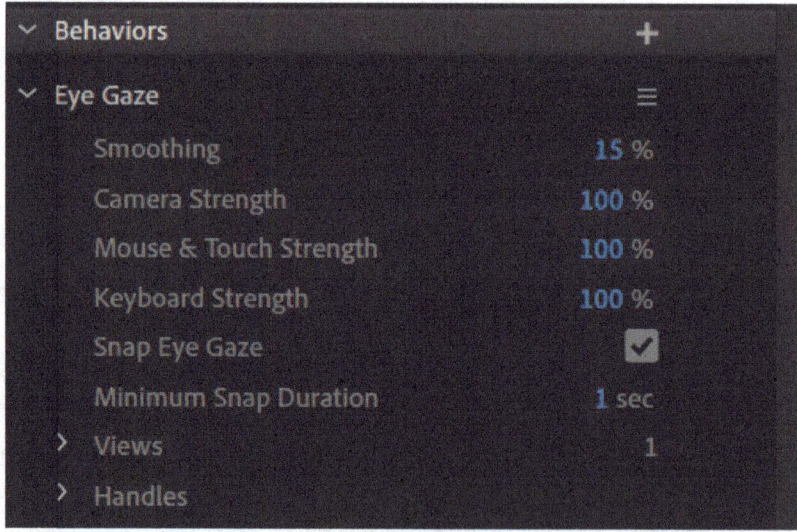

Figure 11.10: You have many options with Eye Gaze

4. Now, go to the **Record** tab.
5. Click **Alien_Guest_v2**.

6. Locate **Eye Gaze [3-4th Head]** and expand it to reveal its options.

7. Ensure only **Keyboard Input** is set to record. This will allow us to control the pupils using our arrow keys. Here, pressing left will move the pupils right and vice versa due to us mirroring the rig on the set.

8. Set **Keyboard Strength** to 70% to keep the eyes from drifting too far.

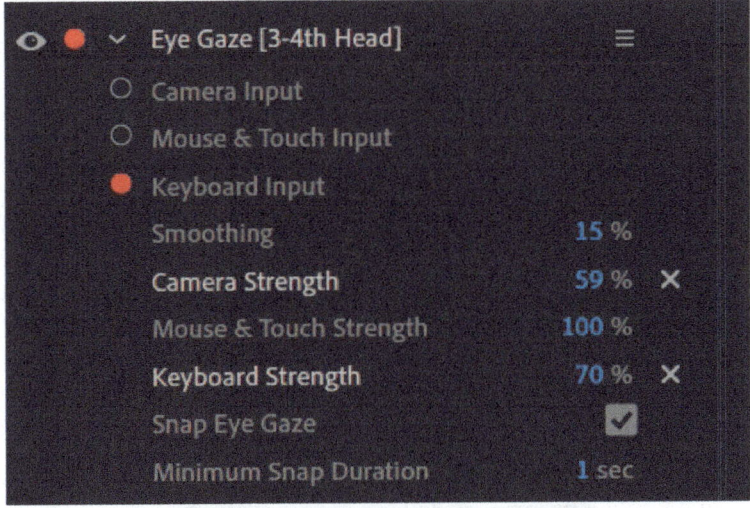

Figure 11.11: Set Keyboard Strength to 70%

9. Set the play head back to **00:00:00**.

10. We are going to record the new eye gaze action. To do this, hold down the left key and then press the **Record** button. Hold the left arrow key until around the beginning of the alien's dialogue. This will allow him to glance at Chaz and then look at the audience as he talks.

Figure 11.12: If everything works correctly, the alien will appear to be looking at Chaz

As we do this, keyframes for **Eye Gaze** will start to record on the timeline.

Figure 11.13: You should see keyframes for Eye Gaze [3-4th Head]

With the gaze set, let's add a bit more life to the eyes. Luckily, there's a built-in behavior that makes this easy.

Setting automatic blinks for the alien

While we could set the blinks to record and use our camera to capture our own blinks, like we did when we recorded Chaz's base actions, we're going to use a special behavior to give you the chance to explore more tools. Here's what we need to do:

1. Go to the **Rig** tab.
2. Click **3-4th Head**.
3. On the bottom right of the **Behaviors** panel, click the + icon and then **Auto Blink**.

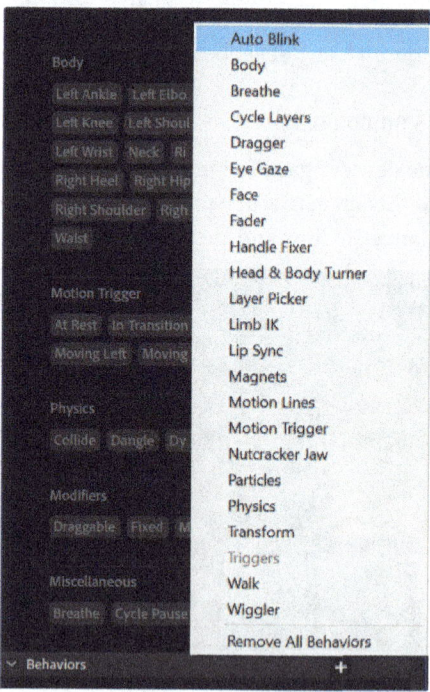

Figure 11.14: Auto Blink is the first behavior on the list

4. Once added, you can adjust three parameters, choosing how many blinks per minute to set, how long a blink lasts, and how random the blink occurrence is. We will leave these at the default settings, but experiment if you wish.

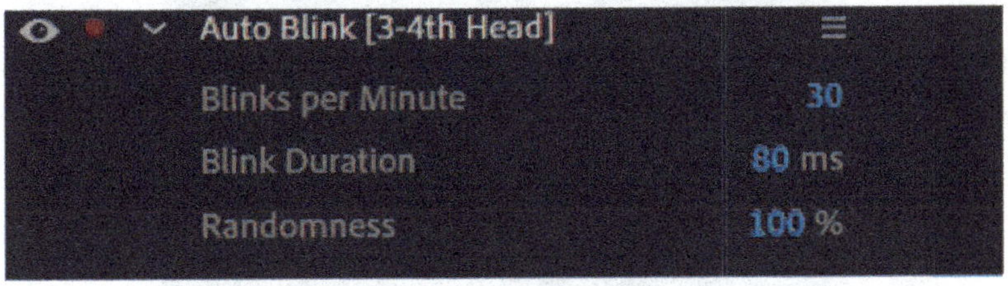

Figure 11.15: These are the default settings, but if you want to adjust the blink animation, feel free

5. Go to the **Record** panel and see the blinks taking hold. Locate **Auto Blink [3-4th Head]** and set it to record. That way, it'll be functioning for preview and exporting purposes.

Preview the scene to see how the blinks add to the conversation and character interactions. Now, we can add a little body movement to the alien to help add even more life to the sequence.

Adding arm movement to the alien

While we have set down keyframes to allow the alien to sit, we can make the sequence more interesting by adding body movements, such as arm gestures. This can be as subtle or extreme as you like. Since we already added **Dragger** keys, let's add a new dragger and isolate it to the left or front arm.

For this purpose, we are going to have the alien raise his arm as he talks:

1. Go to the **Rig** tab and click on **Alien_Guest_v2**.
2. Click on the **Front Arm** group layer.
3. At the bottom right, click the + button next to **Behaviors** and choose **Dragger**.
4. Go to the **Record** tab. Among the behaviors, locate the new dragger for the left arm. Set this to **Record**, leaving all other behaviors unarmed.

194   Rearranging, Polishing, and Enhancing Our Sequence

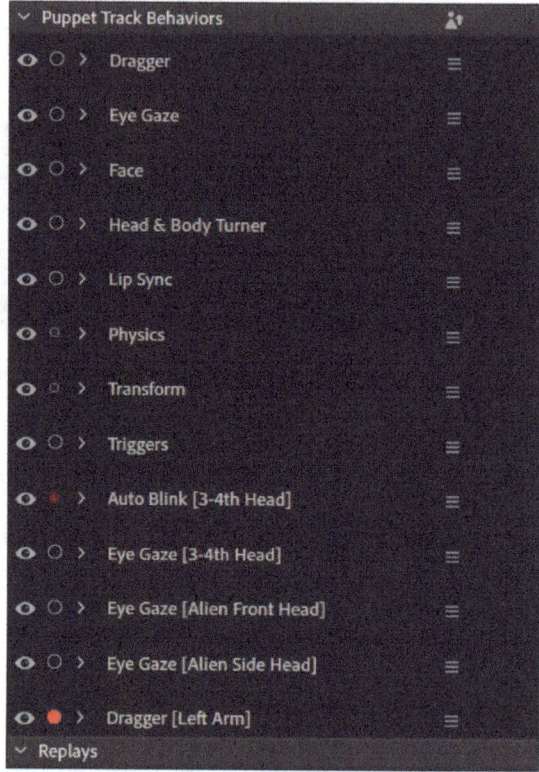

Figure 11.16: Make sure only Dragger [Left Arm] is set for record

5. Click the **Record** button on the timeline. Let the animation play out until the alien speaks. Grab the front wrist and raise it as he talks.

Figure 11.17: Raising the arm as the alien speaks will breathe more life into the conversation

6. Near the end of his line, lower the arm.
7. Once you're finished, press **Stop** and replay the scene. The alien should remain sitting while the arm animates independently from what we previously established.

By now, you should understand how we can build movements using multiple behaviors. But what about Chaz? While we recorded his actions, there may be some issues that cropped up. Luckily, we can edit these actions after the fact to make the animation more pleasing.

> **Note**
> The alien's tags will be flipped (left arm and leg being on the right and vice versa). This is due to changing the **Scale X** to -100 in the previous chapter. We can counter this by flipping the character before setting up and tagging the rig.

Arranging character actions in sequence

When we recorded our character actions in the previous chapter, we didn't pay attention to proper ordering. That's fine, as we were only focusing on getting the audio and basic keys laid down.

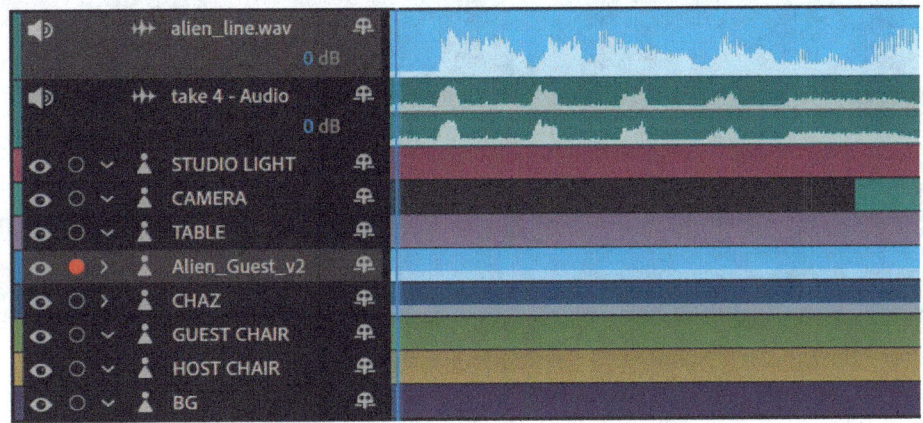

Figure 11.18: As it stands right now, the timeline is a mess

But right now, if we play the animation, it will appear as a jumbled mess. The first thing we should do to work through this is pull up our script or outline from the previous chapter that lays out the scene. We can use this as a blueprint for timeline ordering:

We will start with a zoom-in on the stage as the audience cheers.

Chaz laughs and welcomes the audience back from the commercial break:

"Welcome back to Chatting with Chaz! I am, of course, your adoring host, Chaz, and today we have a special guest!"

Cut to show alien.

"An alien from outer space! How are you doing, sir?"

The alien replies: "Oh, you know, just sort of hanging out, planning to take over Earth, that sort of thing."

"Well, that's great, I... wait, what?"

Suddenly, three more aliens transport onto the set!

The first line suggests we have a moment for the audience to react before Chaz speaks. This means we should push any of Chaz's and the alien's actions forward on the timeline to create space for the audience's reaction. Let's push everything up by 1 second except for the audience. To do this, take the following steps:

1. While on **Record**, starting with **alien_line.wav** and **take 4 - Audio** at the top of the timeline, click and drag each of those layers 1 second to the right.

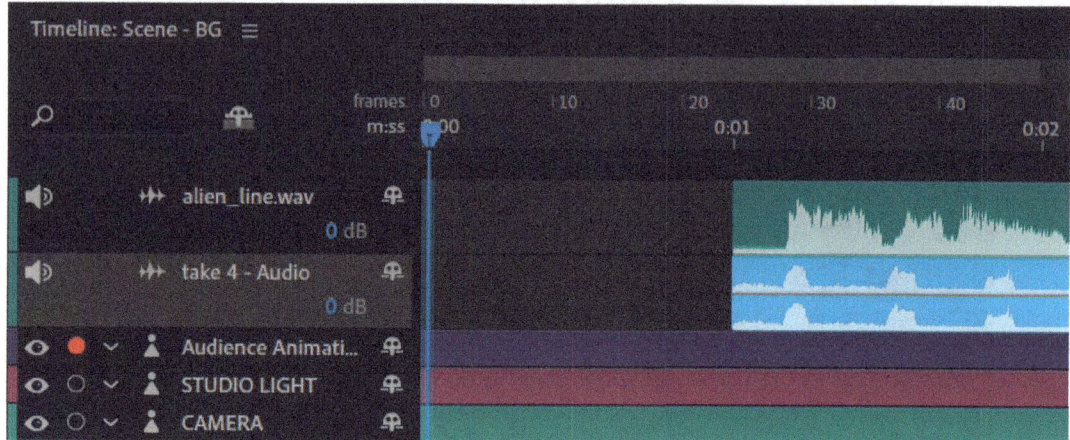

Figure 11.19: Both audio files should start at 0:01

2. We will need to move Chaz and the alien's actions forward as well to match. Starting with **CHAZ**, click the drop-down arrow to reveal all the keyframes.

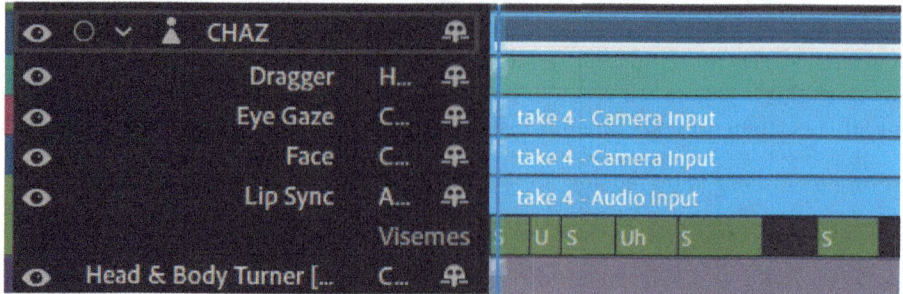

Figure 11.20: Expand the CHAZ layer to access the recorded behavior

3. We want to move most of these actions to the 1-second mark so we can match the audio. The exception here is **Dragger**. We used **Dragger** to set the character at his desk. We want to keep him there at the start of the animation. So, move **Eye Gaze**, **Face**, **Lip Sync**, and **Head & Body Turner** over to the 1-second mark.

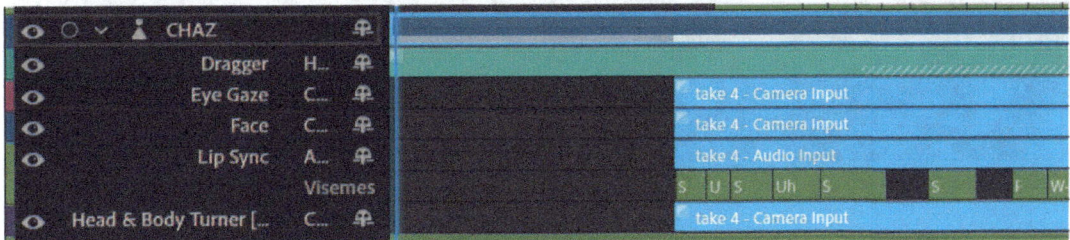

Figure 11.21: Move Chaz's actions up by 1 second to match his audio file

Finally, we need to properly sequence the alien's interaction with Chaz. While giving the scene a second to establish itself is good, having both characters talk at the same time makes no sense. We will also need to create some space for the alien's line to play out before Chaz answers him. Here's how to make the adjustments:

1. Starting with the audio, select **take 4 - Audio**.
2. Use ⌘ or *Ctrl* + *D* to duplicate the layer.

Figure 11.22: We will be duplicating the audio file to split the lines up

3. Trim the top audio file to remove the dialogue *"Well, that's great, I... wait, what?"*.
4. For the bottom **take 4 - Audio** layer, trim from the beginning, and remove everything except for *"Well, that's great, I... wait, what?"*. This will create a space to add the alien's reaction.

Figure 11.23: Trimming the audio files provides us with more freedom when arranging actions

5. Now, arrange the lines so that the **alien_line.wav** layer sits in between the two **take 4 - Audio** files.

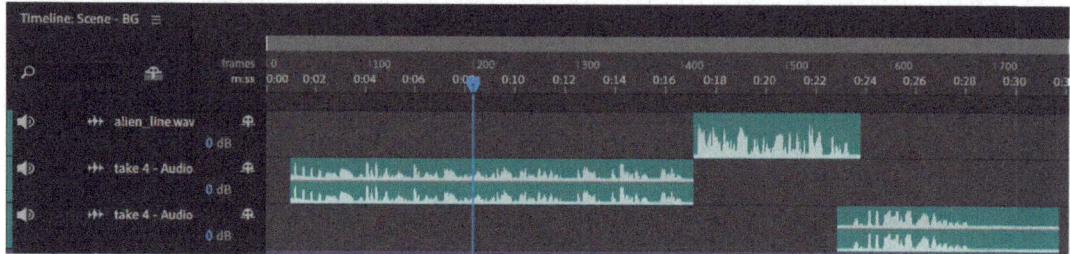

Figure 11.24: We need to place the alien's line between Chaz's split audio file

This will offset the character actions with the audio. Therefore, we need to rearrange the recorded actions for both characters so they match the new audio locations on the timeline. Let's relocate the alien's actions first:

1. Expand **Alien_Guest_2** and locate **Lip Sync**.
2. Select the **Lip Sync** and **Visemes** keys.
3. Drag them over to the left to match the audio for the alien. The start frame should be at around `00:17:03`.

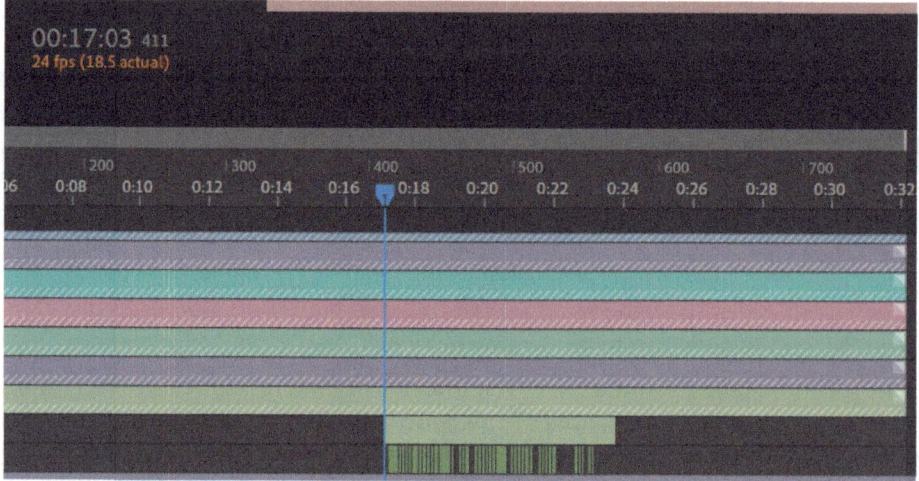

Figure 11.25: Drag the Lip Sync and Visemes keys up to 00:17:03

We also need to account for the **Dragger** behavior we added to the alien arm. As it stands right now, he will speak and then raise his arm. We want the alien to raise his arm as he speaks:

1. Locate **Dragger [Left Arm] [Alien_v2]** and drag it to the left.
2. Move it a little at a time and test the animation until the arm is raising with his dialogue.

Arranging character actions in sequence   199

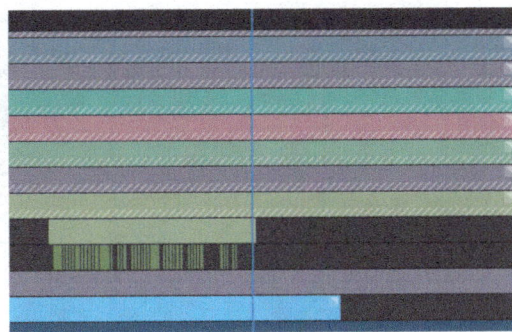

Figure 11.26: Moving the keys will change when the animation starts

Once that is set, we need to account for Chaz's last line. This means we need to arrange his mouth and body actions as well:

1. Collapse the **Alien_Guest_v2** layer for easier viewing.
2. Expand the **CHAZ** layer to see the recorded actions.
3. Starting with **Lip Sync**, click and drag the sequence so that it matches the end of the last audio file on the timeline.

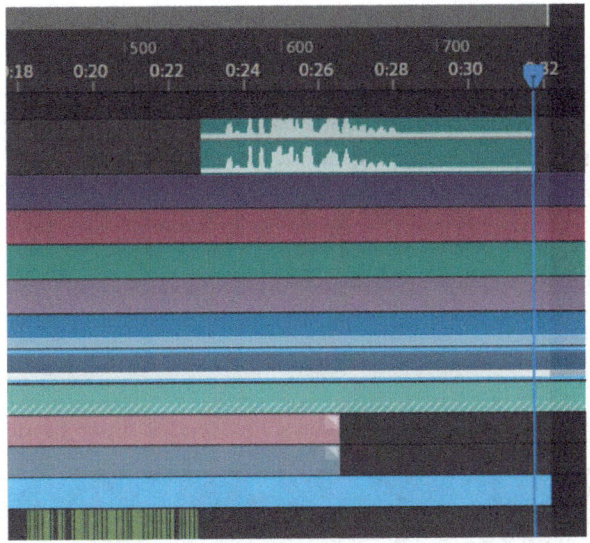

Figure 11.27: By extending the Lip Sync behavior, we can add the visemes closer to the end of where the line now is

4. Then, grab the visemes starting at 00:18:03 and move them over to match the audio file at the start of 00:22:20.

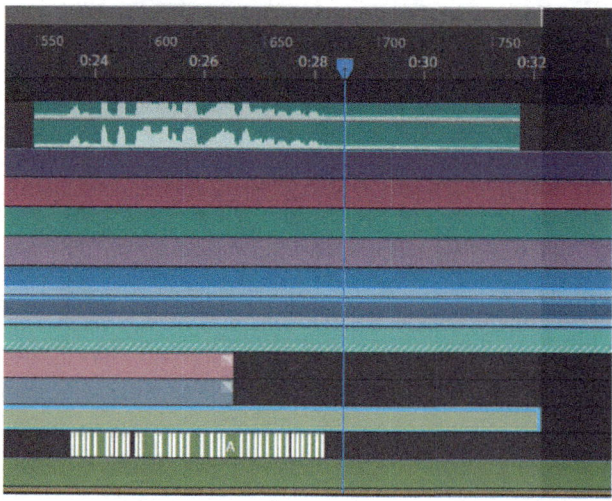

Figure 11.28: Move the visemes up to match the start of the audio file

With these changes, playing the animation back should now reveal a scene in the correct order, with no overlapping dialogue, and proper lip-syncing. Now, we can add a bit more life to the character actions.

Correcting flaws and enhancing animations

While using the camera is a great way to lie down animation quickly, you may find some anomalies pop up. In our case, the character's head is turning but the actions are random in duration and appearance. Don't worry, this is where the script comes in. By using it as a guide, we can plan out when to turn the head and for how long.

So, to add refined head turns to Chaz's actions:

1. Go to the **Record** tab.
2. Expand the **CHAZ** layer.
3. Click on the **take 4 - Camera Input** sequence for **Head & Body Turner**.

Figure 11.29: Locate the Head & Body Turner behavior for CHAZ

4. Remove it by pressing the *Delete* key on your keyboard.

We are now going to re-apply the head-turn animation. We can do this using the webcam or with triggers. But we're only going to focus on turning the head. To do this, let's break down Chaz's dialogue and plan out when we should turn his head:

"Welcome back to Chatting with Chaz! I am, of course, your adoring host, Chaz, and today we have a special guest!... An alien from outer space!"

During these lines, we will want to have our character face the audience.

"How are you doing, sir?... Well, that's great, I... wait, what?"

With these lines, Chaz should face the alien guest. Once those lines end, we can have Chaz go back to the 3/4th view.

With that in mind, here's what you need to do:

1. Turn your webcam on if it's not already.
2. Ensure **CHAZ** is still selected.
3. Make sure **Head & Body Turner [Heads]** is the only behavior set for recording.

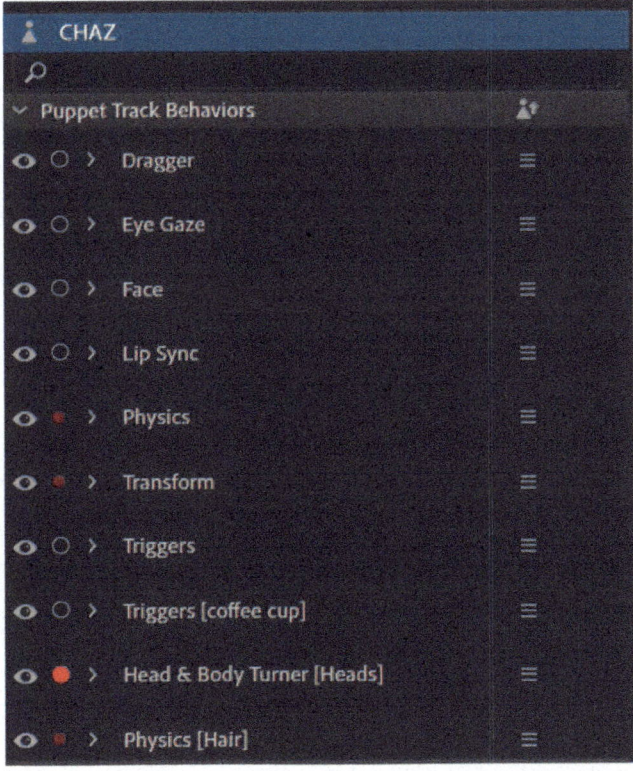

Figure 11.30: We're only focusing on the head turns for this part

4. Bring the play head back to 00 : 00 : 00.
5. Press **Record**.
6. After the countdown, turn your head to the right to have the character face the audience.

Figure 11.31: Since the default position for our head is the 3/4th view when looking directly at the camera, turning right will activate the front view

As you make your movements, the puppet will react accordingly:

Figure 11.32: Chaz should react according to your head movement. In this case, he's facing the camera

7. After he introduces the alien, turn your head to the left.

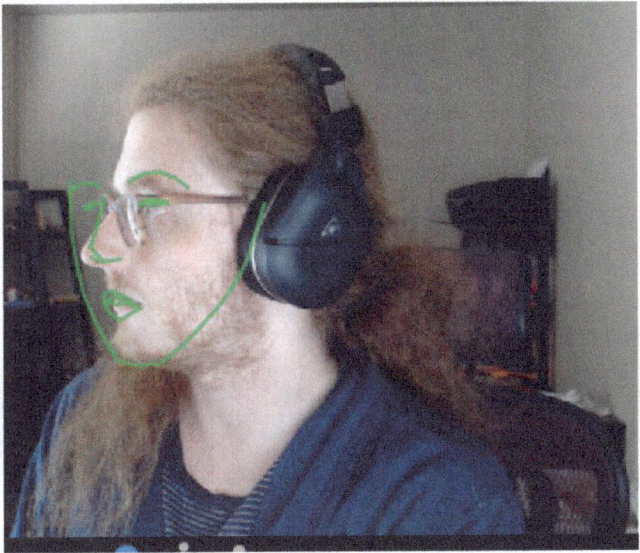

Figure 11.33: Looking left will also activate the left-head phase

The puppet should match the left-facing head:

Figure 11.34: Chaz faces left, just like what you see in the webcam preview window

8. When Chaz says his next line, face the camera to go back to his default 3/4th position.

Figure 11.35: Looking forward will activate the default 3/4th view

Facing forward will activate the default view, which in our case is the 3/4th shot:

Figure 11.36: Chaz's default head view

9. Once the recording is complete, press **Stop** or the *spacebar* and replay the recording to see whether the head actions line up. If needed, you can delete the keys and try again until you get it right.

From here, look at the gaze and make sure it's lining up. If the eyes are drifting, you can choose to re-record the action. The same goes for anything else you've recorded. Remember, you can apply manual controls if you need even more refinement.

Summary

While Character Animator allows you to press a record button and create an animation, the results may sometimes not transfer the way you intended. You can add, change, and remove actions. Being able to isolate specific actions to fine-tune them is very helpful. Even if you can't record an animation in sequence, the timeline is powerful enough to allow for isolating actions and rearranging them to create a cohesive narrative. Finally, don't forget you can add outside animations using the PNG sequence behavior built into the app. The more you try out these behaviors, the more possibilities you'll find.

So, what's next? There are several ways we can edit and enhance our production. In the next chapter, we will be exporting our work to be shared, visually enhanced through After Effects, and tightened up in Premiere.

12
Exporting, Editing, and Sharing Your Character Animator Sequence

With a complete sequence animated in Character Animator, we can take it to the next step. You can choose to export the sequence as is to share it with friends or on social media, or you can take it over to After Effects or Premiere to add effects or make edits to help with the flow. We can use Character Animator for many projects, so we will try to cover as much ground as logically possible.

In this chapter, we will cover the following:

- Export options in Character Animator
- Editing in After Effects with Dynamic Link
- Editing in Premiere

Technical requirements

In addition to Character Animator, we will be using After Effects, Premiere, and Media Encoder for this chapter. There are a few files we will be referencing (you can download them from the Chapter 12 folder):

- Chat_with_Chaz.chproj (Character Animator project file)
- Chat with Chaz.prproj (Premiere project file)
- Chat_with_Chaz_AE_File.aep (After Effects project file)
- Chat with Chaz Title.png
- Scene 01 - Chaz with Alien Guest.mp4

- `Scene 01 - Chaz with Alien Guest-AE-RENDER.mp4`
- `Scene 01 - Chaz with Alien Guest-PR-RENDER.mp4`
- The `AudienceAnimation` PNG sequence (from *Chapter 11*'s files)
- `BG.png` (from *Chapter 10*'s files)
- `CAMERA.png` (from *Chapter 10*'s files)
- `STUDIO LIGHT.png` (from *Chapter 10*'s files)

So, with that said, let's look at what we can do to bring our animation into other applications.

Export options in Character Animator

While Character Animator is a fully featured animation suite, there are some tasks best left to other applications – tasks such as integrating visual effects, and filters, cutting out unneeded frames, and editing sequences together. Before we get too ahead of ourselves, let's look at our options for exporting and sharing media with other Adobe apps.

Setting export duration

Before we export our file, let's make sure we have the timeline set up to render only what we need. There's no need, for example, to render several seconds of the scene after the keyframes we animated. This is easy to correct:

1. Make sure you're on the **Record** tab with access to the timeline.
2. At the top of the timeline, above and to the right of the text frames, is a dark gray or, if selected, a light gray bar.

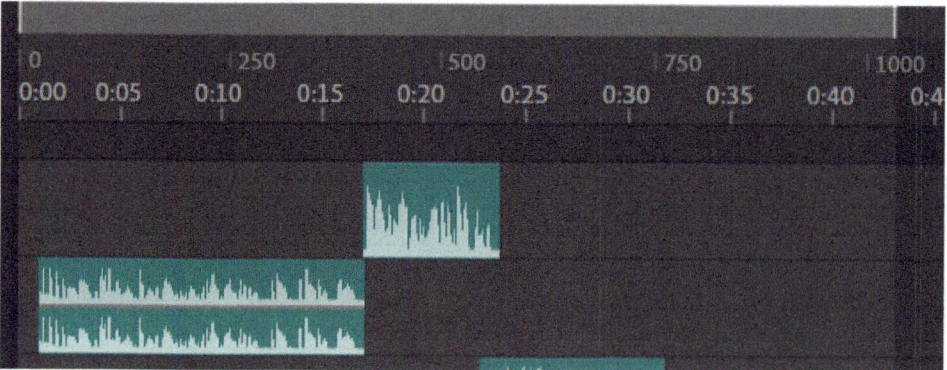

Figure 12.1: The light gray bar at the top of the timeline shows us what will be exported

3. Go to the end of the bar and click and drag the end of the bar back to **00:31:20**.

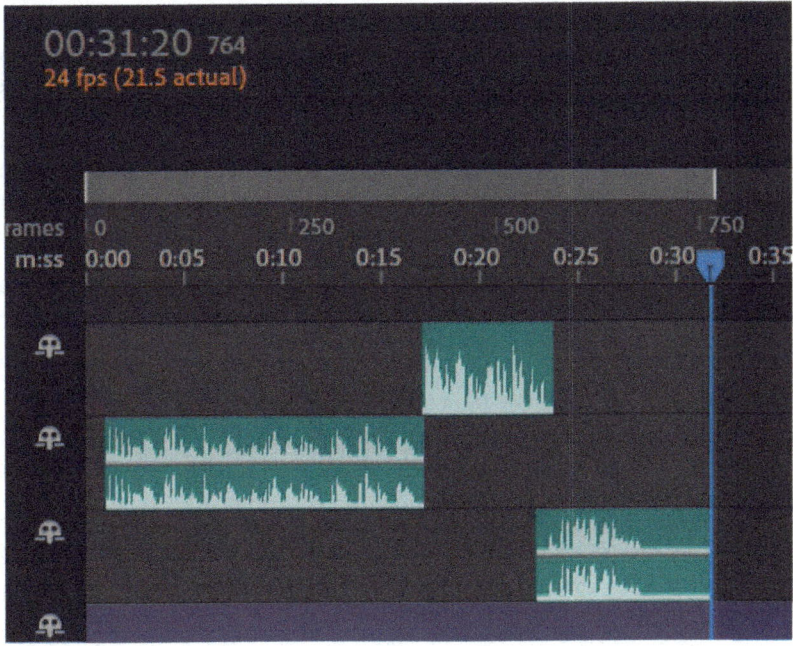

Figure 12.2: Trimming the duration eliminates dead space we don't need

With that, we should now be ready to export our files.

How to export files

There are a few options to create media files for your sequences in Character Animator. You can find these options when going to **File** > **Export**.

Video via Adobe Media Encoder...	Ctrl+M
Video with Alpha via Adobe Media Encoder...	
PNG Sequence and WAV...	Ctrl+Alt+M
Adobe Dynamic Link...	
Frame...	
Puppet...	
Live Options...	

Figure 12.3: The list of export options available in Character Animator

Here is what each of these options does:

- **Video via Adobe Media Encoder...**: This allows us to bring the sequence into Media Encoder and use its tools and presets to render the video as we choose. We will learn more about Media Encoder throughout this chapter.

- **Video with Alpha via Adobe Media Encoder...**: If you have alpha effects, you can choose this option to include this effect when you bring the sequence to Media Encoder to export.

- **PNG Sequence and WAV...**: Export the sequence as a series of images with the audio sequences compressed into a .wav file. This is like the audience image sequence we imported in the previous chapter.

- **Adobe Dynamic Link...**: Dynamic Link refers to the Adobe suite's ability to import project files from one app to another without having to render media first. This actually doesn't require us to export anything from Character Animator. Instead, this option under **Export** launches the Adobe website, giving you more information on exporting with Character Animator.

- **Frame...**: Exports the current frame on the timeline as an image. This is nice if you want to export an image quickly to share with friends or perhaps use it for promotional purposes.

- **Puppet...**: This allows you to select a puppet on the timeline and export it to be used in other Character Animator projects.

- **Live Options...**: This launches the Adobe website, giving you more information on streaming with Character Animator. We will go over streaming in the next chapter.

With an idea of our export options, let's start by exporting the current scene as a video.

Exporting Character Animator scenes as videos

Exporting a video of your scene serves multiple purposes, such as creating a file that can be shared with friends, edited in another app, or uploaded online. Here is how we can do that:

1. First, let's rename our scene to something more specific. Locate `Scene - BG` in the **Project** panel.
2. Right-click and rename `Scene - BG` `Scene 01 - Chaz with Alien Guest`.

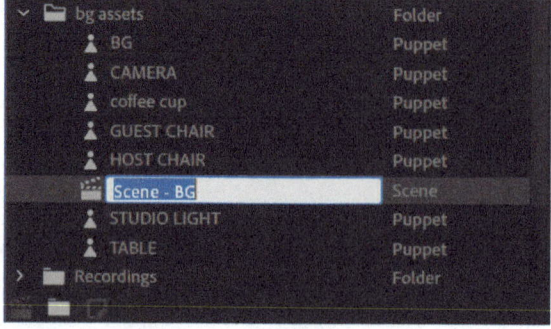

Figure 12.4: It's best to rename files to keep things as organized as possible

3. Go to **File** > **Export** and choose **Video via Media Encoder...**, or you can use *Ctrl + M* or *⌘ + M*.

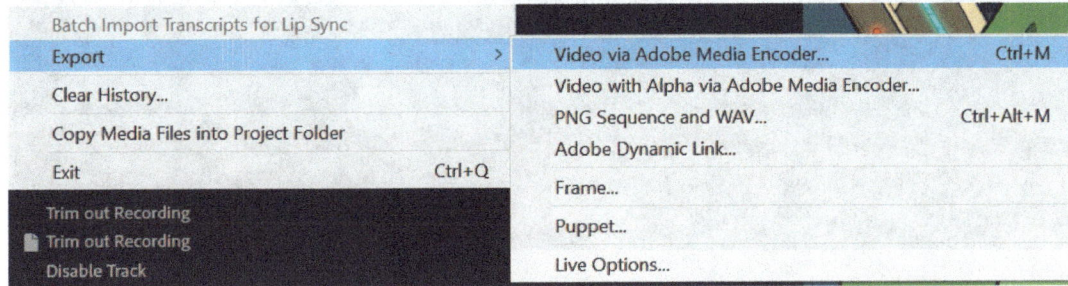

Figure 12.5: Exporting with Media Encoder is the first option on the Export list

4. This will launch an **Export Scene** window. Choose where you want to save your video using the file browser.

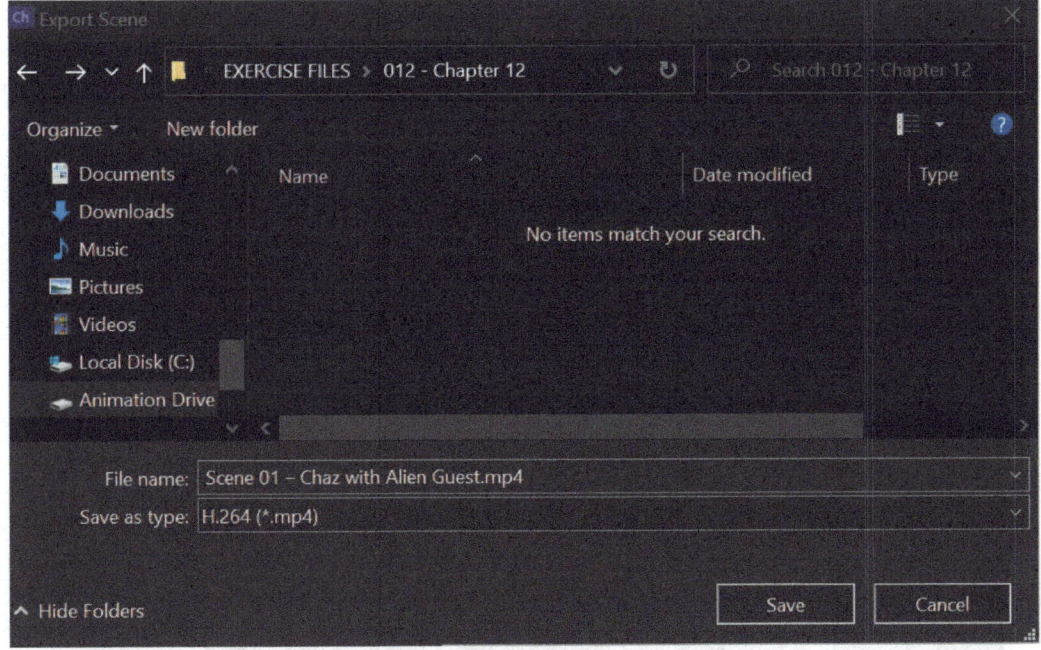

Figure 12.6: Exporting with Media Encoder is the first option on the Export list

5. Pressing **Save** on the bottom right will prepare the scene to be sent to Adobe Media Encoder. Be patient during this time, as it may take some time for the file to be ready to render.
6. Once Adobe Media Encoder launches, you will see `Scene 01 - Chaz with Alien Guest` appear in the **Queue** tab.

212   Exporting, Editing, and Sharing Your Character Animator Sequence

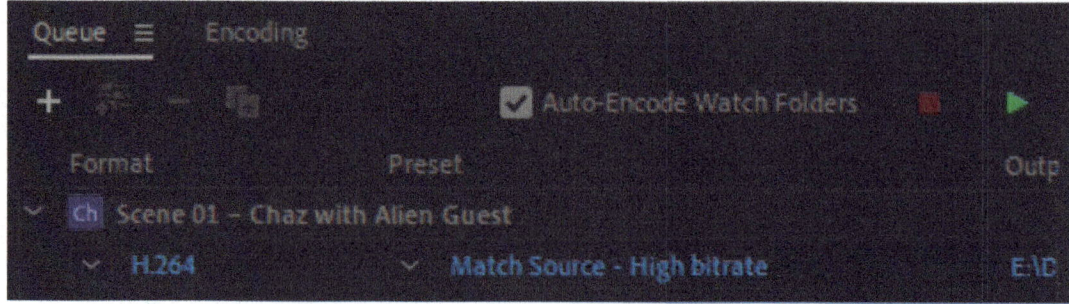

Figure 12.7: Your project listed in Adobe Media Encoder

The preset defaults to **H.264** with a **Match Source - High bitrate** preset. This is a good option if you want to export a video that keeps as much quality as possible while making the file size manageable. So, we will go with that. Here are some other popular formats for your reference:

- **Animated GIF**: Creates a sharable `.gif` image that shows the animated frames from the export
- **JPEG, BMP, PNG**, and **TIFF**: Allows you to export every frame as an image, using your desired format, to be re-compiled into an animated sequence elsewhere
- **ACC AUDIO, AIFF, MP3**, and **Waveform Audio**: Exports an audio file using your desired format

You will find the **Preset** list changes depending on what format you have selected. You can explore that on your own. For now, let's move on to exporting our video.

Make sure **Format** is set to **H.264** and **Preset to Match Source - High bitrate**:

1. Click the **Output File** link.

Figure 12.8: Clicking the file link allows you to choose where to save your files

2. Choose where you want to save the video using the file browser.
3. Hit **Save**.
4. Finally, click the green **Start Queue** button to render the video.

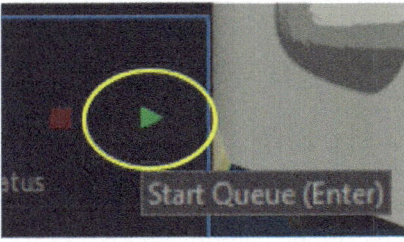

Figure 12.9: The green Start Queue button will start the exporting process

You will see the **Status** bar appear. As the animation renders, this bar will show its progress.

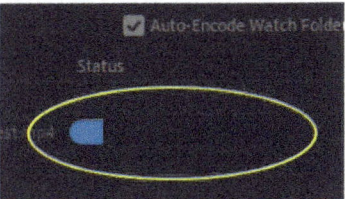

Figure 12.10: Exporting can take some time; it will depend on the animation duration and detail

From here, sit back and relax. Once the file has finished rendering, go to your computer's file browser and preview the video using your media player of choice.

Figure 12.11: Watching renders is a good way to spot errors or areas that need more work

While we could use this file to edit our scene in Premiere or After Effects, we will be using Dynamic Link to show another way of working with these files.

Editing in After Effects with Dynamic Link

The good thing about working with the Adobe Dynamic Link option is that it's all automated for us. We really don't have to do anything beyond importing the Character Animator project file into After Effects and getting to work.

Why use After Effects?

Let's briefly discuss After Effects before we dive into editing with Dynamic Link. After Effects is an incredibly deep program with limitless uses. And one thing it's good at is allowing us to apply visual effects quickly and easily, something that would be more difficult to pull off in Character Animator alone.

Do we need these visual effects? Not necessarily. As stated before, you could use what we exported in the preceding section as your completed piece of art. However, since we have access to After Effects, why not see what it can do to enhance the scene?

Importing and understanding Dynamic Link

Here is what we need to do to get going:

1. Launch After Effects. You will find it included in the Adobe Creative Cloud app you used to install Character Animator.

2. On the welcome screen, press **New project** on the upper left.

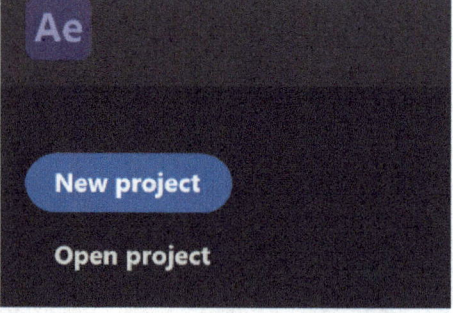

Figure 12.12: Click New project to begin your After Effects work

3. Once launched, make sure you're using the **Default** workspace. This is on the upper right of the app window.

Figure 12.13: The Default workspace is a good starting point when using After Effects

4. On the left side is our **Project** panel, similar to Character Animator. Double-click inside the **Project** panel to prompt an import.
5. Locate `Chat_With_Chaz.chproj`, the Character Animator project file, and choose **Import**.

Figure 12.14: The Character Animator file should appear in the import list

6. Once you do this, the app will ask which scene you'd like to import into After Effects. Select `Scene 01 - Chaz with Alien Guest` and choose **OK**.

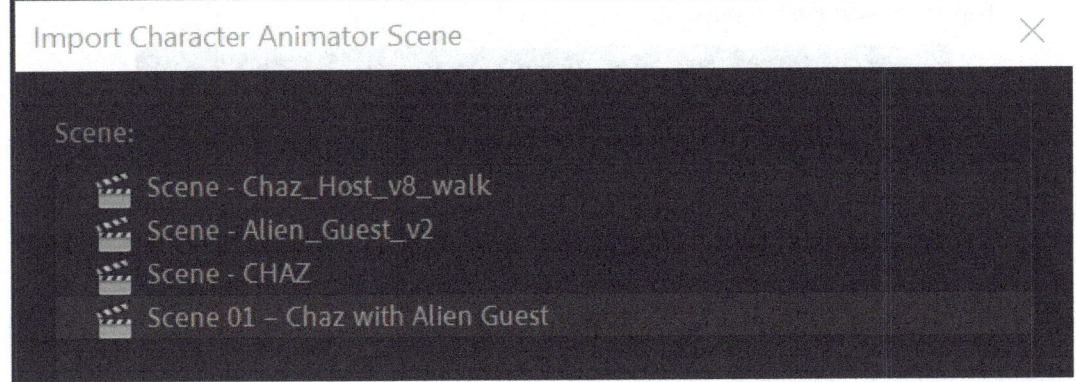

Figure 12.15: Choose the animation scene we worked on in Character Animator

7. This may take a few moments. Once it finishes importing, the file will appear in the **Project** panel.

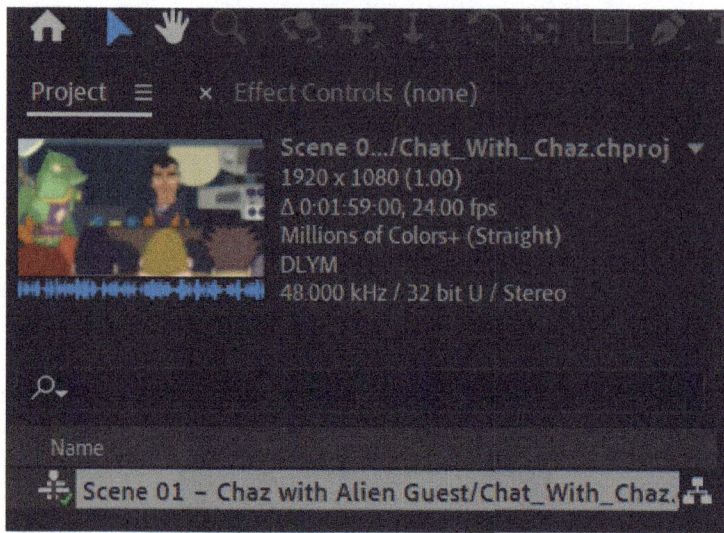

Figure 12.16: Dynamic Link saves time by cutting out the exporting process

8. To easily bring this animation into a composition, click and drag `Scene 01 - Chaz with Alien Guest` down to the **New Composition** button, which looks like a frame with three shapes in it near the bottom of the app.

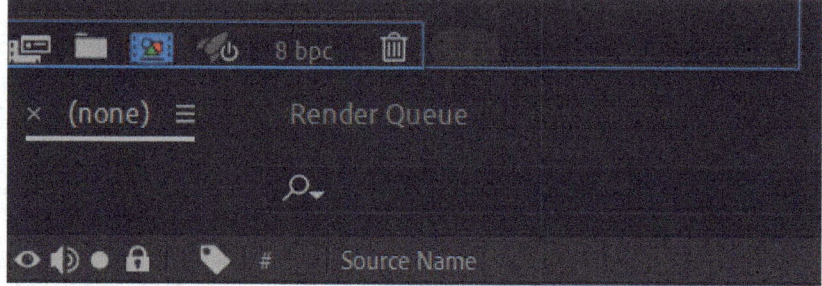

Figure 12.17: Drag the file right on top of the New Composition button

Once you release the mouse button, the footage should create a new composition that matches the duration and frame rate of the Character Animator file.

Editing in After Effects with Dynamic Link 217

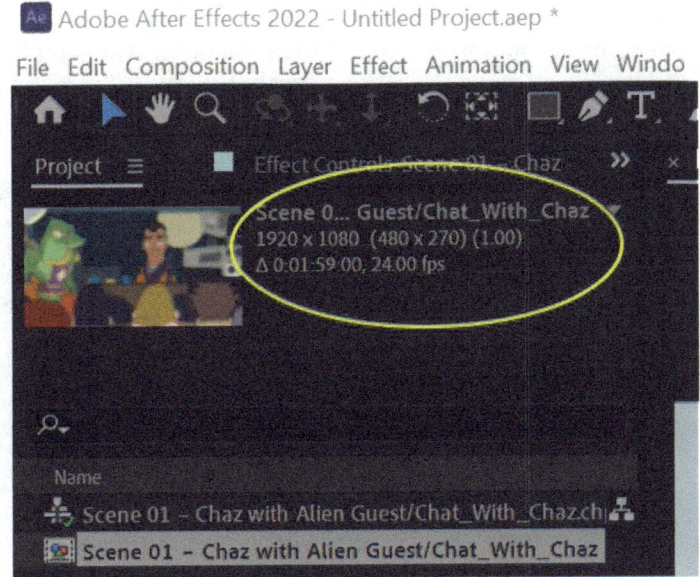

Figure 12.18: The good thing about Dynamic Link is it saves the resolution and frame rate

With that now set up, we can move over and focus on properly layering the assets and preparing to add effects.

Layering

In order to add effects, we first need to establish proper layer ordering. As of right now, with this imported scene, it's all on one layer. But with a combination of Dynamic Link and rebuilding some of the scene, we will get the most use out of this technique.

The most important part of the Character Animator file is Chaz and the Alien. Everything else we can add back in through After Effects. So, how do we isolate the characters? Here is one quick way to accomplish this:

1. Launch Character Animator and load the `Chatting_With_Chaz` project file.
2. Make sure you have `Scene 01 - Chaz with Alien Guest` open, as well.
3. Hide every layer in the Character Animator scene except for Chaz, the Alien, the two chairs, and the table.
4. Go back to After Effects. You should now see the two characters interacting on a black background.

This is the power of Adobe Dynamic Link. Any changes made in Character Animator will update in After Effects.

218 Exporting, Editing, and Sharing Your Character Animator Sequence

> **Note**
> For more granular control, you can also import each Character Animator layer as its own composition into After Effects and work back and forth that way. Play around with different workflows to see what works for you!

Figure 12.19: Making changes to any part of Dynamic Link will update instantly

Now, let's rebuild the set so that we can add our special effects. To start this process, we will need to import our assets:

1. In After Effects, double-click the **Project** panel to prompt an import.

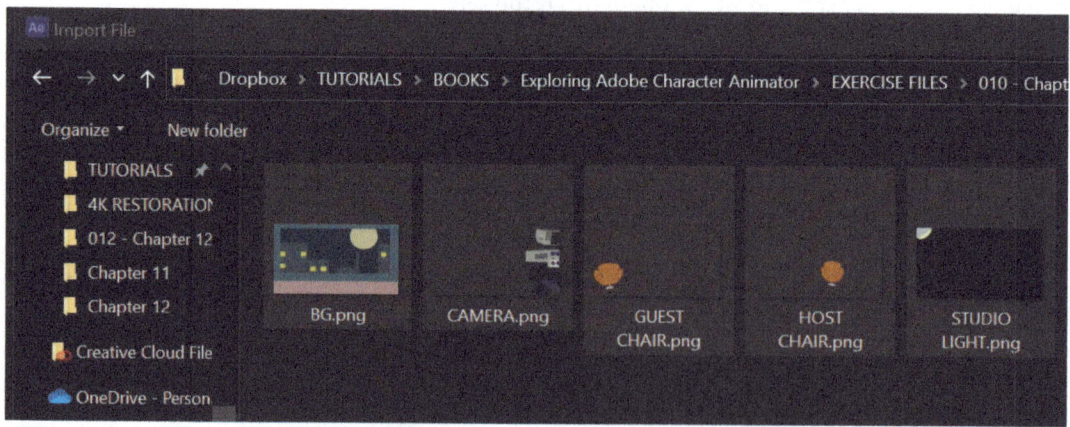

Figure 12.20: The background assets from Chapter 10

2. Locate the background assets we used to build the set in Character Animator in *Chapter 10* and import them.

Figure 12.21: Drag STUDIO LIGHT.png, CAMERA.png, and BG.png to the timeline

3. With those assets selected, drag them over to the **Composition** panel. This will add them to the timeline.

Finally, rearrange the layers on the timeline so that the order is the same as how we arranged it in Character Animator:

1. `CAMERA.png`
2. `STUDIO LIGHT.png`
3. `Scene 01 - Chaz with Alien Guest/Chat With Chaz.chproj`
4. `BG.png`

The following image also shows this order.

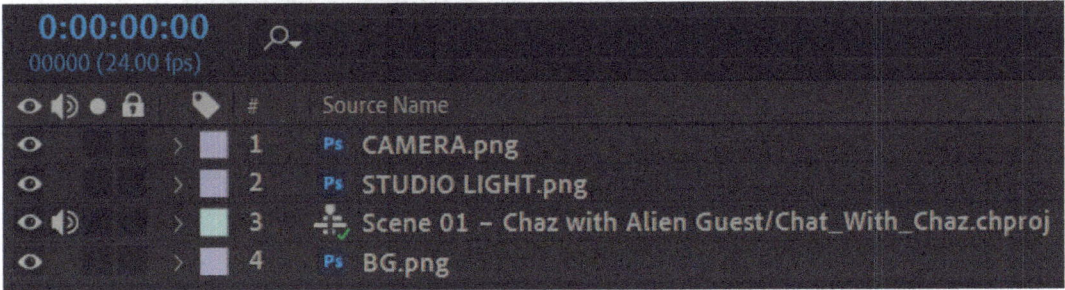

Figure 12.22: Properly reordering the layers is key to building effects properly

We also need to add the audience back in. This will require a different way of importing the files compared to the background assets:

1. Double-click the **Project** panel to import the files.
2. Locate the `AudienceAnimation` folder from *Chapter 11*, which contains the `AudienceAnimation.png` files we used in Character Animator in the previous chapter.
3. Select the first image, `AudienceAnimation_00001.png`, from the list of images.

Figure 12.23: Like Character Animator, After Effects can build animated sequences from a series of images

4. Before importing, ensure **PNG Sequence** at the bottom of the panel is checked.

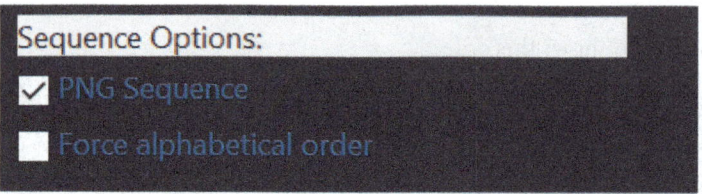

Figure 12.24: Selecting PNG Sequence is important when you don't want just still images to be imported

5. Click **Import**.
6. Once in the **Project** panel, drag `AudienceAnimation_p[00001-00060].png` into the scene.

Figure 12.25: The audience will appear too high up in the shot initially

7. With the audience still selected, use your *down arrow key* on the keyboard to move the audience down, as we did in Character Animator in the previous chapter.

Figure 12.26: The audience should be low enough so that we can see Chaz and the Alien

8. Finally, right-click on the `AudienceAnimation_p[00001-00060].png` layer and go to **Time** > **Freeze on Last Frame**. This will ensure that the audience stops moving and stays in the frame once the animation ends.

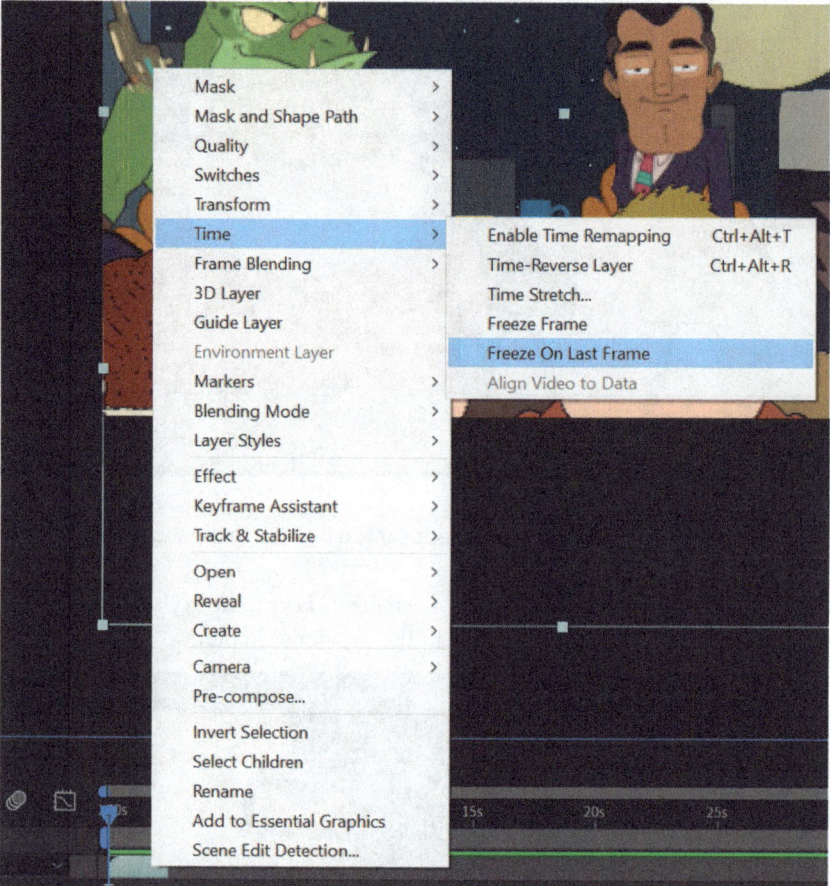

Figure 12.27: Freeze On Last Frame will prevent the audience from disappearing after they stop cheering

Adding special effects

With all the assets now in place, we can add our special effects! Let's start with something simple: adding a blur effect to the audience. This will help to focus on Chaz and the Alien. To do this, follow these steps:

1. Locate the **Effects & Presets** tab on the right side of the screen.
2. At the top of the **Effects & Presets** panel is a search bar.

3. Search for `blur`.

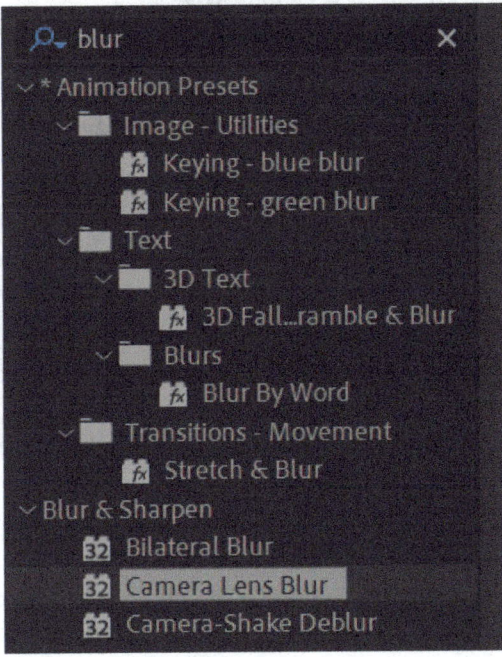

Figure 12.28: The search bar can help with finding specific effects

4. Select **Camera Lens Blur** from the list on the panel; click and drag it over to the `AudienceAnimation_p[00001-00060].png` layer on the timeline.
5. With the effect in place, the **Effect Controls** panel will open on the left.
6. The first option on the panel, **Blur Radius**, by default, is set to **5**. Adjust it to **15**.

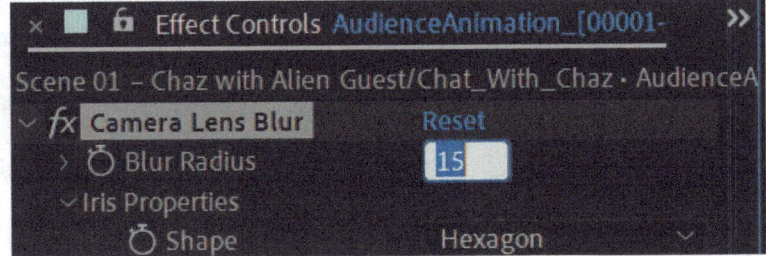

Figure 12.29: Effect Controls allows you to adjust any effect on the selected layer

The result on the **Composition** panel should be evident, with the audience appearing a bit out of focus.

Figure 12.30: Creating the illusion of depth of field can be a nice way to separate elements in the scene

We have a bit more to do. Let's focus on the background next.

7. Grab the **Camera Lens Blur** effect from the **Effects & Presets** panel and place it on the **BG** layer on the timeline.

8. Set **Blur Radius** to 7, giving the background a softer appearance.

Figure 12.31: It may be hard to tell in this image but the background is slightly out of focus

9. Now, let's search for another effect on the **Effect & Presets** panel. This time, we will search for `Brightness`. The only effect that should appear is **Brightness & Contrast**.

Figure 12.32: The search function comes in handy; use it when you can

10. Drag the effect over to the `AudienceAnimation_p[00001-00060].png` layer.
11. Under the **Effect Controls** panel on the left, you should see **Brightness & Contrast** listed under **Camera Lens Blur**.
12. Under **Brightness & Contrast**, change **Brightness** to -106 and **Contrast** to 56.

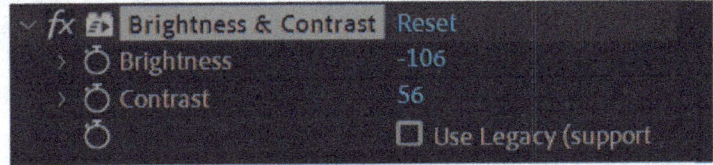

Figure 12.33: Like any parameter, you can drag the number with your mouse or enter it manually with your keyboard

13. Now, go back to the **Effects & Presets** panel, grab **Brightness & Contrast**, and drag it over **BG**.
14. Change the effect values for **Brightness** to -66 and **Contrast** to 49.

Figure 12.34: A lot of these style choices can be altered to your liking; play around if you wish!

Now, let's add a light effect to add a bit more visual appeal to the set. To do this, we will create an adjustment layer to add a lens flare effect. Usually, we would advise you to create your own lens flare, as it's always best to build your own assets when possible. However, since this book isn't going to extensively cover After Effects, we will use a built-in effect. First, let's add that adjustment layer:

1. Click once on the **Timeline** panel.
2. Go up to **Layer** > **New** > **Adjustment Layer** or press *Ctrl* or ⌘ + *Alt* + *Y*.
3. Drag the new layer below **STUDIO LIGHT.png** onto the timeline.
4. With the new layer still selected, press *Enter* on the keyboard to rename the new layer from `Adjustment Layer` to `Flare`.

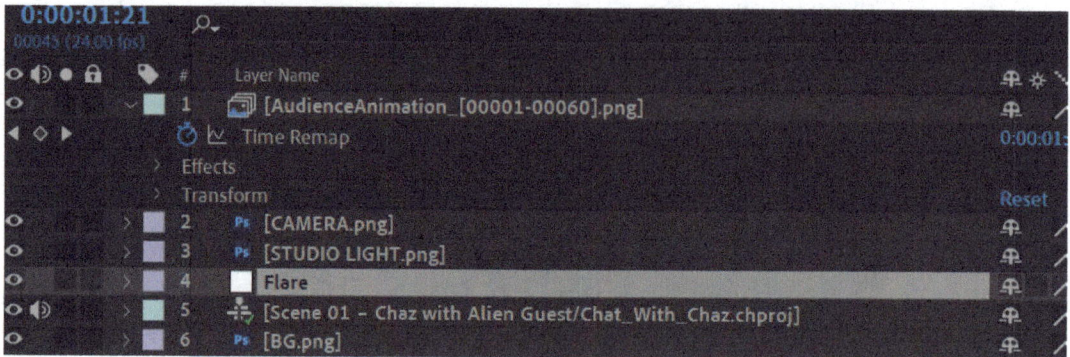

Figure 12.35: Renaming and keeping layers organized helps with any task

5. Now, under the **Effects & Presets** panel, search for `Lens Flare`.
6. Drag the **Lens Flare** effect over to the **Flare** adjustment layer.
7. With the **Flare** layer still selected, make the following adjustments under **Effect Controls**:

    - **Flare Center**: `137.0,122.0`
    - **Flare Brightness**: `93%`
    - **Lens Type: 105mm Prime**
    - **Blend with Original**: `19%`

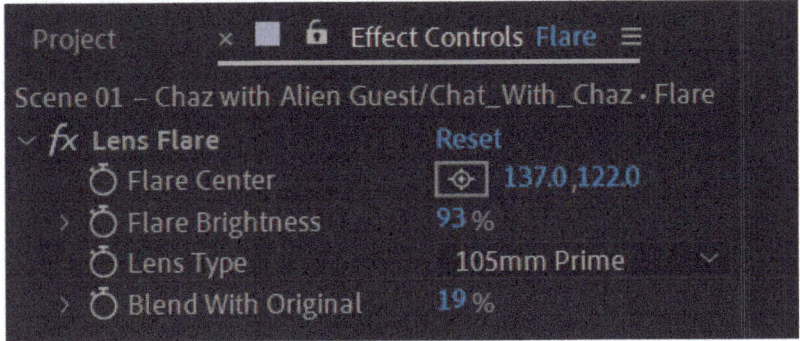

Figure 12.36: Feel free to change the Lens Flare parameters if something else appeals to you

As you adjust these Len Flare parameters, you will see the visuals update in the Composition panel.

Figure 12.37: The lens flare adds a bit more punch to the scene

Now, let's add a little motion blur to the moving assets. This, like any effect, comes down to choice. You may not like how the motion blur looks, and that's perfectly fine. However, if you wish to add it, follow these steps:

1. Search for `Pixel Motion Blur` under **Effects & Presets**.
2. Drag **Pixel Motion Blur** over to `Scene 01 - Chaz with Alien Guest` and `[AudienceAnimation]_[00001 - 00060].png`.

3. If you lose your **Brightness** effect for the audience, click on the layer, and under **Effects & Presets**, make sure **Pixel Motion Blur** is the first effect on the list. Drag it up if it's not.

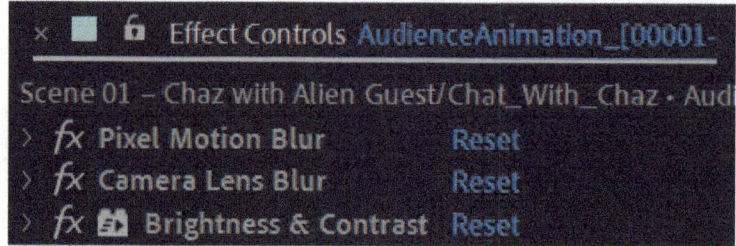

Figure 12.38: The order of your effects will change how the layer looks

Test the effect by playing the sequence. You should see a motion blur take place during the animation.

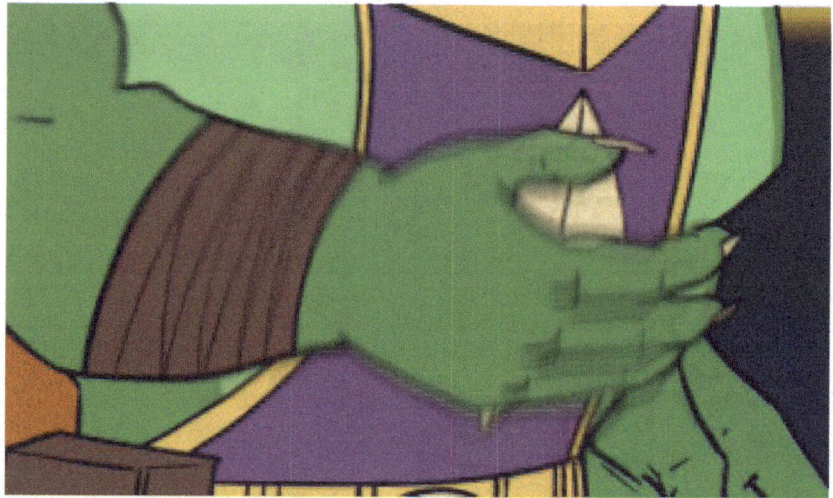

Figure 12.39: Motion blur can be as subtle or extreme as you like

Pixel Motion Blur, like any effect, can be adjusted. However, we will just use the default settings for this book.

Adding camera features

So, what about camera pans, cuts, and zooms? We can do that in After Effects as well. What's important here is we create a logical pace, such as the camera pointing and zooming in on where an important event is happening in the scene.

There is a caveat to this. If you use the camera to zoom past the original resolution of the Character Animator scene, your assets will appear blurry or pixelated. This is a good reason to create assets bigger than the scene you plan to render.

As an example, we are working with a composition that contains our assets that is set to 1920 x 1080 px. We designed the scene in Character Animator to be this resolution as well. So, zooming in past that resolution will degrade the quality, but we can work around this by shrinking the scene down.

This means we will take our 1080p scene and turn it into a 720p resolution sequence. If you want a higher resolution with camera zooms, then it's best to plan around this. If you want to export your scene at 4K, then designing the assets and scene to be around 8K is recommended.

We have been using a smaller resolution to keep the book's file sizes manageable. So, here's how we can set up our composition for a 720p scene:

1. Click the **Project** tab on the top left so you can see your imported assets:

    - Click and drag the `Scene 01 - Chaz with Alien Guest/Chat` composition with `Chaz.chproj` from the **Project** panel down to the **New Composition** button. Remember, this looks like a frame with three shapes in the middle. *Ctrl* or ⌘ + *Shift* + *C* also creates a new composition for any selected asset(s).

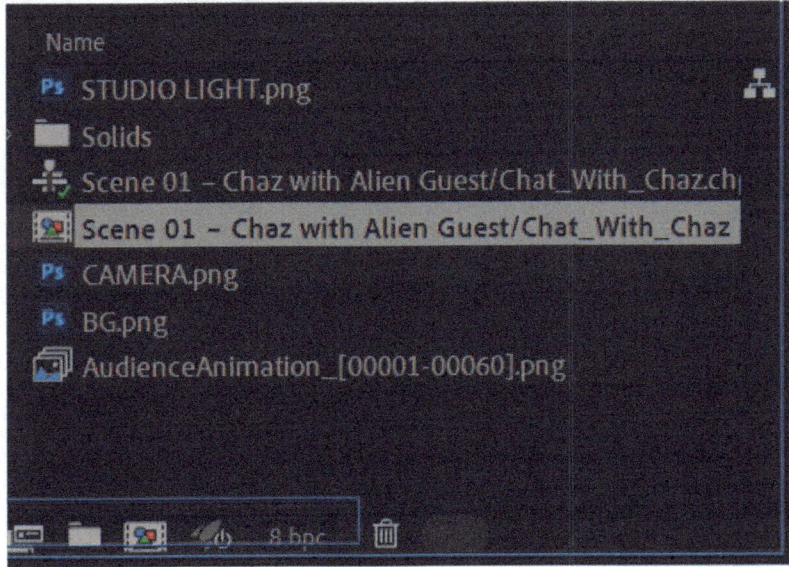

Figure 12.40: Dragging a composition on top of the New Composition button will create a new composition within a composition

What this will do is create a new composition, placing your old composition as the only layer on the timeline.

Figure 12.41: Having a composition within a composition allows us to move the entire scene without worrying about the individual set layers

In order to use the **Camera** tool, we need to ensure our layers are 3D. Since we created a new composition to do this, we only have one layer to worry about.

2. To do this, click the **3D** cube icon next to the layer on the timeline.

Figure 12.42: Clicking the 3D cube makes a layer interact in 3D space

3. Next, to add the camera, go up to **Layer** > **New** > **Camera**.
4. A new window will allow you to adjust **Camera Settings**. Just press **OK**.

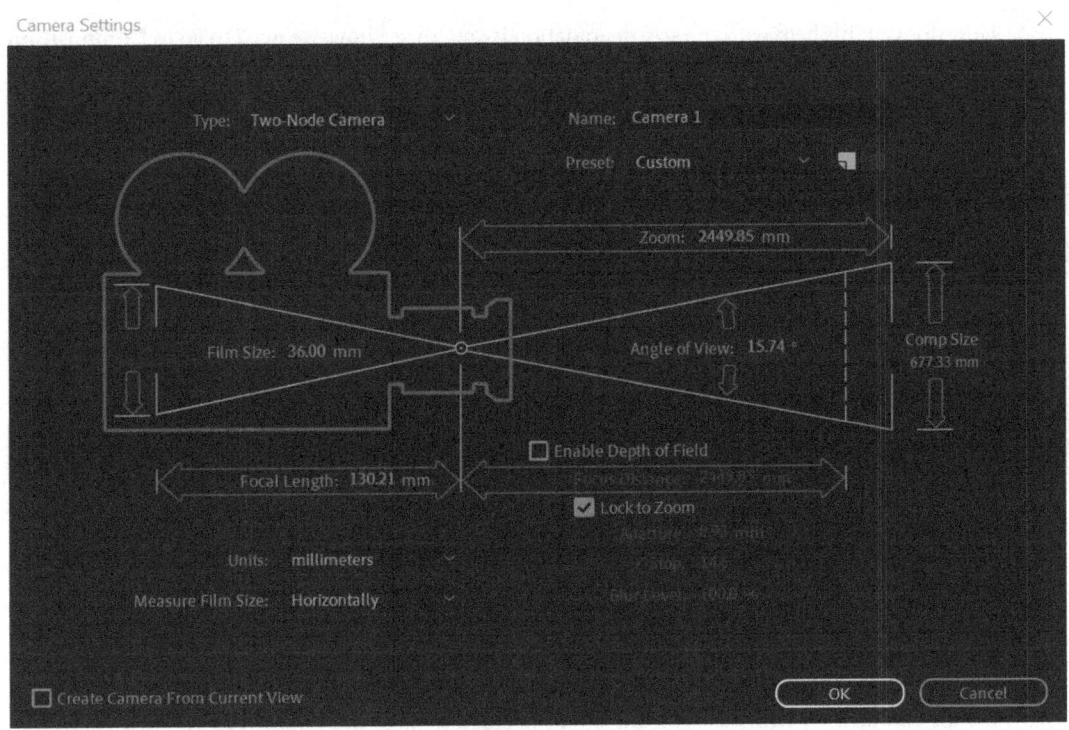

Figure 12.43: You can adjust many things with the camera layers

5. A layer called **Camera 1** will now be added to the timeline. Click the down arrow next to the layer to expand its options.
6. Then, click **Camera Options** to see what options we have.

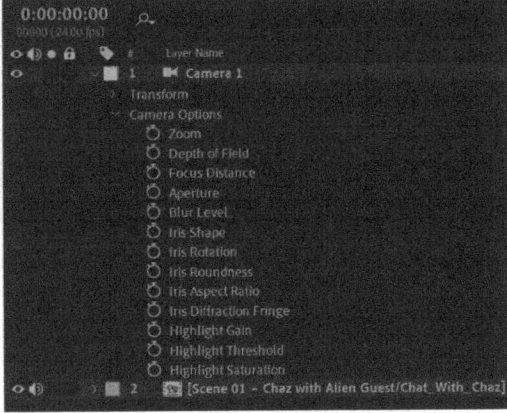

Figure 12.44: You can access many different camera parameters when working in 3D space

232 | Exporting, Editing, and Sharing Your Character Animator Sequence

7. How does all this help with the size degradation issue? To see how, we need to go to **Composition Settings** using *Ctrl* or *⌘ + K*.

8. Change **Width** to 1280 px and **Height** to 720 px.

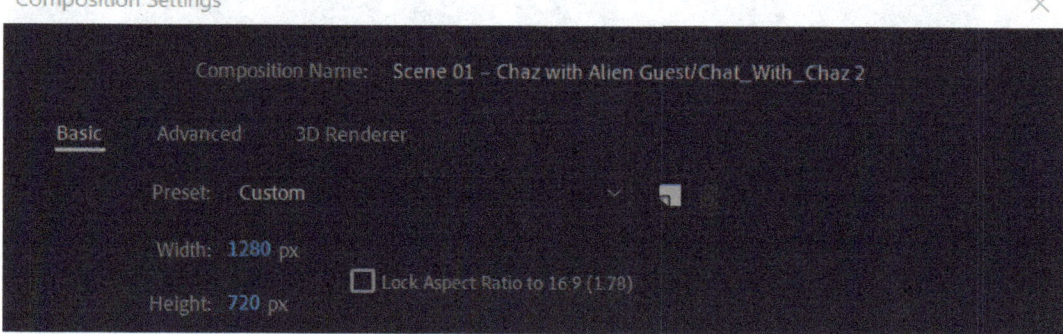

Figure 12.45: You can change the size of a composition at any time

Your sequence will now appear cut off, but we can animate the camera to fix this:

1. Go to **0:00:00:00** on the timeline.

2. Under **Camera Options** for **Zoom**, click the clock icon to the left of it to create a keyframe. This will allow us to create animation, similar to how we created frames in Character Animator for our characters.

Figure 12.46: The clock to the left of any effect allows you to turn on the animation

3. For **Zoom**, set the value to 4660.4 pixels. This will shrink the scene back so that everything is in view.

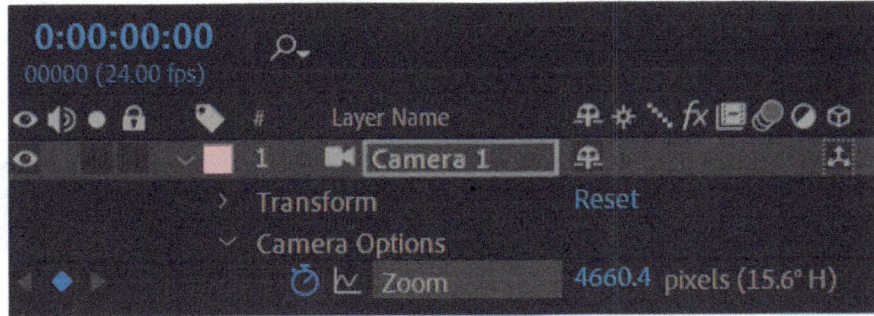

Figure 12.47: When you adjust a parameter with the stopwatch turned on, keyframes will automatically be created

4. Expand **Transform** under **Camera 1**.
5. Keyframe **Point of Interest** by clicking the clock to the left of it.

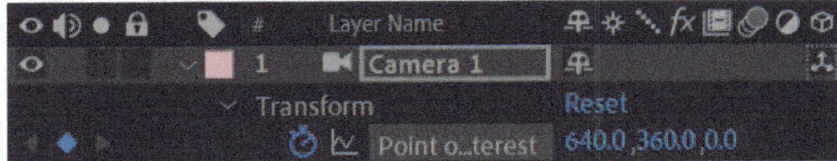

Figure 12.48: Point of Interest allows us to pan the camera around the set

6. Now, advance to **0:00:11:21** on the timeline.
7. Change the **Zoom** value to `6615.4`.
8. Change **Point of Interest** to `898.0, 318.0, 0.0`. This will frame the camera to focus on Chaz. However, if we scroll back to frame 1, we also now have an animated zoom effect.

Figure 12.49: Animating your camera can really add life to an otherwise static scene

9. Now, go to `0:00:17:00`.
10. Click the add keyframe button for **Zoom**. This looks like a diamond to the left of the setting. This will lock down our zoom animation at this spot.

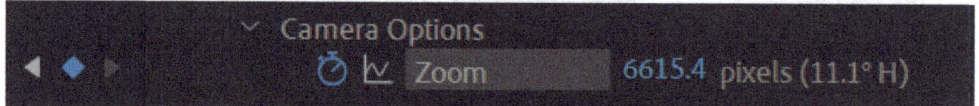

Figure 12.50: The diamond shape on the left, when blue, indicates a keyframe

11. Now, change **Point of Interest** to `367.0, 318.0, 0.0` to center the frame on both characters.

Figure 12.51: Laying down one keyframe after another allows us to create a quick cut with no zoom

12. Go to **0:00:25:00**.
13. Click the add keyframe button for both **Point of Interest** and **Zoom**.
14. Advance forward one frame to `0:00:25:01`.
15. Set the camera keys back to how they were on frame 1. To easily do this, you can drag a lasso around the two keyframes on frame 1, copy with *Ctrl* or ⌘ + *C*, and then go to **0:00:25:01** and paste with *Ctrl* or ⌘ + *V*.
16. Once you have finished, save the file with *Ctrl* or ⌘ + *S*.

When you play the animation now, we should see the camera zoom in on Chaz, pan over to the Alien, and then cut back out. Adding a little camera movement to any animation can breathe additional life into the scene. It's an excellent technique to keep in mind.

You can also reference the complete video in your book files by accessing `Scene 01 - Chaz with Alien Guest-AE-RENDER.mp4`.

As you can see, it's pretty simple to add a wide range of effects using After Effects. There are so many things we can do to enhance this further. But the purpose here is to give a crash course on the benefits After Effects brings to any Character Animator project. Add more effects and continue to explore the app. Once you are ready, we can move over and work on our animation in Premiere.

Editing in Premiere

While After Effects is best used to create special effects, or even build animations, Premiere is best for piecing footage together, adding transitions, basic titles, audio, color grading, and much more. In this book, we will focus on a few basics and export the video.

To get started, be sure to have Premiere ready:

1. Once on the **Welcome** screen, click **New Project**.

Figure 12.52: The New Project button is in the same spot in Premiere as it is in After Effects

2. At the top, name the project `Chat_With_Chaz` and choose a location on your computer for the Premiere files.

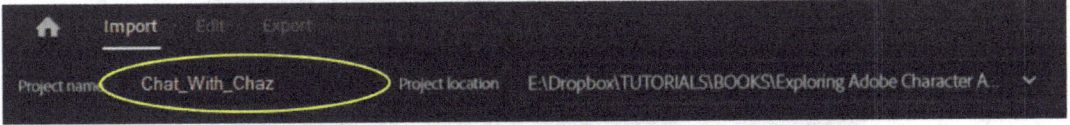

Figure 12.53: You need to create a project before any work can be done

3. On the bottom right, click **Create**.
4. On the top-left **Project** panel, double-click to import the `Chat_With_Chaz_AE_File` file.

5. It will then ask you which composition to import. Choose the second scene, `Scene 01 - Chaz with Alien Guest/Chat_with_Chaz 2`.

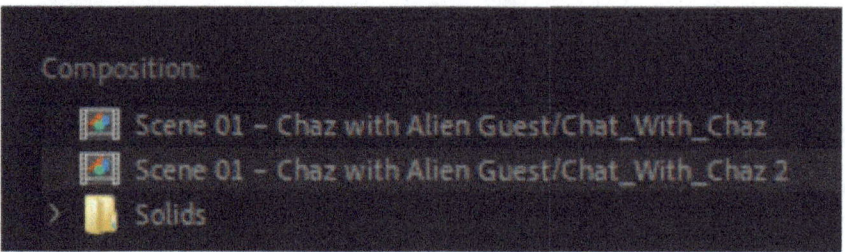

Figure 12.54: Select the second item on the list to import

6. Once the composition is imported into the **Project** panel, grab the file and drag it to the bottom blank timeline. This will create a Premiere sequence for us that matches the After Effects composition settings.

Figure 12.55: Luckily, the Timeline and Project panels appear in the same spot between all three apps; this makes learning how to use the interface less problematic

This also means Dynamic Link is working between the three apps. If you were to go back to Character Animator and make changes, they would also reflect in Premiere through the After Effects sequence. This also applies to hiding layers. Hopefully, such a workflow is showing its benefits.

Going back to the task at hand, let's start by trimming the sequence. As it stands now, it has a lot of extra space we don't need:

1. Place the timeline playhead at **0:00:32:15**.
2. Place the cursor at the right end of the clip.
3. Drag it back to the **0:00:32:15** mark. This will trim the sequence and remove the dead space we left in After Effects.

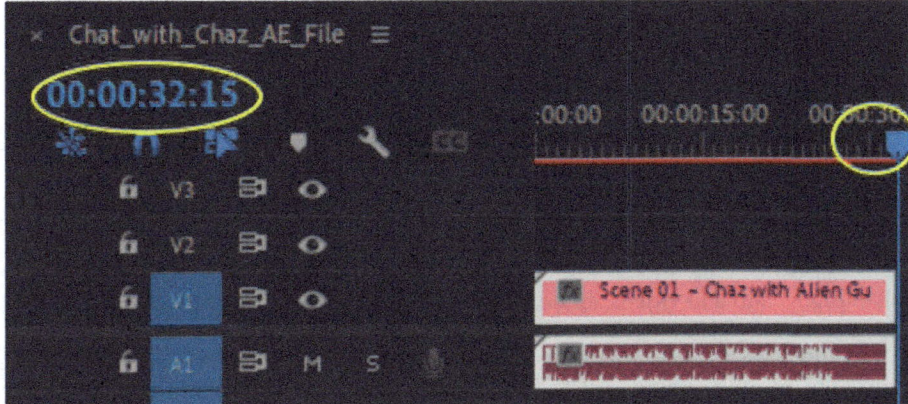

Figure 12.56: You could trim the sequence in After Effects or Character Animator as well

4. Let's bring an image in to add to the sequence. Double-click your **Project** panel and import `Chat_with_Chaz_Title.png`.
5. Go back to the timeline, and click and drag the scene clip so that it starts at **0:00:03:00**.
6. Drag `Chat_with_Chaz_Title.png` from the **Project** panel and place it above the scene layer.

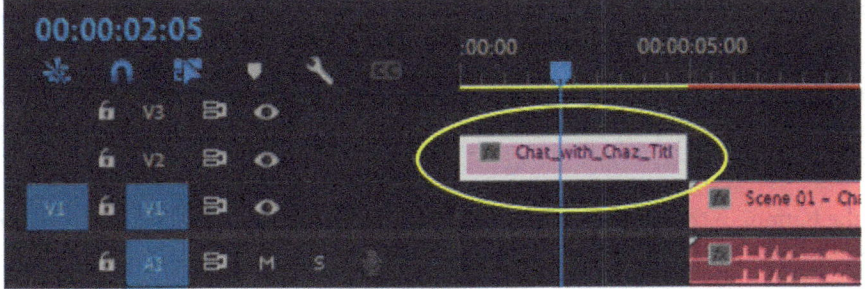

Figure 12.57: Adding images or other media through Premiere is an easy task

7. Now, trim the new layer so that it ends at **0:00:03:00**, when the scene begins.
8. Then, drag the title layer down to the scene channel, as shown here.

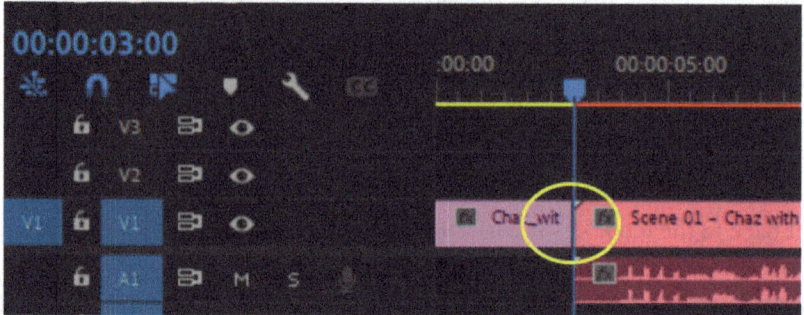

Figure 12.58: The two clips will now play back to back

9. Right-click the title image on the timeline and choose **Scale to Frame Size** to shrink the image into view.

Now, when you play the content, we will see the title, followed by the animated scene. This is a simple example of how you can build more complex sequences. While we are using an image for this example, you can also import and add videos, audio files, PNG sequences, and more.

Speaking of audio files, adding music and sounds, such as the audience cheering, can really help breathe more life into the sequence. It's advised you seek these audio files on your own as we can't include other artists' works in the book files because of various copyright issues.

However, there are plenty of free and paid options out there. Just be sure to pay attention to the copyright parameters before adding any outside media to your production, as some artists and services have specific rules for using their work.

Before we wrap up, let's look at one more feature that Premiere offers.

Color grading and filters

Color grading and filters allow you to change the overall look of footage to help various visuals pop or even create a mood for the scene. While After Effects can grade your footage, Premiere has a feature set that can be quickly and easily applied to perform this task. Let's create an adjustment layer. This acts as the After Effects variant, allowing us to add effects to the sequence easily:

1. At the bottom of the timeline is the **New Item** icon. Click it and choose **Adjustment Layer...** from the list.

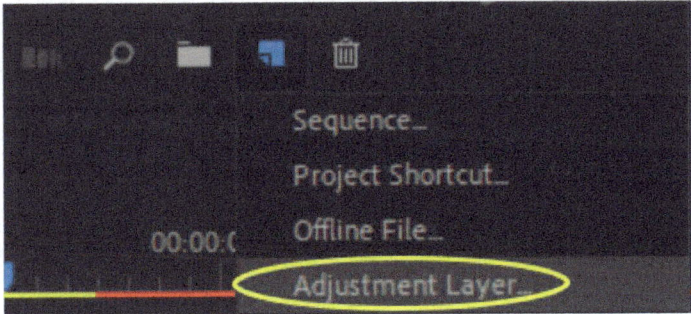

Figure 12.59: There are many items you can create in Premiere

2. A new window will pop up confirming the adjustment layer. The default options should be fine, so just click **OK** to continue.

3. The adjustment layer will now appear in our **Project** panel. Click and drag it to the **V2** channel, the one above our sequence, on the timeline.

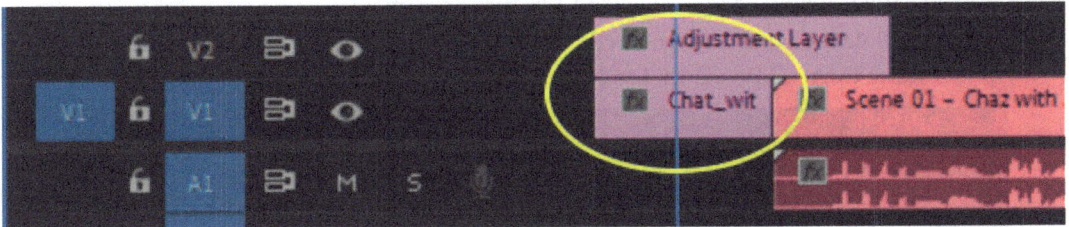

Figure 12.60: You can layer items on top of one another for more complex workflows

4. Place your cursor on the right end of the adjustment layer and drag it to the right until you match the duration of the animated sequence.

Figure 12.61: Adjustment layers are great for adding effects in any Adobe app

5. Switch the workspace to **Color** by going to **Window > Workspaces > Color**.

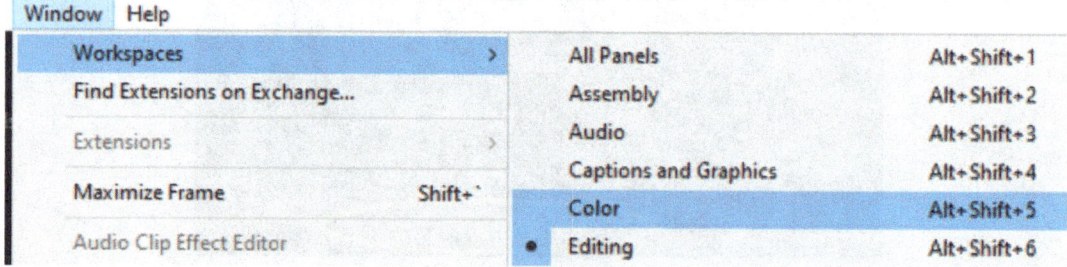

Figure 12.62: You can switch workspaces to fit the task at hand anytime

6. At the top right should be a panel labeled **Lumetri Color**. Select it to open the panel.
7. Here, you will see a wealth of options. You can adjust the colors in a wide range of ways, choose a **Creative** template, add a vignette, and so much more. Experiment with all the options to see whether you can find a look you like for the scene.
8. Use the following screenshots to reference the settings we will use for the book files. To start, under **Basic Correction**, adjust **Temperature** to **–49.5** and **Tint** to **4.3**.

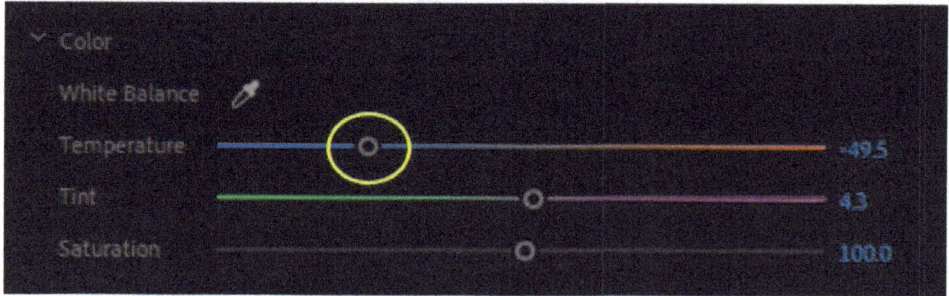

Figure 12.63: You can make footage look warmer or cooler by dragging the Temperature dial

9. Under **Creative** is a drop-down menu labeled **Look**. Choose **SL CLEAN STRAIGHT NDR** from the list.

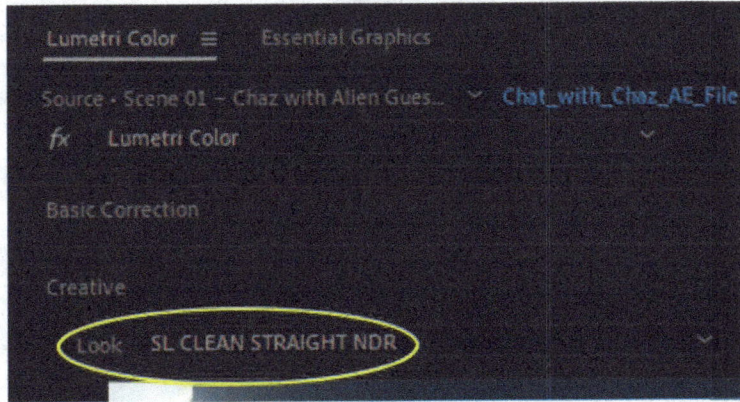

Figure 12.64: You have many options for creative looks in Premiere

10. The last option on the panel, **Vignette**, adds a shadow effect around the frame. Change this to **–3.0** for **Amount**.

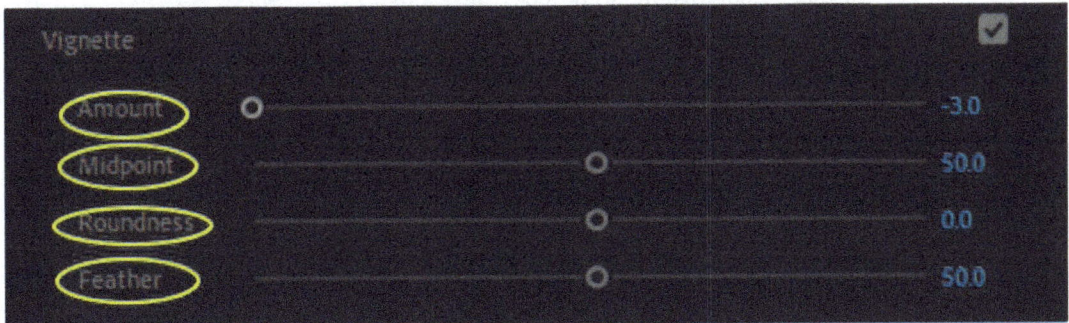

Figure 12.65: You can make the vignette light or dark, as well as many other options

The final result creates a cooler-looking image that adds a bit more contrast to the original look.

Figure 12.66: What the scene looks like before the color effects

The result gives the scene a more blue or cool look.

Figure 12.67: What the scene looks like with the color effects applied

Once you are satisfied with your production, you can export the sequence through Adobe Media Encoder, just like we did at the beginning of the chapter. To do this, simply have the sequence you wish to export open in Premiere and then go to **File** > **Export** > **Media** or *Ctrl* or ⌘ + *M*.

Figure 12.68: You can export with many options, just like Adobe Media Encoder

Here, you can export directly from Premiere or choose **Send to Media Encoder**. Sending to Media Encoder will open up the app and allow you to queue up and adjust settings for clips you wish to export, just like we did before.

If you want to just export this clip, using the export feature in Premiere should work just fine as it contains the same features as Media Encoder, minus the ability to queue multiple files for export.

For this book, we will use the default setting, **H.264** with **Match Source - Adaptive High Bitrate**

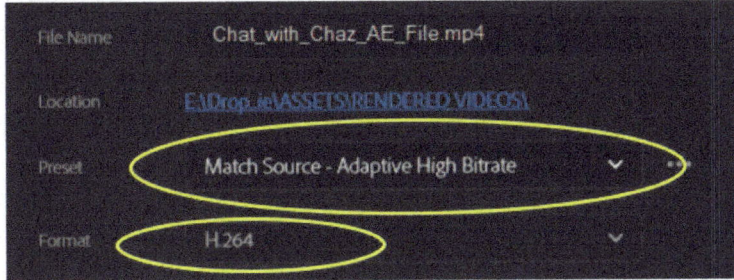

Figure 12.69: The default preset and format settings should be suitable

Once you are satisfied with the file settings, you can press **Export** on the bottom right.

Figure 12.70: You can export or add the sequence to Media Encoder

You can also reference the complete video in your book files by accessing `Scene 01 - Chaz with Alien Guest-PR-RENDER.mp4`.

Premiere offers a lot of features, and what we have done here doesn't even scratch the surface. Hopefully, trimming clips, piecing footage together, color grading, and exporting your sequence gave a good crash course on how the app works.

Summary

There is understandably a lot to take in with this chapter. The thing to keep in mind is there is no right or wrong process. If you feel the animation you created in Character Animator is sufficient, you don't need to take the process any further. Using After Effects for simple or complex effects is a great option. If you need to piece clips together, add audio or other media, or even do some quick color grading, Premiere is the best pick. Having access to Adobe Creative Cloud has many benefits, including being able to dynamically link to all these files as you work. Finally, Adobe Media Encoder allows us to export in a variety of formats, as well as queue up multiple clips at once.

Next, we are going to go over some additional features that didn't fit into our original workflow. This includes Puppet Maker, body turns, streaming, and much more!

13
Additional Character Animator Tools and Features

While we have covered a lot of what Character Animator offers, there are still more features to explore. At the time of writing this book, some of these features didn't work within the planned workflow. Character Animator even introduced some features as the book was being written, which is a great example of how Adobe supports its products. So, we want to highlight these features as they can enhance your animations, save time, or even help you to perform live on a variety of streaming platforms.

In this chapter, we are going to cover the following topics:

- Puppet Maker
- Character Animator scene cameras
- Tracking body movements
- Tracking body turns
- Using the Stream workspace

Technical requirements

We will use unique assets for this chapter compared to what we built previously. We will separate the topics to make them easier to digest. We will reference `Chapter_13_Additional_Features.chproj` but feel free to create your own project to follow along if you wish. `BENIK_FRONT.psd` and `BENIK_BODY_TURN.psd` will also be referenced in the body tracking sections.

With that said, let's open up Character Animator and get started with **Puppet Maker**, a feature that allows us to build ready-to-animate puppets with a few clicks.

Puppet Maker

Puppet Maker is a feature that allows us to get up and run quickly with Character Animator. You can generate a puppet using a series of parameters that are ready to be controlled using your mouse, camera, mic, and **Behaviors**. This process is similar to **Characterizer** but provides more control without using photos or our faces to generate a result.

This feature is easy to launch and use. Here is what we need to do:

1. With Character Animator open, make sure you're on the **Home** screen:

Figure 13.1: The welcome screen for Character Animator

2. Click **New Project** so that we can keep this separated from the `Chat_with_Chaz.chproj` file we were working with.

3. Name the new file `Chapter_13_Additional_Features.chproj` and find a safe place for it. Click **Save**.

4. Go to **File** > **Open Puppet Maker…**:

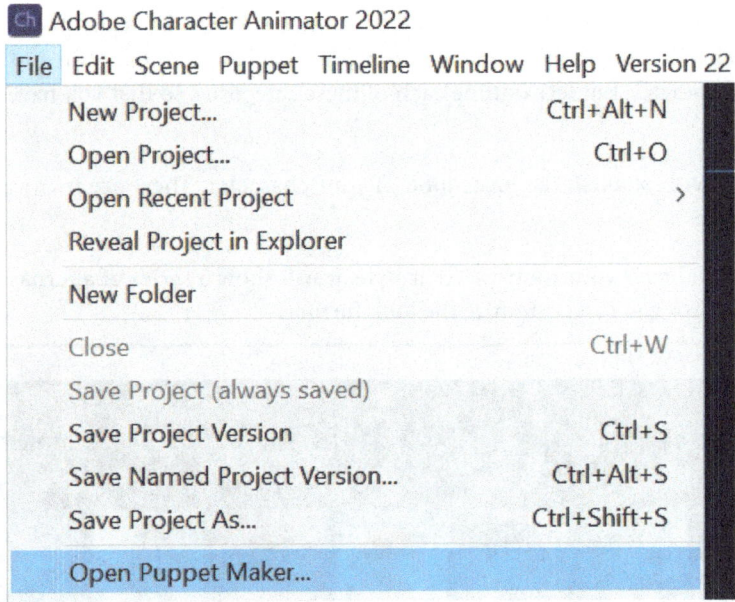

Figure 13.2: You can access Puppet Maker at any time to add new puppets to a project

A new window will appear with a host of colorful options. If you've ever used a character creator in a video game or online social app, this should feel familiar:

Figure 13.3: Each style not only looks different but has unique customization options

On the left, you have the categories of parameters you can adjust. The right-hand side provides a preview of the character as you make changes to it. The goal here is to have fun and select what you want to create a character. But let's outline each of these categories so that you have a better idea of what to expect:

- **Style**: This will establish the basic look of your character. There are many artistic styles to choose from:

    - When you hover your mouse over a style, it will show a series of alternate thumbnails to indicate how you can customize the look further:

Figure 13.4: If you don't see a style you like, Adobe has other options you can download

- Click on a thumbnail to see the character's look updated on the right
- You can change **Style** even after changing the **Customize** options
- The **See more** button will launch your browser and point you to a page for you to download additional styles for the app

- **Customize**: The subcategories for this will vary, depending on your **Style**. Some categories will offer **Hair** styles or **Face** shapes, while others will have unique features not available to other styles. It may be best to explore all these **Styles** to see what each style offers in terms of customization:

Figure 13.5: Compare this to the Customize options below; each Style can be customized completely differently

Don't forget to scroll down when viewing the **Customize** settings as some styles can contain more options:

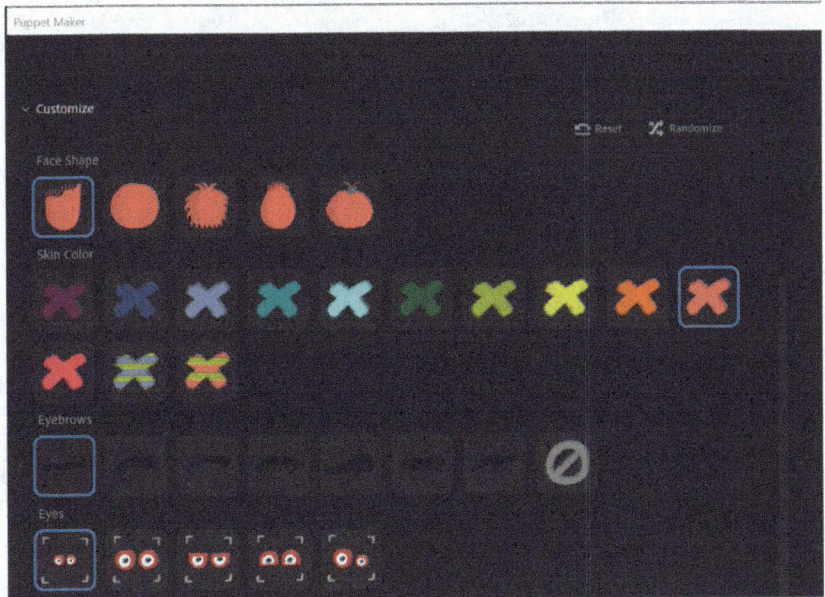

Figure 13.6: This particular style has head shapes and hairstyles, as one example

- **Play**: Here, you can play with the rig to see the different hand and eye phases, preview simple animations, and sample backgrounds to get a better feel for the rig you're creating:

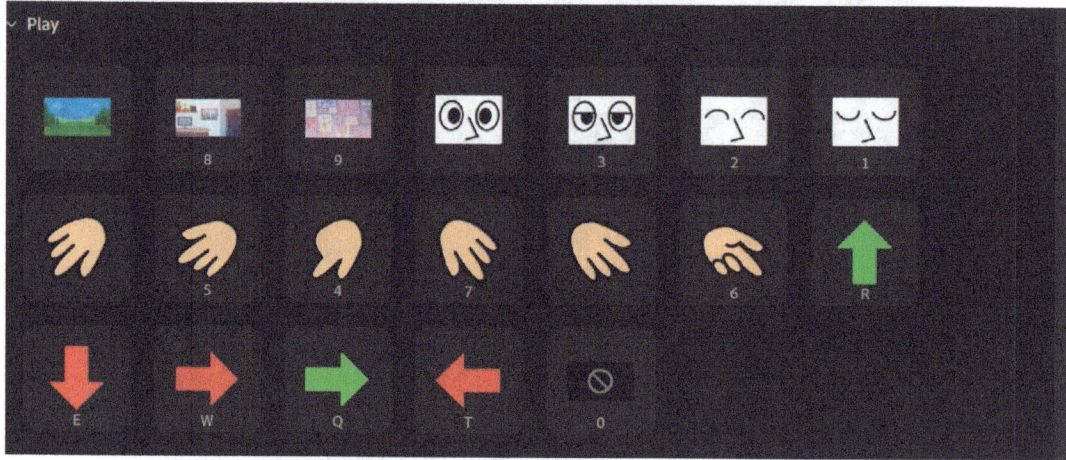

Figure 13.7: The Play panel will have different animation options, depending on your Style choice

Click a thumbnail to see the change on the right. You can also press the keyboard keys under each **Play** thumbnail to preview the action:

Figure 13.8: As you interact with the Play panel, you will see the results in the Puppet Maker panel

Once you have your puppet set up visually, you can test your actions and animation further by enabling your **webcam**, **body tracking**, and **microphone**:

1. You will find these options at the bottom right of the **Puppet Maker** panel:

Figure 13.9: You can test out the webcam and mic functions as you build the puppet

These icons should seem familiar since we used them to calibrate and record animation in the previous chapters of this book. Try enabling these three options and then choose to **Calibrate**.

2. After the countdown, move your head and even raise your arms to see the puppet's preview animation in action. If the puppet has lip-syncing, you can preview that by talking into the mic:

Figure 13.10: Calibrating the camera and moving your arms should yield a similar result on the screen

3. Once you're satisfied with the puppet and the animations you're seeing, navigate to the top right, where the **Name** field is. Name your character and then click the **Generate** button:

Figure 13.11: You can name the puppet before generating it into a new scene

4. This will bring you to the **Record** tab, with your puppet ready to go. You may wish to calibrate your camera again since you can now see the camera preview and reference yourself in the frame.

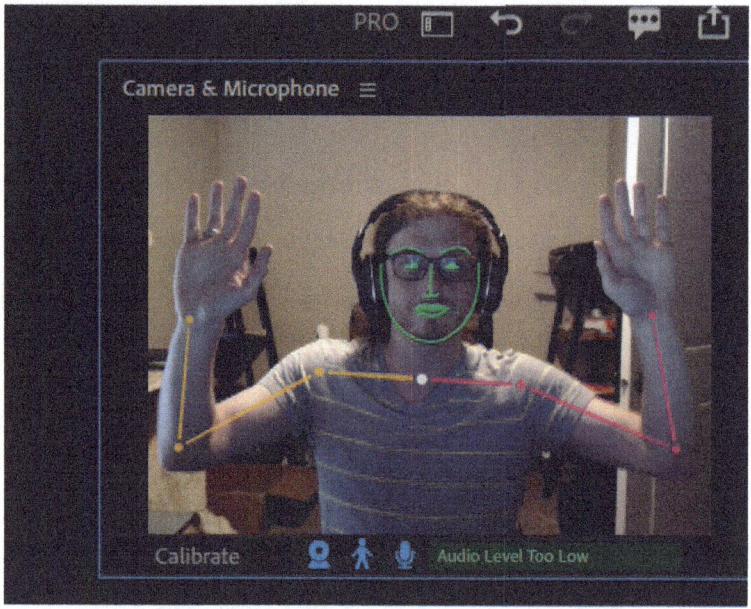

Figure 13.12: When tracking body animation, the points you're affecting will overlay over the actor to show how the puppet may react

This puppet has body-tracking controls, so raising your arms will raise the arms of the puppet. Neat!

Figure 13.13: The result should be reflected by the puppet on the screen

5. From here, you can continue to build the animation as you see fit. You can even go to the **Rig** tab and alter the puppet using methods taught in the prior chapters.
6. You're also not just limited to one puppet from **Puppet Maker**. If you want to add additional characters, simply go back to **File** > **Open Puppet Maker...** and generate a new character.
7. This will put the new puppet into a new scene, like the first one. However, you can simply grab and drag the new puppet from the **Project** panel to the first scene you generated to build a scene with multiple characters. Just note that if the new puppet has a background layer, hide or remove it:

Figure 13.14: You can add as many puppets as needed using Puppet Maker

Puppet Maker is a prominent feature if you want to get up and running with animation with little fuss. It's also a great tool for beginners to dive into pre-made rigs and dissect, analyze, and learn from them. Being able to control these puppets with your body is a great alternative to traditional animation. What's better is that we can add this **Behavior** to any puppet and use an actor's full body on camera to record animation from head to toe.

We will be learning more about body tracking soon. But first, since we have this basic Puppet Maker scene already set up, let's use it to learn about scene cameras.

Character Animator scene cameras

When we created the Chatting with Chat animation, we used After Effects' camera system to add zooms, closeups, and cuts to the scene. This benefited us since we used After Effects for more than just the camera. But what if you want to use a camera and skip using After Effects entirely? We can do that with **Scene Camera** in Character Animator.

For a quick example, let's keep `Chapter_13_Additional_Features.chproj` open. To add a camera to the scene, follow these steps:

1. Make sure **Scene – Pirate Chad** is still open.
2. Go to **Scene** > **New Scene Camera** (*Ctrl* or *Command* + *Alt* + *Shift* + *C*):

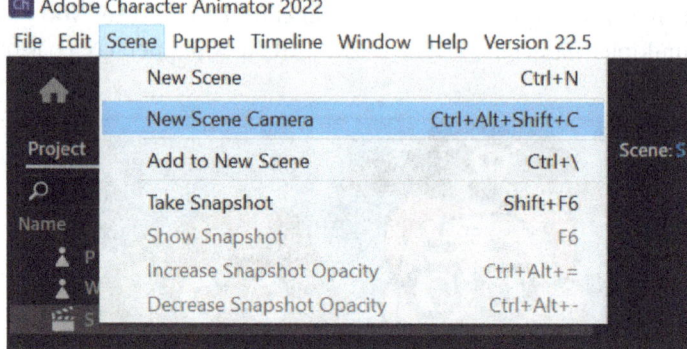

Figure 13.15: You will find that the camera tool is more simple than After Effects' but is still effective

3. This will create an additional layer designated as the camera, labeled **Camera 1**. If you click this layer, the **Camera Track Behaviors** panel will appear on the right:

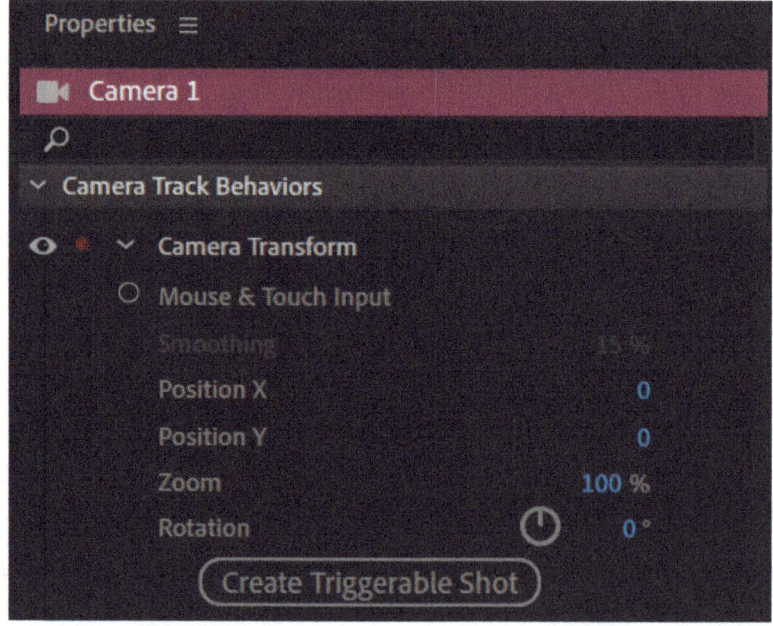

Figure 13.16: While you can't work in 3D space, panning, zooming, and rotating are still very useful for helping pace a scene

You have the following options for controlling the camera:

- **Position X**: Moves the camera left or right
- **Position Y**: Moves the camera up or down
- **Zoom**: Zooms the camera in
- **Rotation**: Rotates the camera

You also have **Create Triggerable Shot**. But let's focus on learning to animate the camera first. There are *two* ways to animate the camera.

The *first* is to enable **Mouse & Touch Input**. Clicking the red icon next to the parameter will arm it, like any other behavior in the app:

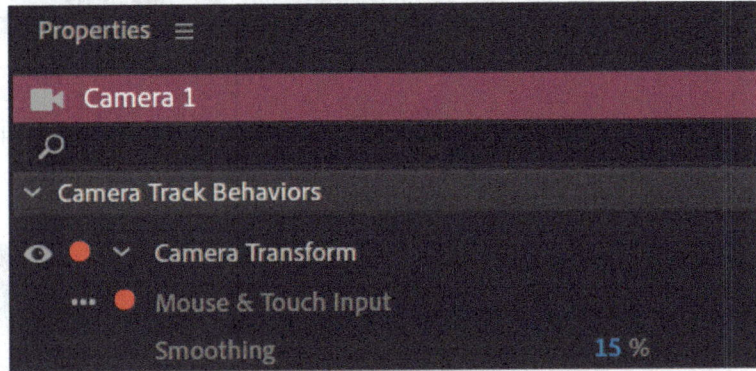

Figure 13.17: Mouse & Touch Input allows you to move the camera live during recording, like how we animated our characters in previous chapters

4. Now, if you press **Record** on the timeline, as the playhead moves, you can click and drag to move the camera and even use a mouse wheel to zoom in and out. You can also use the *Alt* key to move the workspace if needed, as opposed to what the camera sees.

5. To see the result of **Mouse & Touch Input**, press **Stop**, go back to the beginning, and hit **Play**; you'll see the camera animate following what you did with the mouse.

6. Hitting the down arrow next to **Camera 1** will reveal the recorded keyframes:

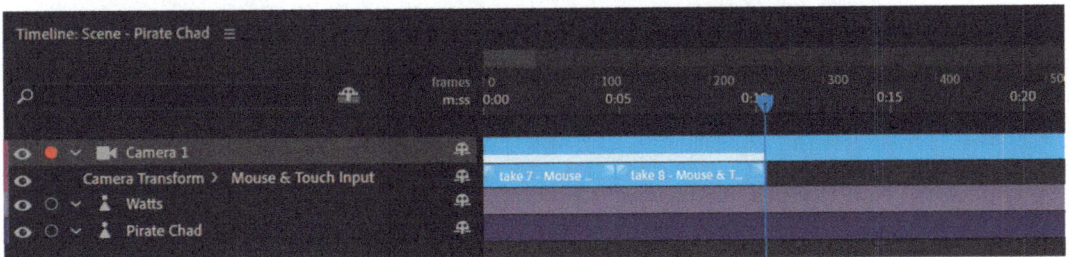

Figure 13.18: You will see what's been recorded, again like any animated item in the app

The *second* way to animate a camera allows you to animate using the panel parameters and separate each item into its own set of keyframes. These items won't animate by default:

1. You will need to enable the **Stopwatch** option next to the parameter you'd like to animate:

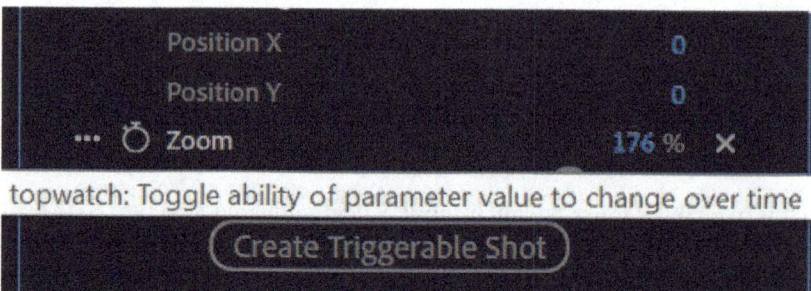

Figure 13.19 Stopwatches are not only available for the camera but for other behaviors as wel.

2. Once you have triggered the parameters you'd like to animate, you can go through the timeline, without hitting **Record**, to place cuts, pans, and zooms using a similar keyframe setup to what we saw in After Effects:

Figure 13.20: Using keyframes like this makes animation work similar to After Effects

So, what about that **Create Triggerable Shot** button? What you can do with this is create keyboard triggers for certain shots. Let's say you want a certain keyboard key to focus on one character, with an alternate focusing on the second character, while a third trigger could be for a wide shot. This is a simple example, but let's set it up for a bit of practice:

1. First, clear all the keyframes on **Camera 1** so that we can work with a clean slate.
2. Using the **Camera Transform** panel, put **Position X**, **Position Y**, and **Rotation** to 0 and **Zoom** to 100%. This will act as our default view:

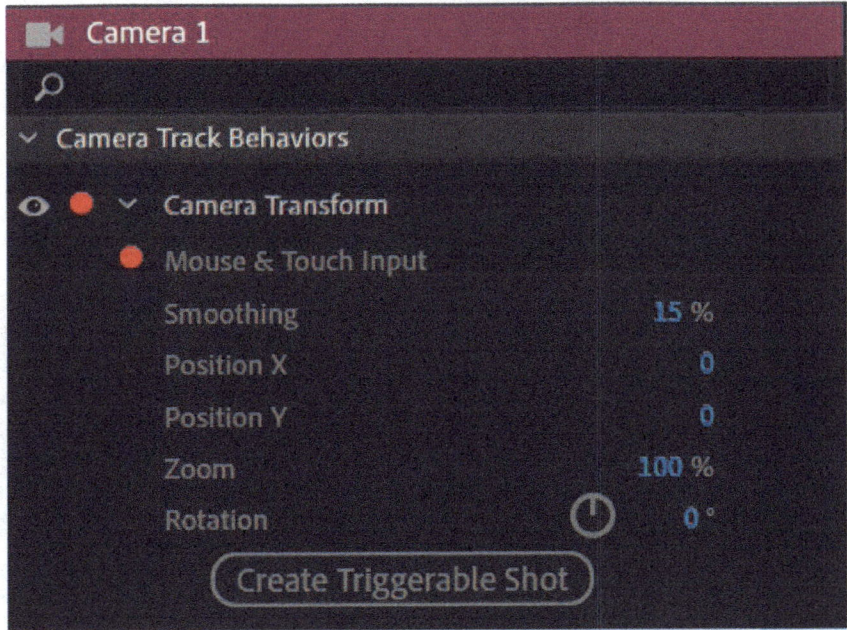

Figure 13.21: You can adjust these parameters and create a new shot without needing to add keyframes

3. Now, click the **Create Triggerable Shot** button.
4. Under **Triggers** on the left, **Shot 1** will appear, allowing you to control it like any other trigger.
5. Enter 1 for the shortcut:

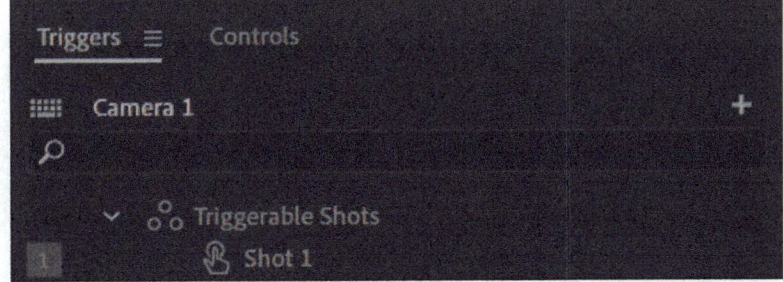

Figure 13.22: Shots can be triggered, just like any other item in Character Animator

6. Now, go back to the **Camera Track Behaviors** panel and zoom in on the **Pirate Chad** character. You can easily do this by entering 4 for **Position X**, -115 for **Position Y**, and setting **Zoom** to 196%.
7. Then, click **Create Triggerable Shot**:

Figure 13.23: Clicking this will always create a new shot using the current parameters

8. For **Shot 2** on the **Triggers** panel, enter 2 for the keyboard trigger.
9. Go back to the **Camera Track Behaviors** panel one more time.
10. Enter 700 for **Position X** and click **Create Triggerable Shot**:

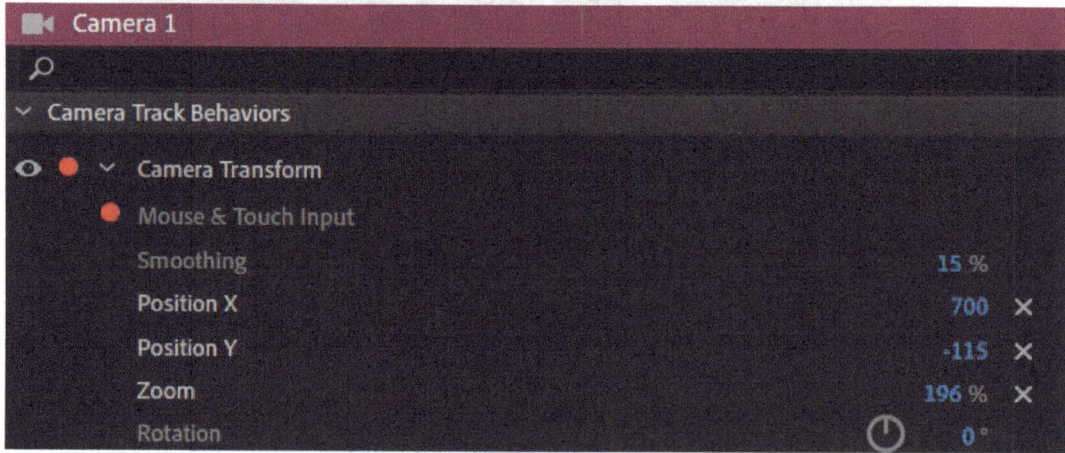

Figure 13.24: This turns animating with Character Animator more into an application like After Effects

11. Under **Triggerable Shots**, trigger **Shot 3** with keyboard key 3:

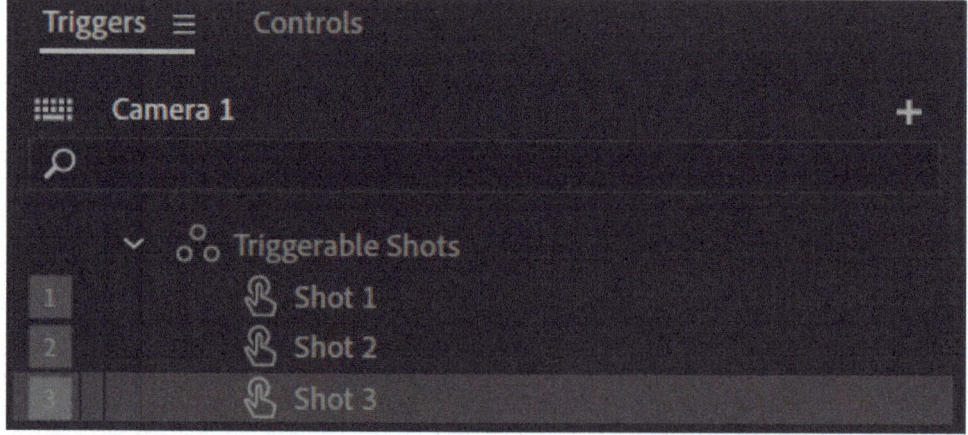

Figure 13.25: You can have as many shots as needed

12. Now, try pressing trigger key *1*, *2*, or *3*; you should see the camera change based on what you set down for the trigger. Here, **1** will be a wide shot, **2** will be a closeup of **Pirate Chad**, and **3** will show **Watts**. If you press **Record** while doing this, you will see the keyframes record on the timeline, just like any other animated action:

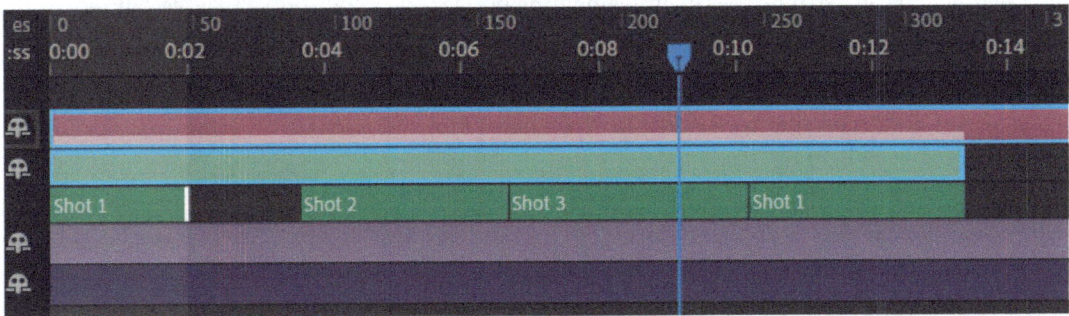

Figure 13.26: Shots will appear in the timeline for you to shorten or extend if needed

13. You can also preview any of the camera shots by referencing a **Shot** of your choice. These will be located under **Replays**. Click and holding will show the shot in the **Scene** panel:

Figure 13.27: You can check the Replays panel to preview the shots

As you can see, **Scene Camera** can be quite useful for framing shots and adding more focus to a sequence. It's good to know it's there, especially if you plan to forgo using After Effects or other apps for post-production.

One more thing to note is that you can add more than one camera to any sequence. Perhaps you want one camera just to focus on close-ups while the other is for various wide shots. The possibilities are open to you. It just depends on how you want to tackle the content.

Now, let's swing back and talk more about being able to control a custom rig using your web camera and body.

Tracking body animations

As we observed when setting up our **Puppet Maker** rigs, we can track our body with the webcam to record animation. We used this tracker for head turns when animating the Chatting with Chaz scene. But now, let's take it a step further by implementing body tracker controls so that we can move our limbs using only the camera.

We will use a new forward-facing custom rig for this example as it will best show this feature. Also, if you plan to do this on your own, make sure you have plenty of room for the webcam to track your body and nice, even lighting.

With `Chapter_13_Additional_Features.chproj` still open, follow these steps:

1. Direct your attention to the `BENIK_FRONT_TRACKING` rig in the **Project** panel and double-click to open it.

2. Note that the rig setup is more simplified – for example, it's lacking mouth, eye, and hand poses. We have tagged all the points on the body for animation as we just want to focus on that:

Figure 13.28: This new character has been tagged for body animation

3. So, how do we set up the **Body** tracker? On the **Puppet** panel, click the **Add Behavior** button to the right of the puppet label and choose **Body** from the list:

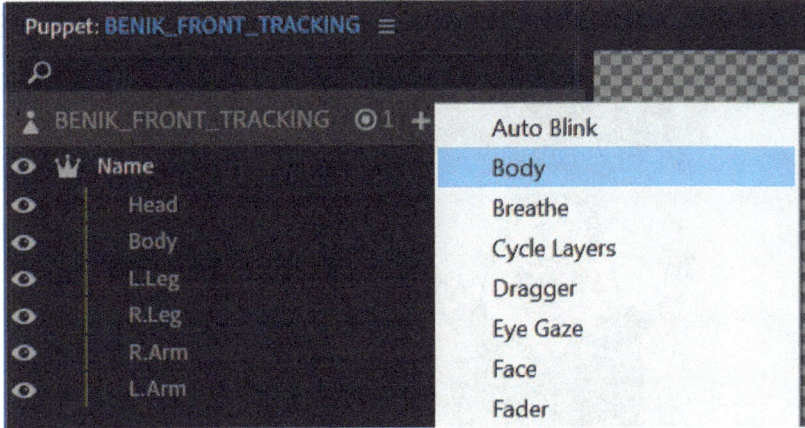

Figure 13.29: Adding the body behavior will allow us to control the body with our camera

4. Now, on the right, under **Behaviors**, we have a similar-looking list of settings that we saw when working with the **Puppet Maker** rigs. Pressing the down arrow next to **Tracked Handles** will reveal a list of checkboxes associated with a tagged limb:

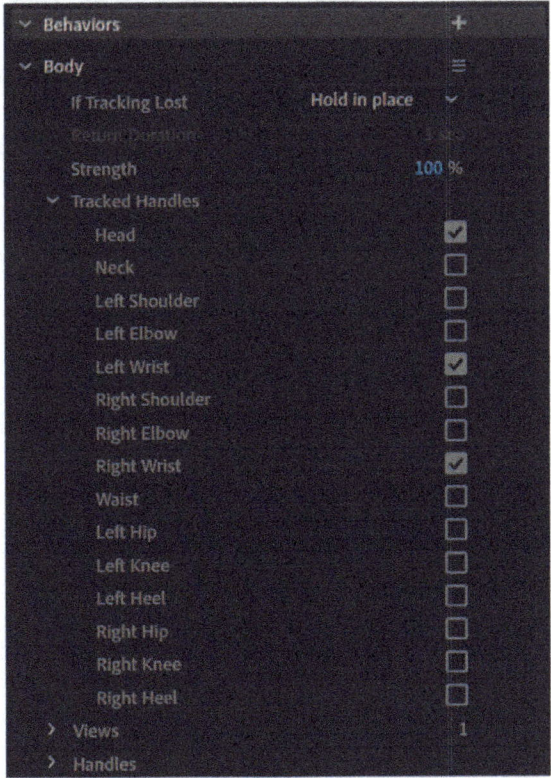

Figure 13.30: The body behavior will track the head and wrists by default

5. Now, if you go to **Record**, **Calibrate** your camera, and raise your arms as we did previously, you should see a familiar pose to what was set up with the **Puppet Maker** rigs:

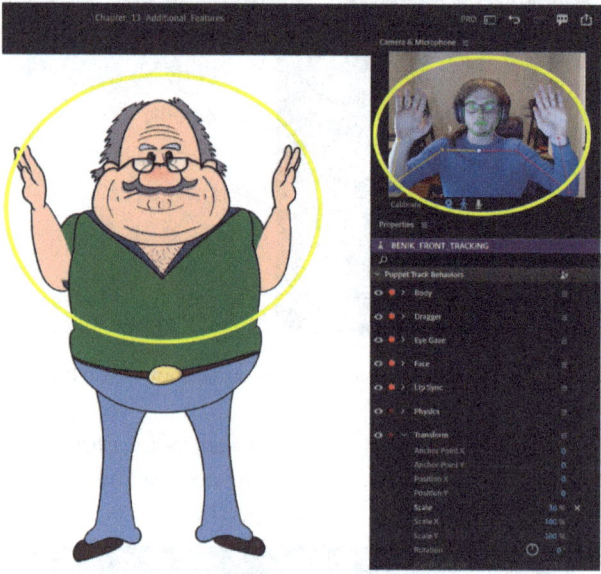

Figure 13.31: The rig should react to your head and hand positions

6. But what about those other checkboxes we left alone? Go back to the **Rig** tab and try enabling them all:

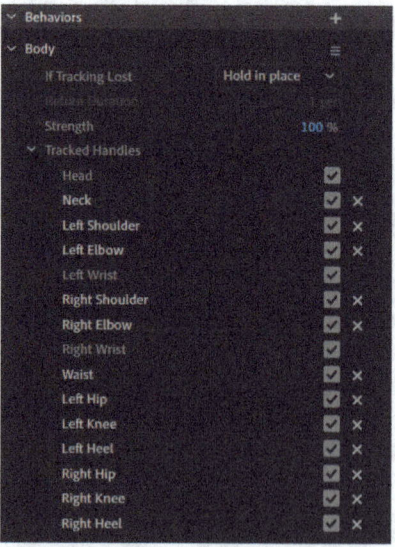

Figure 13.32: So long as you've properly tagged the puppet, you should be able to enable whichever handle you wish

7. Now, go back to **Record** and try to give yourself as much room as possible. **Calibrate** and then try moving your body. You should see the rig respond to whatever you're doing on camera:

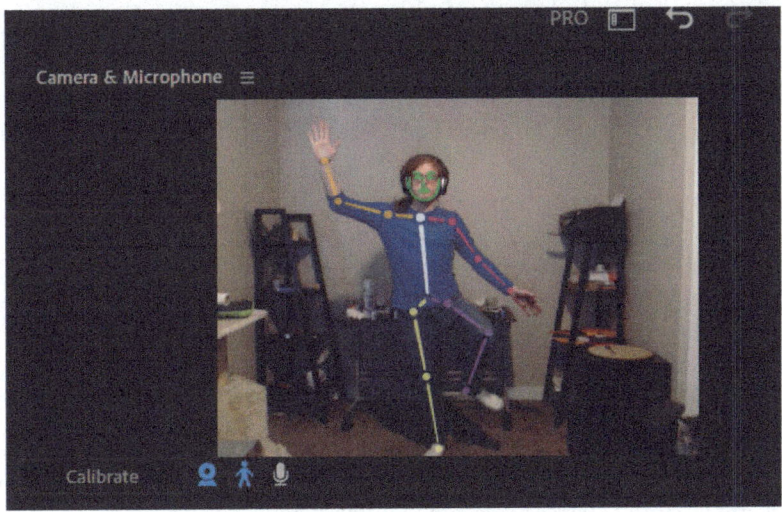

Figure 13.33: If you wish to track your full body, be sure to have plenty of room

Depending on how you move, you may encounter minor tracking or art errors. Depending on the rig, you may need to adjust your `.psd` or rigging layout to make things look right:

Figure 13.34: It may take some calibration and rig adjustment to get everything to work properly

Keep in mind that you can also limit what is being tracked. If you're having issues with a certain point, try unchecking it from the list to see if it helps. Also, depending on what you want the rig to do, check what layers are independent and where they link.

Having full body tracking to control a character is a fantastic addition to an already full suite of animation tools. What other features can we explore? Well, what about turning the body? We've already learned that we can turn a character's head. Creating a body turn is a very similar process.

Tracking body turns

Setting up a body turn is quite similar to setting up a head turn. You will need to have a rig set up with more than one body position for this to work. For this example, we will use `Scene - BENIK_BODY_TURN` inside the `Chapter_13_Additional_Features` project file.

This rig hasn't been set up for animation since we went through that process previously. Here, we just want to show the body turn switch:

1. To create the body turn, it's advised you group each phase into its own folder. In our example, the front and left profile views are grouped individually:

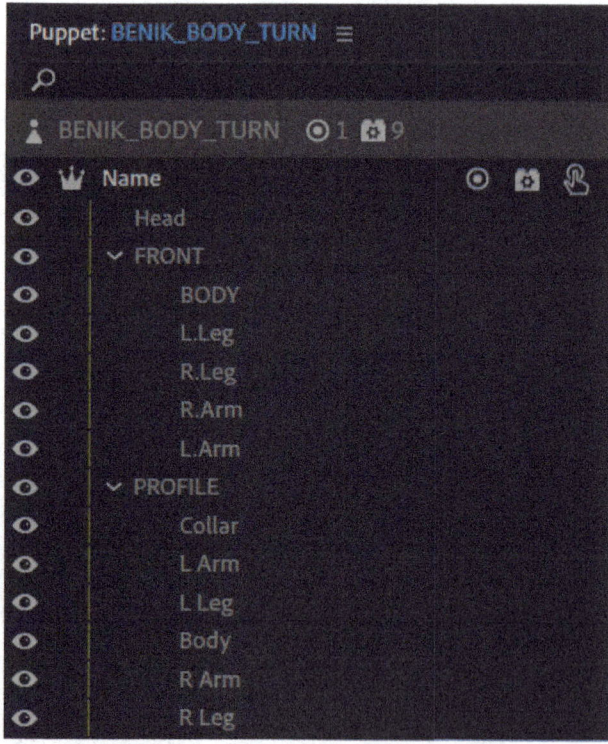

Figure 13.35: This rig setup is simple, but showcases how you could organize the body phases

2. Now, to create the turn, you will need to add **Head & Body Turner** to your puppet. Do this by clicking the **Add Behavior** icon next to BENIK_BODY_TURN and choosing **Head & Body Turner** from the list:

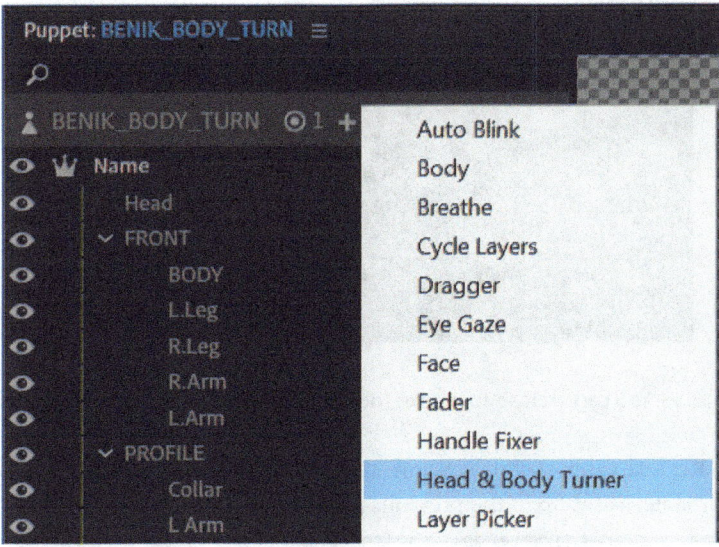

Figure 13.36: If you wish to track your full body, be sure that you have plenty of room

3. You will need to label the phases so that the turner behavior knows when to call what group up. This is like identifying your head phases. To do this, follow these steps:

    I. Click the **FRONT** group.

    II. On the right, click the **Frontal** face view.

    III. Click **PROFILE** and then click the **Left Profile** face icon:

Figure 13.37: The face icons can also be used to assign body phases

As we discovered when animating Chaz, we can control head turns with the webcam. The same goes for body turns. You can set this up so that when you turn your head or body on camera, the layer switches appropriately.

4. The **Body & Turner** option allows you to start the turn by either using your head or body. For now, we will keep it set to **Head** for a more simplified tracking solution. Within the panel, you should also see that both **Front** and **Left Profile** have a **1** next to them, indicating they each have a phase defined:

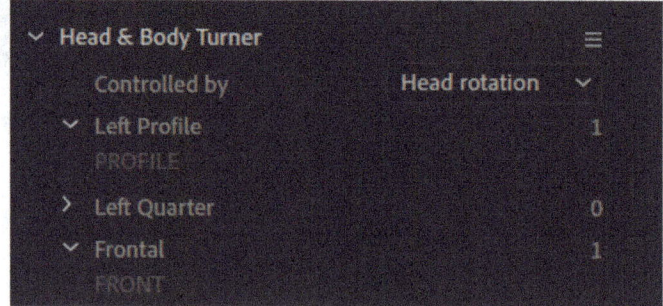

Figure 13.38: You can choose to invoke the turn using your head or body on camera

5. Now, go to **Record**, calibrate the webcam, and turn your head to the left. The body should shift to its profile state, as set up in the previous panel:

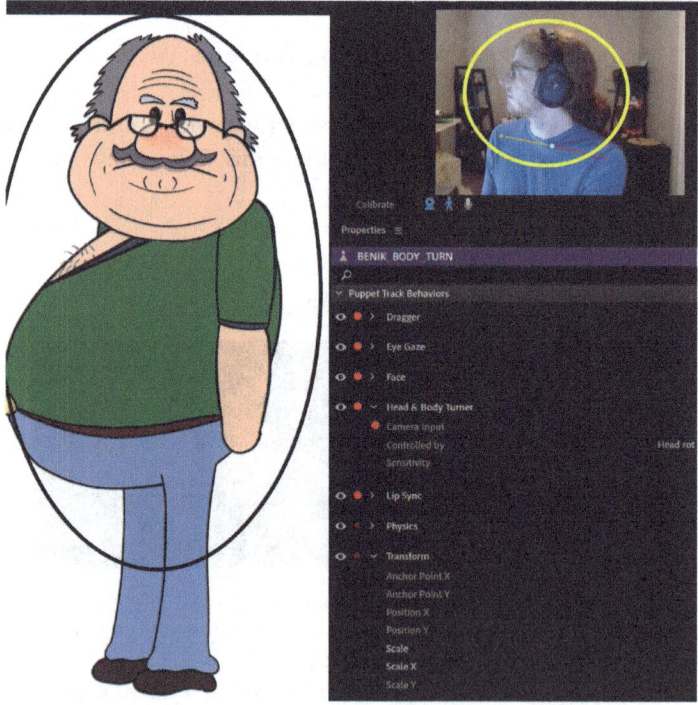

Figure 13.39: As you can see, we set this up so that when the actor turns their head, the body will switch to its new pose

Setting up body turns is a simple matter of grouping your body parts into views and tagging them appropriately. There is a lot of power here, between the camera tracking and keyboard and mouse controls. Hopefully, with everything we learned throughout the book, your imagination is soaring with possibilities.

Finally, let's talk about how we can set Character Animator up to be friendly for a streaming environment.

Using the Stream workspace

The **Stream** workspace doesn't offer much other than a clean area to help you display and animate a character with a streaming application. You will find no timeline, just any controls and behaviors you need to access to animate. The idea here is to take a complete puppet, point your streaming app to Character Animator, set up your visuals in the streaming app, and then perform them.

The **Stream** workspace offers a couple of options you will find near the bottom right of the **Scene** window:

Figure 13.40: The Stream options are limited but useful

Let's go over these icons from left to right:

- The first icon, **Refresh**, will reload your scene and rig in the event you're having issues with changes appearing in the **Stream** workspace.
- The **Show Mesh** icon will display the mesh of the puppet. This could be useful for testing.
- The **Stream Live** option is useful if you have multiple monitors. By ticking the **Enable Mercury Transmit** box, you can display just the Character Animator scene on the desired monitor, making it easier for you to capture the output using your streaming application. If you don't have multiple displays, you can still perform and see the results in the application window itself. Clicking the icon will enable or disable the feature while using *Ctrl* or *Command* and then clicking will take you to your list of monitors:

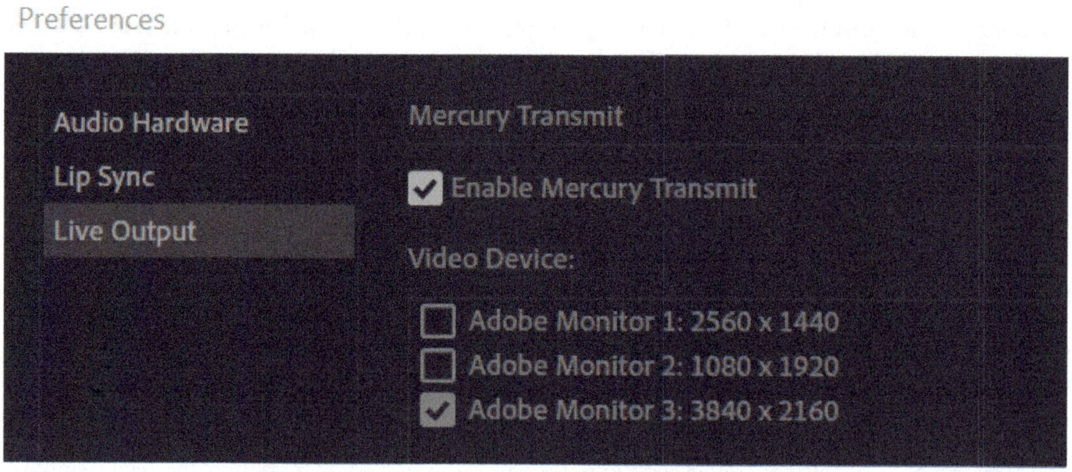

Preferences

Figure 13.41: Available monitors will be listed once you check the Enable Mercury Transmit box

- **Background,** the last icon next to the **Zoom** level, allows you to create a background quickly for your character. This can have its uses, depending on how and what you're streaming. You may also opt for a solid color to chroma key in your streaming application, to overlay the character over other graphics and information:

Figure 13.42: Available backgrounds for the Stream workspace

Once you have these options set to how you want, the next steps will take place in your streaming app of choice. But typically, this involves setting the app to point at the monitor displaying the character animation, cropping it, chroma keying the background if desired, adding text and other effects, and perhaps a window displaying another stream (think a video game or other activity).

The possibilities here are limitless and it's an exciting way to share information and entertain. If you're a streamer looking to spice up your creative routine, Character Animator is an outstanding addition to your toolset.

Summary

As stated previously, Character Animator is a robust piece of software with lots of ways to tackle the animation process. There is no right or wrong in choosing your path. So long as you're making progress and taking advantage of features that suit you, that's what counts. But with everything you've learned in this book, it's good to know you can quickly produce puppets with **Puppet Maker**, control puppet bodies with your camera, and even set up a stream-friendly environment. And with Adobe updating Character Animator regularly, there's always something new to look forward to and explore.

Above all else, have fun with your productions. Don't be afraid to put your complete self into it. The creative process can be an unwieldy ride, but those who see it through will find exceptional rewards, both personal and professional. Happy animating!

Index

A

Adobe After Effects 34
  capability, expanding 36
  compositing 35
  editing, with Dynamic Link 214
  effective areas 34
  grading media 35
  history 34
  motion graphics 35, 36
  need for 214
  toolset, expanding 36
  using, with Character Animator productions 36
Adobe Animate 21
  history 22, 23
Adobe Animate, features 24
  drawing tools 26
  frame-by-frame animation 24
  symbols 25
alien guest
  importing 175-177
  positioning 175-177
alien's dialogue
  importing 179-181
  lip-syncing 179-181
Animate
  assets, designing 26
  characters, designing 26
  using, with Character Animator productions 26
Animate art
  importing, into Character Animator 27-30
Animate content
  exporting, for Character Animator 31-33
  importing, for Character Animator 31-33
animation
  creating 31
  recording 16
  refining, with meshes 128-130
animation apps 36
assets
  layering 217-222

Index

B

Blender 36
body animations
　tracking 260-264
body layers
　tagging 92-97
body turns
　tracking 264-267
breathing behavior
　animating 148-150

C

camera features
　adding 228-235
character
　designing 39, 40
character actions
　adding 190
　alien's gaze, adjusting 190-192
　animations, enhancing 200-204
　arm movement, adding to alien 193-195
　arranging, in sequence 195-200
　automatic blinks, setting for alien 192, 193
　flaws, correcting 200-204
Character Animator
　Animate art, importing into 27-30
　Animate content, exporting
　　and importing 31-33
　body animations, tracking 260-264
　body turns, tracking 264-267
　character, designing 39, 40
　Chaz, importing 76, 77
　downloading 4-7
　equipment, calibrating 8
　export options 208
　eyebrow phases, adding 60-62
　eye groups, arranging 62-65
　functioning 14
　hair, separating out 66-69
　layer changes, making 77-81
　layers, streamlining and renaming 41, 42
　left tag 85, 86
　main groups, creating 58-60
　normal and independent
　　groups, organizing 57
　Pro, versus Starter 7, 8
　PSD layers, cleaning up 69, 71
　PSD versions, creating 81-83
　Puppet Maker 246-253
　rig, adjusting 75
　right tag 85, 86
　scene cameras 253-259
　Stream workspace, using 267, 268
　system requirements 3, 4
Character Animator productions
　Adobe After Effects, using with 36
　Animate, using with 26
Character Animator scenes
　exporting, as videos 210-214
Characterizer
　animating with 17-19
characters
　positioning, in scene 172
Chaz
　dialogue, recording 177-179
　importing 173-175
　positioning 173-175
Cinema 4D 36
Cycle Layers behavior
　adding, to PNG sequences 186-188

D

danglers
   adding 121-124
dialogue, recording 177
   screenplay or outline, using 177
dragger controls
   adding, to modifiers 102-108
Dynamic Link
   After Effects, editing with 214
   importing 214-217

E

effects
   creating 31
equipment calibration 8, 9
   microphone, testing 13, 14
   new project, creating 9
   project versions, loading 10, 11
   project versions, renaming 10, 11
   project versions, saving 9, 10
   webcam, testing 11-13
export options 208
   duration, setting 208
   used, for exporting files 209, 210
eyelids
   animating 143, 144
   character, importing with 144, 145
   tagging 145-148

H

head layers
   tagging 87-91
head turns
   implementing 150
   phases, tagging 151, 152
   testing 152, 153

I

independent groups
   layers, assigning to 108-110
   linking 108
   welding, to body 110-114

J

jaw behavior
   animating 148-150

L

layers
   character group, creating 43
   eye layers, reorganizing 49-57
   limbs, merging 45-49
   limbs, renaming 45-49
   unneeded layers, removing 44, 45
layer-specific behaviors
   creating 127, 128
limbs
   refining, with stick tool 114-116
   rotation, adjusting 116-119

M

meshes
  animation, refining with 128-130
modifiers
  adding, to mouse control 99, 100
  dragger controls, adding 102-104
  Fixed modifier, adding 105-108
  layer and mesh properties, adjusting 101, 102
Moho
  URL 36
mouse control
  modifiers, adding 99, 100
mouth layers
  tagging 91, 92

O

OpenToonz
  URL 36

P

physics
  adding 121-124
PNG sequences
  audience, adding in scene 188-190
  Cycle Layers behavior, adding 186-188
  importing 184-186
  using, for external animations 183
Premiere
  color grading and filters 238-244
  editing 235-238
props
  importing 132-134
  triggers, creating 131

PSD layers
  cleaning up 69, 71
puppet handle 92
Puppet Maker 246- 253

S

sample rig
  playing with 14, 15
set
  assembling 170
  background assets, importing 170
  building 171, 172
special effects
  adding 222- 228
stick tool
  limbs, refining with 114-116
Stream workspace
  using 267-269
swap set
  setting up, for changing hand poses 137-140
  using, tips 142

T

tag view
  switching 84, 85
timeline
  walk animation, mixing on 166, 167
Toon Boom 36
triggers
  creating 135-137
  creating, for props 131
  using, tips 142
  visual controls, creating 140-142
TVPaint Animation
  URL 36

U

universal behaviors
   modifying 124-127

V

visual controls
   creating, for triggers 140-142

W

walk cycle
   creating 157-164
   modifying 164-166

Packt.com

Subscribe to our online digital library for full access to over 7,000 books and videos, as well as industry leading tools to help you plan your personal development and advance your career. For more information, please visit our website.

Why subscribe?

- Spend less time learning and more time coding with practical eBooks and Videos from over 4,000 industry professionals
- Improve your learning with Skill Plans built especially for you
- Get a free eBook or video every month
- Fully searchable for easy access to vital information
- Copy and paste, print, and bookmark content

Did you know that Packt offers eBook versions of every book published, with PDF and ePub files available? You can upgrade to the eBook version at packt.com and as a print book customer, you are entitled to a discount on the eBook copy. Get in touch with us at customercare@packtpub.com for more details.

At www.packt.com, you can also read a collection of free technical articles, sign up for a range of free newsletters, and receive exclusive discounts and offers on Packt books and eBooks.

Other Books You May Enjoy

If you enjoyed this book, you may be interested in these other books by Packt:

Mastering Adobe Animate 2021

Joseph Labrecque

ISBN: 978-1-80107-416-2

- Gain a solid understanding of Adobe Animate foundations and new features
- Understand the nuances associated with publishing and exporting rich media content for various platforms
- Make use of advanced layering and rigging techniques to create engaging motion content
- Create dynamic motion by using the camera and variable layer depth techniques
- Develop web-based games, virtual reality experiences, and multiplatform mobile applications
- Extend Animate with extensions, application-level scripting, and the creation of custom integrated tutorials

Mastering Adobe Photoshop Elements

Robin Nichols

ISBN: 978-1-78980-815-5

- Understand the latest Photoshop tools to add life to your photos
- Add graphic elements to any composition, photograph, or illustration
- Tackle challenges in editing multi-layered images for your photography projects
- Develop illustrative skills with Photoshop Elements' variety of drawing tools
- Understand techniques for professional photo retouching
- Work with online and local templates to create calendars, greeting cards, and other projects

Packt is searching for authors like you

If you're interested in becoming an author for Packt, please visit `authors.packtpub.com` and apply today. We have worked with thousands of developers and tech professionals, just like you, to help them share their insight with the global tech community. You can make a general application, apply for a specific hot topic that we are recruiting an author for, or submit your own idea.

Hi!

Chad Troftgruben here, author of the book you just read. I hope you had an enjoyable and productive time following along and animating with me. It would mean a lot if you could leave a review on Amazon and share your experience. Thank you and happy animating!

Go to the link below or scan the QR code to leave your review:

https://packt.link/r/1803246944

Your review will help us to understand what's worked well in this book, and what could be improved upon for future editions, so it really is appreciated.

Best wishes,

Download a free PDF copy of this book

Thanks for purchasing this book!

Do you like to read on the go but are unable to carry your print books everywhere? Is your eBook purchase not compatible with the device of your choice?

Don't worry, now with every Packt book you get a DRM-free PDF version of that book at no cost.

Read anywhere, any place, on any device. Search, copy, and paste code from your favorite technical books directly into your application.

The perks don't stop there, you can get exclusive access to discounts, newsletters, and great free content in your inbox daily

Follow these simple steps to get the benefits:

1. Scan the QR code or visit the link below

`packt.link/free-ebook/9781803246949`

2. Submit your proof of purchase
3. That's it! We'll send your free PDF and other benefits to your email directly

Made in the USA
Las Vegas, NV
08 October 2023